D0795759

eCommerce

ISBN 0-13-019844-7

90000

9 780130 198440

In an increasingly competitive world, it is quality
of thinking that gives an edge. An idea that opens new
doors, a technique that solves a problem, or an insight
that simply helps make sense of it all.

We must work with leading authors in the fields of
management and finance to bring cutting-edge thinking
and best learning practice to a global market.

Under a range of leading imprints, including
Financial Times Prentice Hall, we create world-class
print publications and electronic products giving readers
knowledge and understanding which can then be
applied, whether studying or at work.

To find out more about our business and professional
products, you can visit us at www.phptr.com

eCommerce

Formulation of Strategy

Robert T. Plant

Prentice Hall PTR
Upper Saddle River, NJ 07458
www.phptr.com

Library of Congress Cataloging-in-Publication Data

```
Plant, Robert (Robert T.)
     eCommerce : formulation of strategy / Robert Plant.
       p. cm.
     Includes bibliographical references and index.
     ISBN 0-13-019844-7 (pbk.)
     1. Electronic commerce—Case studies.  2. Business
     planning—Case studies.  I. Title.
HF5548.32 .P58 2000
658.4'012—dc21                                        00-033996
```

Editorial/production supervision: *BooksCraft, Inc., Indianapolis, IN*
Acquisitions editor: *Mike Meehan*
Editorial assistant: *Linda Ramagnano*
Marketing manager: *Bryan Gambrel*
Manufacturing manager: *Maura Goldstaub*
Cover design director: *Jerry Votta*
Cover designer: *Talar Agasyan*
Project coordinator: *Anne Trowbridge*

© 2000 by Prentice Hall PTR
Prentice-Hall, Inc.
Upper Saddle River, NJ 07458

Prentice Hall books are widely used by corporations and government agencies for training, marketing, and resale.

The publisher offers discounts on this book when ordered in bulk quantities.
For more information, contact:
Corporate Sales Department
Phone: 800-382-3419   Fax: 201-236-7141
E-mail: corpsales@prenhall.com

Or write:
Prentice Hall PTR
Corporate Sales Department
One Lake Street
Upper Saddle River, NJ 07458

All product names mentioned herein are the trademarks of their respective owners.

Quotations from representatives of IBM on pages 1 and 227 and the patent information on page 228 are reprinted with permission from IBM Website (www.ibm.com), © 1999 by International Business Machines Corporation, Internet Division, Somers, NY.

All rights reserved. No part of this book may be reproduced, in any form or by any means, without permission in writing from the publisher.

Printed in the United States of America

10 9 8 7 6 5 4 3 2 1

ISBN: 0-13-019844-7

Prentice-Hall International (UK) Limited, *London*
Prentice-Hall of Australia Pty. Limited, *Sydney*
Prentice-Hall Canada Inc., *Toronto*
Prentice-Hall Hispanoamericana, S.A., *Mexico*
Prentice-Hall of India Private Limited, *New Delhi*
Prentice-Hall of Japan, Inc., *Tokyo*
Pearson Education Asia Pte. Ltd.
Editora Prentice-Hall do Brasil, Ltda., *Rio de Janeiro*

About the Author

Dr. Plant is an associate professor at the School of Business Administration, University of Miami, Coral Gables, Florida. He obtained his Ph.D. in Computer Science at The University of Liverpool, England. Dr. Plant is a Microsoft Certified Systems Engineer and an MCP + I. He holds visiting teaching and research positions at Templeton College, Oxford University, England; Universidad Gabriela Mistral, Santiago, Chile; and Victoria University of Wellington, New Zealand. In addition, he has taught in executive MBA programs at IBM, Motorola, Pratt & Whitney, Office Depot, American Express, W. R. Grace, Siemens, and other *Fortune* 500 companies.

Dr. Plant's consulting and research interests are in e-commerce, virtual organizations, and the role of information systems in strategic management. He has published over eighty articles in such leading journals as *Financial Times*, *Oxford Executive Research Briefings*, and *Information & Management*.

To Dr. David Bendel Hertz,
visionary, mentor, and friend

Contents

Preface

Even the Super Bowl, the most sacred and most watched sporting event in the United States had succumbed to the Internet and its influence. Victoria's Secret, the lingerie company, was the first to take the initiative with a 15-second slot promoting a live supermodel fashion show on the Internet[1]—an event probably more memorable than the game itself. By Super Bowl XXXIV only two years later in January 2000, with an estimated 130 million viewers the excitement and conversation was centered as much around the "dot-com" advertisements airing during the game as the game itself, each company paying out a record $2.2 million for each 30-second slot.

The message is clear: the Internet is here to stay. But beyond the start-up legends, the intermediaries, infomediaries, and service providers, the Internet is challenging established corporations' relationships with customers. The question they face is: "What will be the impact of the Internet on our business, our competitive strategy, and our information systems strategy?"

In researching this book, I interviewed senior executives at more than 40 major corporations in the United States and Europe. These in-depth interviews revealed diverse approaches to how this question is being approached.

---

1. For further reading, see C. Allbritton, "Victoria's Secret Net Show a Bust," *Associated Press*, February 4, 1999.

☞ Most companies have recognized that they need to create and execute an e-commerce strategy; however, as they look for strategy models to follow, they realize that there are none available, especially for manufacturers in traditional industries. To blindly follow the strategy of the new Internet stars such as Amazon is impossible.

☞ Some companies still feel that they can largely ignore the Internet and that they can offer a token Website with a basic product offering. To executives at these companies, my response is "How quickly could you respond if your strongest competitor came out with a powerful e-commerce strategy tomorrow?"

☞ Other companies, however, have recognized some of the drivers in e-commerce and have adopted one of them to the exclusion of the others—for example, positioning themselves to have a low-cost Internet customer service position. However, this lack of balance between service, branding, technology, and marketing can be extremely detrimental.

☞ Clearly, some organizations are winning in the battle for the Internet marketspace and are creating adaptive, intelligent solutions that will keep them ahead of the competition, build successful barriers to entry against insurgents, and allow them to create new empires as the slow giants of the old economy fight to change course and pick up steam.

Thus, in the face of a barrage of new rules for the information economy, business is finding that the boundaries of strategic thinking, and of competition, have vastly expanded. The challenge is to keep up with the rapid growth in converging technologies and to translate the potential of these technologies into business vision and dynamic competitive strategy.

So, what exactly *is* corporate strategy in the face of e-commerce? We can define corporate strategy as the formulation of a set of directives that, when effectively executed, fulfill the competitive vision set by executive management. In light of that, my consistent finding has been that, to be effective, an e-commerce strategy has to be integrated with the strategic vision of the company as a whole. As an executive from American Express put it, "The Net has to integrate into your core business." However, the approach to the creation of an effective e-commerce strategy is not always clear. True, many classic examples now exist and are very visible—Amazon.com, AOL.com, eBay.com—but these are new organizations, *born on the Web.* What if you're an industrial manufacturer of cyclical products, *how do you proceed?* What if you are a supplier of information-based services and wish to develop an Internet strategy, again, how do you proceed?

Executives can study the successes of the Amazons of the world, but does an Amazon-type strategy translate to other industries or organizations? Probably not. A sample of one type of Internet strategy, even if derived from the best of pure dot-com companies, has severe limitations.

The aim of this book therefore is twofold:

1. To enable CEOs, senior executives, and managers to understand the competitive ramifications of e-commerce within their arenas of corporate competition
2. Through the methodologies presented, to enable executives to take effective action in developing a strong, unique, and effective strategy for their own organizations

Companies and Case Studies

The methodologies presented in this book are based on a series of in-depth interviews and studies with executives and managers at 33 North American and European companies and, through use of public data and case studies, information for 10 additional organizations (see the table). This approach allowed us to get inside the thinking and philosophy of these global marketplace leaders, 16 of which were in their industries' top 10 as defined by *Fortune*. The in-depth interviews, examination of case situations, and discussions with leading practitioners have been distilled into a comprehensive set of frameworks. From these, you will get a clear picture of the dynamics involved in the creation of an Internet strategy and its deployment.

Research Organizations

Company		Industry Categories*
Interview Case Studies		
1	IBM	Comps.Hard
2	Citigroup	Banks-M.C.
3	UPS	Transptn. Services
4	American Express	Fin'l Div
5	Nortel	Comm. Equip
6	Entergy	Elec.Cos
7	Sun Microsystems	Comps.Hard
8	UTC (Pratt & Whitney)	Transport. Equip.
9	Office Depot	Retail-Spec
10	USMedicalSystems†	Medical

Research Organizations (Continued)

Company		Industry Categories*
11	Motorola	Telecommunications
12	FPL	Elec.Cos
13	Ryder	Truckers
14	Dow Jones	Publishing
15	Royal Caribbean	Lodging-Hotels
16	Lennar	Homebuilding
17	ABIG	Insurance-M Line
18	W.R. Grace	Chem.-Spec
19	CSR Rinker	Nonmetallic Minerals
20	Chemical†	Biotec
21	Millipore	Manf. Specialized
22	Sony	Entertainment
23	Priceline.com	Online Retail

Private Companies or Companies That Are Part of a Conglomerate

24	Rover Group	Automobiles
25	BMW	Automobiles
26	Alamo	Svcs.Comm
27	Burger King	Restaurants
28	Holberg (Ameriserve)	Logistics
29	VisualCom.com	Internet Services
30	FAR&WIDE.com	Travel
31	manage.MD	Healthcare Services
32	LightPort.com	Finance

Companies—Public Data and Case Study Information Sources

33	Swiss RE	Insurance Carriers
34	Charles Schwab	Finance
35	Schlumberger	Oil
36	Lockheed	Defense
37	Edmunds	Automotive & Publishing
38	Internet Securities Inc	Finance
39	Ford	Automotive
40	America Online	Internet Service Provider
41	Virtual Vineyards	Wine
42	Co-Op BookShop Australia	Publishing & Distribution
43	GM	Automotive

*Categorization: (S&P)/SIC.

†Anonymous company.

The book is organized in the following fashion.

Chapter 1: *Formulating an Internet Strategy in a Networked World*

The chapter discusses the dynamics of the e-commerce marketspace and the three market positions that organizations and their executives find themselves in—traditional established organizations, new online organizations, and hybrid organizations.

- ☞ New organizations: born on the Net
- ☞ Existing organizations: move to the Net
- ☞ E-consortia: swarm to the Net

The ultimate success of the strategy created and adopted by an organization depends heavily upon early identification of the specific issues and options available in each of these sectors when applied to the individual circumstances of the organization.

Chapter 2: *Creating an Integrated E-commerce Strategy*

In this chapter we discuss the seven dimensions of an e-commerce strategy: The four positional characteristics—*brand, technology, service,* and *market*—and the three bonding factors—*leadership, infrastructure,* and *organizational* learning. Determination of the interrelationships among these factors is key to the creation of a strong yet adaptable e-commerce strategy.

Chapter 3: *Ownership Issues*

The creation of a successful e-commerce strategy is more than just the development of a conceptual product and plan. This chapter considers two critical factors internal to the organization—the organizational structure and the content owners.

Success in the online marketspace requires flexibility and adaptivity on the part of the organization. To facilitate this, new e-centric organizational and management structures need to be adopted. These are structures that have their roots in the world of mass customization where the concept of the *networked cross-functional management group* has been previously successfully deployed. This chapter considers how these structures can be utilized in the online organization and how content owners within the organization play a valuable role in that structure.

The chapter thus considers the key organizational issues that need to be effectively managed to successfully compete in the Internet marketspace, including:

☞ E-centric management structures

☞ Content ownership

Chapter 4: *E-strategy Leadership Through a Technology Focus*

Technology does not work in a vacuum to make an organization world class. In this chapter technology issues are considered in relation to other key drivers—corporate positioning and structure. The chapter describes how these factors, when carefully molded together, combine to create the dynamism found in the world's great companies.

We consider:

☞ The role of the executive champion

☞ The McKinsey Seven S Framework

— Strategy

— Skills

— Staff

— Style

— Systems

— Structure

— Shared values

☞ Enterprise resource planning (ERP)

☞ Data warehousing

☞ Knowledge management

Chapter 5: *Developing a Market Focus*

This chapter considers the issues facing industry types and develops the issues pertaining to the four major segments through case studies of leading organizations in e-commerce strategy and deployment. The chapter also considers the role of partnering in developing a successful online market position and outlines the strengths associated with the e-consortia e-business model.

We look at:

☞ Manufacturing: CA-Chemical

☞ Mixed service and goods: Sony

☞ Mixed service and goods (B2B): USMedicalSystems

☞ Service organization: Charles Schwab

Chapter 6: *Service Leadership Through the Internet Service Value Chain*

The ability to create a meaningful customer relationship at all points of contact is central to doing business on the Internet. However the first generation of models that organizations followed were too simplistic both in their view of the customers' behavior and the metrics that they used. This chapter considers the interaction of customer relationship management through three drivers—*content, format,* and *access*—and discusses e-commerce metrics from a perspective that combines research from the area of knowledge-based systems verification and validation with that of market research analysis. At the end of the day, corporate strategists must know that what they are measuring is both valid and useful!

We consider:

- ☞ Customer acquisition: prepurchase support
- ☞ Customer support: during purchase
- ☞ Customer fulfillment: purchase dispatch
- ☞ Customer continuance: postpurchase support

Chapter 7: *E-branding—the Emergence of New Global Brands*

The power of branding on the Internet cannot be underplayed; the strength of the new online organizations has created significant brand equity very quickly. For traditional organizations moving to the Net, their challenge is to leverage existing brands effectively and move forward in their new chosen marketspaces. This chapter discusses the four major positions that can be adopted:

- ☞ Brand reinforcement
- ☞ Brand creation
- ☞ Brand reposition
- ☞ Brand follower

Chapter 8: *Formulating an Internet Rollout Strategy*

This chapter discusses the issues surrounding developmental choices available to executives—whether to develop the systems internally, externally, or some combination. The issues surrounding development and Web hosting are also explained and discussed through the Charles Schwab case study. The case illustrates at an executive level the major technical issues chief information officers and technologists face regarding server configuration, network topology, and application designs.

We look at:

☞ The internal development route
☞ The external development route
☞ Partnering models
☞ Web hosting options
☞ Case study: Charles Schwab

Chapter 9: *Internet Strategy Effectiveness—A Scorecard Approach*

This chapter develops a set of frameworks that executives and managers can work from in order to gain an understanding of the forces in strategy formulation pertaining to their own individual circumstances. The frameworks contain over 50 questions covering the seven dimensions of strategy formulation. The aim of the chapter is to help executives answer two fundamental questions: What are the strengths and weaknesses of my strategy or proposed strategy? What will I get out of this technology investment?

We consider:

☞ The creation of a metrics program
☞ The Internet effectiveness scorecard
☞ The e-value map: an ownership/manager level analysis

Chapter 10: *Waves of the Future*

This chapter discusses the six major areas in which change will emanate as the environment of e-commerce goes forward in time. The ability to stay ahead in all of these areas is vital to e-commerce strategies, and the chapter highlights critical issues in each: patents, e-consortia, wireless technologies, brand equity valuation models, the threat from the "old economy" industrial giants as they recreate themselves, jurisdiction, copyright, pricing models, the home services station, global markets, market hubs, market segmentation, emerging markets, Latin America, China, the information hub, the visible and invisible hand, the White House, cyber crime, the Eighth Principle.

The areas are:

☞ Technology changes
☞ Branding changes
☞ Market changes

☞ Service changes

☞ Government and political changes

☞ External relationship changes

Chapter 11: *Views from the Edge*

This chapter contains five interviews from executives on the leading edge of strategy and vision. The executives were chosen for their fresh views and their insight into particular industry segments. They reveal issues that are both far reaching yet pragmatic as they run their operations in a day-to-day environment. These interviews may help real-world managers and executives cope with their mainstream environments and organizations more effectively. Not all companies are *Fortune* 100 companies or situated in Silicon Valley as portrayed in most other interviews and texts. The interviews include two dot-com start-ups, a software company transitioning to the Net, a multinational telecommunications company, and a power utility.

The interviewees:

☞ Born on the Net

— FAR&WIDE Travel Corporation—$125 million in start-up funding

— LightPort.com—develops and manages sites for 165,000 clients; $125 billion in assets

☞ Move to the Net

— SoftAid—medical billing goes Internet

— Motorola—telecommunications giant goes online

— Florida Power & Light—a Demming Award holder develops its online strategy

The models are created, based on the research collected for this book, to maximize the strategy potential of all organizations that adopt and adapt them for their own individual circumstances. The book's intent is to help executives in all stages of growth and positioning and for executives globally. All organizations have the opportunity to transform themselves through the Internet and the potential it offers.

Acknowledgments

This book could not have been created without the generous support of the participating organizations, which gave generously of their resources and the time, wisdom, and insights of their executives, and I'm deeply indebted. In this regard I would like to acknowledge those executives who contributed to the major case studies that were the basis for this study. These include Ian Robertson and Carol M. Burrows (BMW); Hamid Mughal (Land Rover); John Nigard (Lennar); Phil Blake, Annette Hogan, and Barry Kaplan (FAR&WIDE Travel); Henry Fiallo (Cabletron); Dennis Klinger (FPL); Donna Demarco and Luiza Aguiar (Sun Microsystems); Suan Tong Foo (Citigroup); Dave Dawson (Ryder Systems); Keith Butler (OfficeDepot.com); Craig Neeb (AmeriServe); Dominick Lombardi (Pratt & Whitney); Maria Villar (IBM); Bob Clinton (Motorola); Winston Estridge and Wayne Higgins (Nortel); Tim Gordon (Priceline.com); Thomas Anderson (Millipore); Gregory Gerdy (Dow Jones); Jonathan Bentley (LightPort.com); Jose Valero and Jim Clark (manage.MD); John Maldonado (UPS); Jack Williams (Royal Caribbean International Cruise Lines); Andre Vanyi-Robin (Visualcom.com).

I also especially thank the many executives, managers, technologists, and others who for various reasons wished not to be named as sources. Without their open and frank discussions of the issues surrounding the formulation of e-commerce strategies this book would have been significantly less complete, and I thank them for letting me be a "fly on the wall."

In addition I would like to thank all of the press offices and media relations offices of the companies with whom I interacted—their assistance and help was invaluable. Also thanks to my graduate and executive students at the University of Miami, Florida, whose discussions in and after class let me formalize the material more clearly. I especially thank Christian Petersmann and Nadine Babell for their assistance. I would also like to thank all my friends, students, and colleagues at the University of Miami, Coral Gables, Florida; the University of Oxford, Oxford, England; and Universidad Gabriela Mistral, Santiago de Chile, for their shared insights and encouragement during this project.

Thanks also to Mike Meehan, my editor at Prentice Hall, whose insistence, drive, and faith in the project were there just when I needed them in order to get the book finished. Thanks also to my production editors Anne Trowbridge and Don MacLaren for straightening out the production issues, and especially to Ruth Frick for her ability to decipher my "English" English and make it readable for all. Thanks also to Neville Hawcock of *Financial Times* and Leslie Willcocks of Templeton College, Oxford, for their encouragement in the early stages of this project.

Finally I would like to thank my wife Annette for all her support during the 18 months of this project. Without her continuous positive encouragement, this work would truly not have been possible.

Formulating an Internet Strategy in a Networked World

The Internet as a Business Solution or Pandora's Box

If you ask investors what most defined Wall Street and investment markets in the late 1990s, only one issue will be raised—technology, or, more specifically, the Internet. It appeared that all you had to do was put ".com" on the end of your name and your stock price went up 10% or 20% or more. Since its deregulation as a data transmission media in the mid-1990s, the Internet has changed all the rules of business and, to a large extent, the lives of everyone on the planet, fundamentally changing the way we as humans can now interact. It has been a true inflection point in society, as important as the industrial revolution or the great socio-technical changes of the past, such as the discovery of DNA sequences by Crick and Watson, developments in particle physics by Einstein, or the breakthrough in celestial thinking by Copernicus.

Louis Gerstner, Chairman and CEO of IBM

Every day it becomes clearer that the Net is taking its place alongside the other great transformational technologies that first challenged, and then fundamentally changed, the way things are done in the world.

Source: www.ibm.com/lvg/ (December 14, 1999).

The day the world changed was December 21, 1994, when in a joint press release the University of Illinois at Urbana-Champaign and Netscape Communications Corporation (formerly known as Mosaic Communications) announced that they had reached an agreement that left Netscape free to market its products independent of the university, its collaborator.[1] Less than 6 months later Netscape announced its initial public offering (IPO) was to take place on August 9, 1995, a moment few technology investors will forget as they scrambled for those first 5 million IPO shares at $28 a share. From that moment on no corporation or executive could ignore the impact that the Internet and the Internet browser would have upon the business landscape.

The Way Forward

The growth of the Internet as a communications vehicle since 1995 has been nothing less than spectacular. The Internet has evolved into potentially the most powerful business channel ever, a sentiment echoed by Michael Dell who forcefully captures the mood of competition on the Internet: "The Internet is like a weapon sitting on a table, ready to be picked up by either you or your competitors."[2]

The rise of the Internet has been spectacular, even in comparison to previous leaps in technology and information provision. Analysts at Morgan Stanley Dean Witter project that the percentage of PC owners worldwide who are connected to the Internet will rise from a figure of 1% in 1993 to approximately 58% by the end of 2000.[3] The implications of this direct access channel to households and eyes all around the globe is enormous. After all, it had taken radio 38 years and television 13 years to reach the coverage that the Net will have reached in only 5 years.

The impact of this on forward-looking organizations has also not been anything less than spectacular. The utilization of the Internet by start-up organizations, many of whom have subsequently gone on to become household

---

1. Press Release: "University of Illinois and Netscape Communications Reach Agreement," Champaign, IL (December 21, 1994), www.netscape.com/newsref/pr/newsrelease9.html

2. Michael Dell's Keynote Address at the DirectConnect Conference, Austin, TX, August 25, 1999.

3. U.S. Investment Research: Technology: Internet/New Media, *Internet Quarterly*, "The Business of the Web...Morgan Stanley Dean Witter," September 23, 1997.

names such as Amazon, eBay, and E*TRADE, is well known, as is their basic model of competitive strategy,[4] based on the principles of low costs, high volumes, and comprehensive service, combined with a product range unapproachable through traditional channels. However, what if you are not a startup? What is the business model that you can adopt? Will an Amazon strategy work for a traditional organization repositioning itself? What strategy should be chosen and how does one add value through this channel? Approaching this problem is extremely difficult for many organizations. IBM chief executive Louis Gerstner recently stated that "We need some new models for how we go about exploring IT [information technology] for competitive advantage. We need a new model for IT infrastructure, how we create it and manage it, and we need a new model for how we acquire, manage and deploy the skills that are needed to run that infrastructure."[5] The aim of this book is to help e-commerce strategists create and formulate these models.

As a first step toward a new model for organizational e-commerce, let's consider the Internet world from three different viewpoints (see Figure 1.1):

☞ The new organization, which was *born on the Internet* in the e-commerce marketspace

☞ Established organizations traditionally positioned in the offline marketspace *moving to the Net*

☞ Those organizations that are coming together in a new organizational form—the *e-consortia*—whose aim is to leverage the unique strengths associated with each company and partner through the "virtual structure" of an online organization

New Organizations: Born on the Net

The brave new world of the Internet-based company is dynamic and flourishing. In fact, the most successful IPO market in history was that of the Internet

---

4. Throughout the text we use the terms *strategy*, *e-commerce strategy*, and *Internet strategy*. While for traditionally structured organizations there may well be some separation in the corporate strategy for the entire organization between its online and offline strategies, the terminology utilized here refers to an organization's online strategy and the terms are used interchangeably unless specifically noted.

5. IBM Executive Conference on Information Systems, Latin America, Miami, FL, September 1, 1998.

Figure 1.1
Established,
Online, and
Consortium
Organizations in
the Marketspace

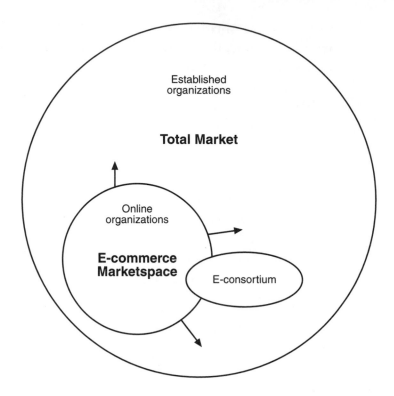

sector in 1998—93% of all IPOs traded up, with the top three generating an amazing 990% average price increase (eBay alone was 1422%) and only three returning negative results. However, after the initial IPO euphoria, the struggle to survive is often intense and fueled by many of the same ingredients that are found in more traditional start-ups and youthful competitive arenas.

Industry growth and competition in the new Internet sector is fast and furious, with the number of competitors increasing daily. However, once again it appears that several traditional paths to, and tenets of, success are still valid even in this "new economic model," as pundits often term it. The premier factor is, as always, *product and market vision.* How successful a new organization will become is founded upon the business concept, in which new vision, concept, or idea equals strong foundation. But clearly, a strong vision is not all it takes—Wall Street is littered with the tombstones of companies founded on bright ideas. However, if we took the time to read the epitaphs on these tombstones we would often find "Bright idea, lousy execution." Remember, corporate strategy has two components: first, the formulation of a winning *conceptual strategy* and, second, delivery of an executable or *operational strategy.*

Conceptual strategy for the new e-commerce sector can itself be broken down into two types:

☞ A company attempting to create *an entirely new product or service concept,* such as America Online, where a new technology is deployed

☞ A company attempting *a new execution of an existing product or service* previously available to the market in an offline form, such as eBay, which, via the Internet, delivers an ancient transactional method of trade, that of the auction house

In both types, companies are subject to traditional rivalry factors, such as the ability to differentiate the product and pressure from competitors when large changes in capacity are augmented to the marketplace or when diversity of the market acts to segment that market. However it is the organizations' ability to react to these forces within the Internet markets that differentiates them and their potential strategic options.

> Differentiation in the new e-commerce sector is the key success factor.

Differentiation in the new e-commerce sector is the key to success, and the degree to which this affects success or failure is remarkable. Those companies that have brought a unique product to market before anyone else have dazzled both Madison Avenue with the speed at which branding has occurred and Wall Street through the valuation levels the investor community has placed upon those newly branded names: eBay, Priceline.com, TheStreet.com, Yahoo!, and Amazon, for example.

> ### What if I'm not first to market?
> Can I, as a start-up, catch up to existing online firms?

However, not everyone was initially prepared for the Internet and not everyone can be first to market. Thus a question frequently raised by executives of start-up companies and some in the Fortune 100 is: *What if I'm not first to market? Can I as a start-up or new entrant catch up?* The answer to that is typically no: if you're not first, rethink your strategy, be different, build your own new sector brand. A CEO of an online brokerage stated that it would take over $600 million to create an online trading company in 1999[6]—a high price

---

6. Interview: CNBC, "Squawk Box," 1999.

for *last mover disadvantage*. So you're not first to market, but second or third to market. Is the first to market such as Amazon destined to rule its market segment forever? The answer again is probably not; however, there is no inconsistency in these two statements. In stating that first mover advantage is king, we simply state that new Internet companies would be advised to define their own branded space on the Internet rather than battle it out with established market leaders and brands. As for the concept that first movers will reign as kings forever, forever is a long time, and, discounting the threat from new start-ups, there is still the major issue of restructuring an established player. As we will discuss later, an established position in the market is no guarantee of future successes. Think of Woolworth's for a second—Woolworth's was a leader, a first mover in the last major shopping paradigm shift that moved the shopping experience from the small neighborhood store to the department store. We all know the name; branded it is, alive it is not.

Just as the Internet has allowed companies to quickly ramp up to a position of dominance, so too do those leading edge organizations understand that the dependence upon one market segment is the weak link in their chain. They could lose that dominance if an even bigger, highly diversified, established industry player gets into the game. For example, when the large traditional brokerages eventually restructure to accommodate the Internet, they may attack the marketspace of the deep discount online broker. If this should happen, as it inevitably will, then the new Internet company, branded or not, could quickly become Woolworth's-type road kill on the information superhighway unless it enacts an aggressive, agile repositioning strategy. Hence the dilemma for the new Internet brand leaders—they want to diversify, but they don't want to dilute the brand. They want to have maximum product scope and coverage, but they don't want to fight many foes on many fronts.

Consider Amazon and eBay, two giants in the branded e-commerce space. Amazon's model was to be a bookseller, a virtual organization based on the premise of selling high volume at low overhead and mass customizing the product offerings to the customer. eBay's model was to provide online auctions, matching buyer and seller in a global classified sales space. While eBay has stayed the pure auction play, Amazon has changed its conceptual strategy, diversifying into multiple market segments—along with books it offers videos, gifts, CDs, e-cards, and now auctions. The winning strategy in the auction arena for eBay is no longer its conceptual strategy. The battle has moved to its execution of that strategy, as Amazon is not the only new entrant coming to the space and offering an auction product. By the spring of 2000 there were over 40 auction sites online competing for customers and items to auction. eBay's brand strength will ensure that it keeps its market share against the no-name start-ups, but other players wait in the wings—potential competitors such as News Corp or the Mirror Group whose global reach may be important in leveling the playing field.

eBay.com and the Competitive Landscape of Auction Houses

Let's examine briefly some of the issues associated with the eBay strategy model. As the competition grows in this arena, the first big battle (after the initial early branding battle) is that of market share. Ultimately this will lead to consolidation through acquisition, the arena being finally composed of several large sites and a few smaller niche players. The driver behind this is that no one wishes to visit a site with no items at auction or place an item where there are no bids.[7] In this competitive arena the brand leverage will play a part, but this is the *Woolworth's factor*[8]—we know who they are and we know what we can get, but are they relevant *to me* the customer? The key is in the execution, because, once the arena becomes a market share game, this will create a battle in two dimensions: the price and the service, a vector of which is *value* in the eyes of the customer. Price will be driven by volume and by operating efficiencies, service by added-value information.

> An e-marketspace is driven by price and service, where
> - Price will be driven by volume and by operating efficiencies.
> - Service will be driven by added-value information.

The magnitude of this price-service proposition has already been felt. On June 10, 1999, due to system failures, eBay suffered a 22-hour auction site outage so that it was unable to add any new items to its auction lists. There were two reactions: that of the customers and that of the financial markets. The auction site lost 300,000 items off its auction lists. The customers' reactions in the press were mixed—some were unhappy; others, perhaps more tech-savvy, were unfazed by this outage; but few wanted a repeat. The clearer measure of the outage was reflected on Wall Street. The stock made its largest-ever one-day

---

7. In e-commerce jargon, this is termed "liquidity."

8. Woolworth's offered low service levels and added little value after price.

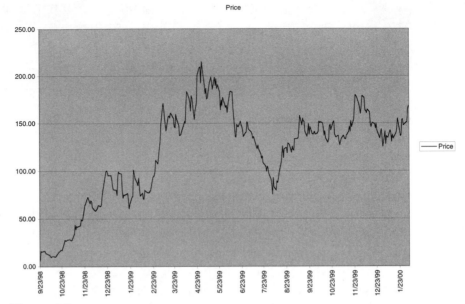

Figure 1.2
eBay's Stock Prices over Time

plunge of $29\frac{7}{8}$ to 136 on a volume of 14.9 million shares, losing more than $4 billion in stock value, or 18 percentage points (see Figure 1.2). This was also based on reports that (98Q1) quarterly sales could fall $3 to $5 million short of consensus revenue estimates of $40 million (the company actually had revenues of only $34 million in the first quarter of 1999, albeit a 469% increase over the $6.0 million reported for the same period the year before[9]). Although the company still has staggering capitalization with astronomical price-to-sales and price-to-earnings ratios, this was a black day and a warning for a one-income-stream online organization. Meg Whitman, the CEO of eBay, wrote to customers, "We know that you expect uninterrupted service from eBay. We believe that this is reasonable, and we know we haven't lived up to your expectations. We want to earn back your trust that we'll provide you with this level of service."[10] Clearly the focus for eBay and other service-driven online organizations has to be on ensuring a fault-tolerant revenue stream from users'

---

9. Press Release: eBay Inc., "Financial Results," San Jose, CA, April 26, 1999, www.ebay.com/community/aboutebay/investor/q1-99.html

10. Scott Ard and Tim Clark, "eBay Blacks Out Yet Again," CNET News.com. June 13, 1999, 11:00 A.M. PT.

transactions. Subsequently, eBay announced that it would delay its new site design and shut down its "My eBay" personalization feature to focus on the reliability issues surrounding its site.

In eBay's experience, we had a classic case of underestimating demand and overestimating the technology, both causing an impact on the stability of the transaction volume, and hence revenues. When the competition really becomes aggressive from a price perspective, this can severely damage a company's ability to compete.

The second dimension of the Woolworth's factor is that of service or of *added value* to the customer beyond pricing. This was also damaged at eBay as a consequence of the outage, and consequently the brand was damaged. According to the market research firm Jupiter Research, of customers who experience an outage

- ☞ 53% make no changes in their behavior.
- ☞ 9% stop using a site altogether.
- ☞ 24% find an alternative site and then continue to use both sites.
- ☞ 13% find a new site but use it only once.[11]

Even though eBay gave free transactions to those customers who lost sales and trade, this post-condition service policy is a mop-up practice at best and generally leaves the customer unsatisfied. It is similar to the airline customers who are offered a $50 pass for a flight on the airline that has just left them sitting in an airport for 18 hours due to problems with locating a flight crew to fly the plane—the next time they just go on another carrier and throw away the $50 token coupon.

The outage at eBay had an even more significant impact on the company than simply losing a few hours of online trading. It forced eBay to reassess its technology leadership strategy, and in fact eBay temporarily had to stop production of the next generation of product offering, which, in an environment where first-mover technology leadership is a powerful competitive weapon, created a valuable opportunity—if only briefly—for its competitors. The second-generation site was intended to encourage customers to personalize their

---

11. Tim Clark, "eBay Outages Nothing New," CNET News.com. June 14, 1999, 1:35 P.M. PT.

interaction with eBay by entering large amounts of personal data. Having done so, customers would be reluctant to repeat the process at a competitor's site—effectively locking customers into eBay's site.

However, concurrently not all is negative and defensive at eBay. With the bread-and-butter transactional issues, eBay is also on the offense. While staying in its vertical auction market, eBay is diversifying across sectors, purchasing Butterfield & Butterfield, an established "bricks-and-mortar" auction house specializing in the appraisal and sale of fine art, antiques, and objects. The company is also a part of the International Auctioneers Network, an alliance of six of the world's largest auction houses. A second investment in the market segmentation strategy was the purchase of a stake in the automobile auction house Kruse International. This moves them toward several positive strategic goals:

☞ It generates greater brand recognition across the industry segments.
☞ It increases the volume of transactions and hence commissions and revenue.
☞ It allows economies of scale in transaction processing costs.
☞ It grows eBay's market share.

All of these benefits contribute to achieving one of the key strategic goals—growth of market share through diversification within the auction market space.

Meanwhile, Amazon has also pursued a growth strategy that aims to grow its brand, its market share, and its sphere of influence in the auction space. At Amazon, the regular "classified-section," which is the equivalent of the eBay.com site, is also aimed at being a high-transaction-based site with an associated revenue stream. To counter the Butterfield & Butterfield dimension of eBay's strategy, Amazon has developed its own premium auction site. This has been achieved through a coalition with Sotheby's, one of the most prestigious auction house brands, a company founded in London in 1744 which today has 104 offices in 41 countries. While not buying Sotheby's completely, Amazon purchased a million shares of Sotheby's stock at \$35.44 a share and an option on a further million shares at \$100 each.[12] This joint venture and

---

12. Press Release: New York, London, Seattle, "Sotheby's and Amazon.com Launch Sothebys.Amazon.com," November 19, 1999.

shared stake in the future of auctioning comes at a time when more choices than ever are available to the customer. The customer is pushing more and more to minimize the costs associated with auction transactions while attempting to maximize the service dimension by forcing organizations to provide ever higher levels of service in order to retain their business. Customers will be interested in low-cost transactions for day-to-day items and will expect auction houses to provide certain basic information-based services as a matter of course: creditworthy ratings on bidders, good-trade ratings on merchants, and so on. Similarly, for premium items, the total *value proposition* will be the dimension that determines if the auction house earns its transaction fee, e.g., product dating assurances from the buyer, currency transactions by sellers, and purchaser verification. In this case Amazon and eBay are buying organizations' skills and attempting to ascend as rapidly as possible up the learning and experience curves, which as we have already stated is a necessity because the first to market is often the only one to market.

Born on the Net: Pillars of Success

From our consideration of eBay and Amazon we see that the born-on-the-Internet organizations have many of the start-up pains that previous generations of technology pioneers had. The Internet arena is similar to that of the computer arena in the 1980s—we might ask ourselves what happened to Osbourne, Commodore, Timex, Sinclair, Tandy, Apricot, Wang, Bull, Prime, Apollo, and on and on? Did they not have the same issues? Osbourne, for example, was first to market with a "portable computer," but its business strategy model was poorly executed and that first-mover advantage was lost.

Examination and research of the strategies of over 40 organizations for this book revealed that those organizations that were born on the Internet and have prospered did so through a strong position in four key pillars of success: technology, marketing, service, and branding (see Table 1.1).

The basic points in Table 1.1 are only a few of the factors that face executives of new online organizations, all of which are attempting to create a winning Internet e-commerce strategy. Few will succeed and many will fail. Throughout this book, we will look at these issues and use the research base to develop solid models to help executives create winning strategies and obtain a deeper knowledge of their own strategic options.

First, however, let's consider the situation in which an existing company needs to reposition its strategy in light of the pressure from Internet e-commerce.

Table 1.1 Leadership Factors for New Internet-based Organizations

Leadership Factor	The Pillars of Success for Organizations Born on the Internet
Technology	• The technology goal must be understood for that organization within its industry and market. • An organization must determine if it is going to be an advanced technology leader or follow a technology agenda that relies upon more stable systems (bleeding versus leading edge). • An organization must determine what is the necessary relationship between the company's technology or product strategy and the operational aspects of that strategy. • The technology employed by an organization must service the customers' needs and expectations from a technology perspective. • Organizations must ask themselves questions such as "Are we a technology company? Can the technology be used to create barriers to entry? Can technology be used to lock in a customer base?" Organizations must have clearly defined the answers to these questions and must work them into their business plan.
Market	• An organization must determine its target market and whether it is still realistically open to new entrants. • An organization must understand how the market is going to segment and grow over the near and longer term and know whether the organization will be able to move rapidly enough to meet those changing needs. • Being born on the Net requires that the organization understand the possible moves from major established organizations and utilize its own nimbleness to counter them.
Service	• An organization must know its customers' expectations regarding service level. • The organization must understand what its value proposition is and how service facilitates or augments it. • An organization must understand its own Internet service value chain, the components of which are — Understanding the relationship between attracting customers and service levels.

Table 1.1 Leadership Factors for New Internet-based Organizations (Continued)

Leadership Factor	The Pillars of Success for Organizations Born on the Internet
Service (continued)	— Understanding how an organization creates service value during a transaction for a customer. — Understanding how service plays a role in the customer fulfillment process, where the purchase is dispatched. — Understanding the role of customer service in retaining customers and maintaining site adhesion.

Brand	• An organization must understand whether it has the ability to create a strong brand.
	
	• An organization must understand the basis of its brand. Is it
	
	  — Technology leadership?
	
	  — Service provision?
	
	  — Market positioning?

Existing Organizations: Move to the Net

The impact of technology change upon organizations and industries can be rapid and dramatic, leaving organizations that are unprepared without a second chance to stay in the game. The enemy of size is change, and the biggest killer in corporate America is *inertia* caused by vested interests, structural inflexibility, and corporate executive blinders. This is obviously not a new phenomenon; it has always been this way. Technology equals change, and certain sectors fear change. For example, in early industrial England the Luddites[13]

---

13. "Luddites: Early 19th-Century workmen who destroyed factory machinery. The name derives from the signature 'Ned Ludd', used on a workmen's manifesto (the original Ned Ludd being reputedly a Leicestershire youth who broke some machinery in 1799). Organized Luddite activity broke out in the textile factories in Nottinghamshire, Derbyshire, Leicestershire, and Yorkshire in 1811–12 and was renewed in 1816. The government fearing a revolutionary conspiracy (and having no effective police forces) repressed Luddite rioting harshly; in 1813 some 17 men were executed at York [England]. Luddism (like earlier machine-smashing episodes) was a desperate attempt to preserve jobs, thought to be threatened by the new machines of the industrial revolution, at a time of economic distress provoked by the Napoleonic War." *The Wordsworth Dictionary of British History*, Market House Books, 1994.

smashed the Spinning Jennies[14] to save their jobs. They lost the jobs anyway, and the wealth creation of the industrial revolution in England powered that nation's economy and world growth, just as today the Internet and technology is powering the productive growth in the American economy and consequent growth in the rest of the world.

> **"Inertia kills."**
> The enemy of size is change; the biggest killer in corporate America is inertia.

A traditional assessment of an organization's competitive position may be made through frameworks such as Michael Porter's five forces model.[15] His model focuses on determination of the power held by buyers and suppliers in an industry, factoring in the threat posed by new entrants as well as the potential of substitute products. Strategists have utilized this model for nearly two decades. However, business plans created using this static snapshot approach are potentially flawed, because their assumptions are based on linear time planning horizons in which everyone's watches run at the same speed. Traditional industries and organizations that have followed and accepted this approach have, as a consequence, potential weaknesses in their management thinking and planning. A Fortune 100 company executive paints this picture:

> Think about being the head of Barnes & Noble, and you have just got promoted after 20 years in the business. You're now the CEO; everything is going great! You have all the high street stores that you're rolling out around the world. Then you open the paper and you read that some guy has started a business to sell books over the Internet at a 40% discount and has claimed that he is now the biggest bookstore with 2.5 million titles. It is impossible for you to ever carry [that many] in your bookstore and he has a level of service that you wish you could have in a physical distribution system. Suddenly your industry has changed forever.[16]

---

14. "Spinning Jenny: A machine patented (1770) by Hargreaves for spinning a number of threads simultaneously. It extended the principle of the spinning wheel by carrying several spindles (ultimately 120) vertically." *The Wordsworth Dictionary of British History*, Market House Books, 1994.

15. Michael E. Porter, *Cases in Competitive Strategy*, Free Press, 1983.

16. Taped conference presentation, Miami, FL, September 1, 1998.

Amazon operates in the domain of Internet time and can ship a book directly to its customer faster than a traditional book company can get that same book to its retail outlet. And often times a store has to order the book and then, upon its arrival from the wholesaler and distributor, call the customer who has to pick it up. The effect of time compression possible with the Internet is visible in the living room and the boardroom of the families and corporations living and operating in the American lifestyle paradigm.

> The Internet does not operate in linear time; the world of e-commerce compresses time.

Time Compression and Adding Value: The Customer's Home

In the living room, customers want everything NOW, no delay, NOW. Perhaps this is an American-led phenomenon, as we truly want all things that we PAY for NOW. Our purchasing decision is an extension of our need to have our capital working for us; hence the immediate demand for goods upon payment is a natural extension of our free market, capitalistic society. "I have $50, and I want to buy a book on the birds of Venezuela. I want it now, not when the store can get it"—that is operating in linear time. "I have $45,000, and I want a black Lincoln Navigator. I want it now, not in 3 weeks. I have the cash; I want the transaction to occur." Customers do not have time to stretch out transactions. Society has focused customers to expect the move from conceptualization of a trade to execution to occur in one step. The Internet is the next time-compression engine of trade or, viewed in a more traditional manner, the engine of productivity growth. It is not a coincidence that the advent of the Internet and the "new economy"[17] has coincided with the longest bull market in American corporate history. The pain of the reengineering efforts of the 1990s facilitating mass customization and huge productivity improvements are finally coming onstream and are facilitated and leveraged through the new Internet channel.

The customer is still not satisfied, however, and wishes to compress time further. A customer who, for example, in the 1980s moved from purchasing home building products at four different stores, each store providing a different part,

---

17. Press Release: The White House, Office of the Press Secretary. "Remarks by the President at Massachusetts Institute of Technology 1998 Commencement, Killian Court Campus of Massachusetts Institute of Technology, Cambridge, Massachusetts," Lincoln, MA, June 5, 1998.

now goes to one megastore such as Home Depot in the United States or the U.K.'s B&Q. However, talk to that customer, and you will hear the time compression dimension in the discussion. He doesn't want to drive to the store every day during a home improvement or building project, search the aisles, stand in line to pay, and hope no one has dinged his car with a cartload of wood in the parking lot. He wants the materials on demand, delivered at low cost. But the logistical dimension adds value in only one way. It is the second dimension of the value proposition where the true earning potential lies. The customer will demand that the organization with whom he is transacting add value through offering information or risk losing the business to a deep discount outlet. He will request greater content—e.g., "How do I install a garbage disposal?" We can easily envisage an online shopping experience for home building products that cannot be far away, where a customer, armed with a portable digital camera and a high-speed wireless data link at his work site, orders through an online catalog, has the product delivered to the door within the hour, and then solves problems online via a *customer contact point* where helpful experts give advice as they monitor the project through the digital camera and Internet linkage.

> Society has focused customers to expect the move from conceptualization of a trade to execution to occur in one step.

Time Compression and Adding Value: The Corporate Boardroom

In the boardroom, the experiences of the customer online have been translated directly into action by several boards of directors. An interesting coincidence was the resignation on April 21, 1999, of Philip M. Pfeffer, CEO of Borders Group Inc., the book-selling chain, following those of Compaq Computer's CEO Eckhard Pfeiffer and CFO Earl Mason on April 19, 1999. Both companies cited "vanilla" reasons for their executives' moves. But careful examination shows that the two companies are undergoing crises at the strategic implementation of an e-commerce strategy.

Borders.com?

Borders is the second largest U.S. bookstore, earning $84.2 million in 1998 on sales of $2.67 billion with a profitability of 3.2%.[18] However, Borders has

---

18. Borders Group Inc., Annual Report, 1998, 1999.

failed not only to keep pace with the growth in sales of its traditional rival Barnes & Noble, but it has also been late coming to the online marketspace. Barnes & Noble, which in 1998 had earnings of $94.3 million on sales of $3.07 billion and profitability of 3.1%,[19] grew over the 5-year period ending in 1999 at a rate of 17.58%, while Borders grew at a modest 13.62%. Even though 5-year sales growth data is not available yet for Amazon, its year-over-year growth is in the range of 200% against 16% for both Barnes & Noble and Borders, leading to a reevaluation of the market dynamics by traditional booksellers.

Borders is suffering significantly from being late to the online arena. It believed that customers would prefer to wait and deal with a known brand through a high-quality Website rather than transact with newcomers. Analysts on Wall Street point to this as a reason for disappointing earnings from Borders' "dot com" division. Borders.com had sales of only $5 million in 1998 against $610 million for Amazon. However, Borders.com by the third quarter of 1999 started to pick up steam, and sales increased 193% to $4.1 million over the same quarter in 1998. Amazon meanwhile had not been standing still and registered net sales of $1.64 billion for the whole of 1999, a 169% increase over its 1998 figures. Of course this war is not yet over and Amazon has not yet turned a profit. But, with a market capitalization approaching $30 billion[20] against $1.7 billion for BarnesandNoble.com and $0.5 billion for Borders it is a powerful adversary.

> **Borders Founder Delivers Groceries**
>
> An interesting and ironic footnote: In 1999 the former chairman and cofounder of Borders, Louis Borders, started his own Web venture—Webvan, a provider of online groceries—backed with $120 million in start-up funds from CBS, Knight-Ridder, and Japan's Softbank. It has a capitalization of $5 billion and 1999 sales of $13.3 million.

While the traditional bricks-and-mortar booksellers have been trying to integrate themselves into an online world, the online book king Amazon has quietly been doing the reverse, growing its warehousing capacity. This has been a disturbing trend for some analysts who worry that the disappearance of the

---

19. Barnes & Noble, Annual Report, 1998, 1999.
20. Barnes & Noble, February 2000.

frictionless economic model of the virtual company will bring associated real transaction costs. However, the proposition is not necessarily so dark as they envisage; while traditional vendors are attempting to reengineer their existing processes, Amazon is creating its processes from scratch and in a way that matches its business model. The reason that Amazon has to create this infrastructure is that, for a virtual organization to function effectively, all organizations associated with that organization need to have highly efficient value chains based upon information technology. Unfortunately, Amazon has found that this is not the case, and the place where the "rubber meets the road" is the wholesaler, whose inventory management and logistics systems are designed to service bulk shipments to retail outlets—shipping, for example, 50 copies of each of the New York Times top 10 to all the stores of Borders, Barnes & Noble, etc. Wholesalers' systems are not geared to supply one copy each of 150,000 titles every day to Amazon and then on to different shipping addresses. Hence the need for Amazon to create a warehouse distribution network. Once the wholesaler becomes efficient, then Amazon may choose to discard its warehouses, but that raises an interesting point. What is then to prevent the wholesalers from backward integrating and taking on Amazon direct? Answer: Amazon has branded the customers' experience and has passed through the learning curve with respect to the lead time for ordering books; if the publishers could actually publish to order, the wholesaler might also feel a stress from that aspect of the supply chain. However this gives us a further insight into Amazon's strength and strategy. Amazon is not as vulnerable as a traditional retailer is; its relationships are its strength. The publishers cannot undermine Amazon's position with its customers because, as stated before, customers wish to consolidate their time and expenditure of effort; hence they will rarely look to a publisher directly as a point of purchase because each publisher will generally list only its own books. Amazon cannot be undermined by the wholesalers because Amazon has developed one of, if not *the*, online brand, a brand that will be very difficult, bar a catastrophic event, to overcome.

Compaq.com?

Compaq Computer Corporation, whose recent strategy has been growth through acquisition, purchasing Tandem Computers (parallel performance machines for high-end fault-tolerant applications), Cray (supercomputers), Altavista (Internet search engine), and Digital Equipment Corporation (PCs to superservers to reduced instruction set computers [RISC] machines). However, Compaq's strategy for PC sales has been subject to significant market pressure.

The largest volume PC maker in 1994,[21] Compaq was slow to adopt a direct Internet-based sales channel, remaining loyal to its physical retail outlets but not effectively leveraging that retail presence. Compaq also had difficulty changing its inventory model to the direct order model used by leading competitors, such as Dell. The cost of not moving to the mass customization, build-on-demand philosophy has been high. While Compaq's annual report for 1998 acknowledges the need to be nimble, again the conceptual and operational strategies are not aligned.

> Business cycles that used to be measured in years or months are now measured in days, hours or minutes. One-size-fits-all is out. One-size-fits-one is in. On the Web, big is not better. Speed, agility, flexibility and responsiveness are. The Internet is even reshaping our old notions of time. The Internet economy is a non-stop, 24-hour-a-day, 7-day-a-week environment. These are not small changes. They are fundamental changes that are transforming information technology from a back-office function to a strategic asset—one that allows companies to build a competitive advantage.[22]

Compaq's own operational execution lacked the speed, agility, flexibility, and responsiveness that it recognizes as vital. This lack of vision can be fatal. The impact of the Internet is not just limited to its PC sales division. In August 1999, Compaq sold 83% of the advanced search engine Altavista, originally created by DEC, to CMGI. These issues combined with the loss of the CEO and the general uncertainty of strategic direction creates unease in the minds of financial industry analysts. The sale of such a prime, once-in-a-lifetime asset at a time when a company has no permanent CEO may jeopardize the company's future ability to create the low-cost, information-based value proposition customers desire. Ultimately the organization may see this day as the day its fate was decided.

Move to the Net: Pillars of Success

In researching and examining the e-commerce strategies employed by traditional, established organizations, the four key pillars of success again surfaced—technology, marketing, service, and branding (see Table 1.2). As was the case

---

21. Compaq Computer Corporation, Annual Report, 1998, www.compaq.com/corporate/1998ar/letter/english03_nf.html

22. Ibid.

Table 1.2 Leadership Factors for Established Organizations

Leadership Factor	*The Pillars of Success for Traditional Established Organizations*
Technology	• An organization must understand what the total technology implications are for that organization—Internet, enterprise resource planning, data warehouse, etc.
	• Organizations must know whether their processes are aligned to an Internet technology-based approach.
	• An organization must understand how its customers view and use technology within the marketspace and must leverage that knowledge to build an effective infrastructure that facilitates an agile and flexible e-commerce strategy.
	• An organization must assess its internal value chain as well as those of its suppliers and build to minimize costs and maximize efficiencies.
Market	• An organization must understand what the implications of e-commerce and technology are for the marketspace in which the organization is to compete in terms of:
	— Branding
	— Relationship management
	• An organization must determine whether its target market is the same as its traditional bricks-and-mortar marketspace or if it has moved.
	• If its core marketspace has moved, is it still realistically open to traditional organizations moving onto the Net?
	• An organization must understand how the market is going to segment and grow over the near future due to the impact of the Internet and must determine whether the organization will be able to move rapidly enough to meet those changing needs.
	• Organizations must assess the impact of pure Internet-based organizations and use their own traditional core strengths—market knowledge and product knowledge—to offset Internet-based companies' nimbleness.
Service	• An organization must determine the new service level expectations of the customer.
	• An organization must understand what the customers' new value proposition requirements are in terms of cost, service level expectations, and information-based service.

Table 1.2 Leadership Factors for Established Organizations (Continued)

Leadership Factor	The Pillars of Success for Traditional Established Organizations
Service (continued)	• Organizations must reassess their service value chain.
	— How are we going to acquire customers?
	— How are we going to develop customer relationships through the new medium?
	— How can we best fulfill the customers' needs—bricks and mortar, clicks and mortar, or online?
	— How do we support our customers during purchase and through order fulfillment?
	— How do we retain customers between orders?
Brand	• Organizations need to determine how to best leverage their existing brand.
	— Do we have the ability to create a strong dot-com brand?
	— What is the basis of that brand?
	— What are the implications for our brand in terms of the technology we employ, develop, or use?
	— What are the challenges for creating a new dot-com brand
	— Does the Internet demand an amendment or a completely new service provision?
	— Will new brand positioning change our existing brand?

with the born-on-the-Net organizations, within these leadership areas, many issues need to be considered, faced, and integrated in order to create a successful e-commerce strategy.

Again, these basic questions are only a few of those that face organizations attempting to reposition themselves and create winning Internet e-commerce strategies. However, we can see from our initial study of Borders, Compaq Computers, and Barnes & Noble that three other important dimensions play a role in the success of e-commerce strategies.

☞ Leadership

☞ Infrastructure

☞ Organizational learning

Let's consider the basic issues in these areas before developing them in depth throughout the remainder of the book (see Table 1.3).

Table 1.3 Bonding Factors Toward the Development of an E-commerce Strategy

Bonding Factors	Issues
Leadership	• Does the CEO have a vision for e-commerce?
	• Does the CEO have a track record of taking technology change in stride?
	• Do the senior executives share a technology vision? Also, do they understand its impact upon their functional area and the organization as a whole?
	• Is the leadership stable or in a continual state of flux?
Infrastructure	• Can the organization's technology infrastructure support the new model of e-business?
	• Can the organization's technology infrastructure support the move to mass customization?
	• What are the implications for the organizational changes needed to be competitive in an e-commerce environment?
	• Does the organization's infrastructure interface with the infrastructures of their suppliers and customers in the electronic marketspace?
Organizational Learning	• Does the organization support internal learning?
	— Scanning the technology horizon for change and then adopting that change where appropriate
	— Developing a self-awareness inside the boundaries of the organization to drive practice and process change
	• Can the learning of the organization with respect to markets, product, technology, processes, etc., be quickly refocused into a new technology-based method of production?

This book will examine all these issues in depth and create solid models to help executives obtain a deeper knowledge of their own strategic options, so that they can go on to develop winning Internet strategies.

Infomediaries and Business-to-Business Consortia

E-consortia: Swarming to the Net

The marketspace of the Internet is no longer composed of just two organizational types—the online born-on-the-Net organization and the established traditional organizational form that is attempting to move to the Internet. A third competitive force has evolved—the *e-consortium*—in which a set of organizations form a consortium to create an online entity in an area in which their individual strengths can be better leveraged to create future value. The effect of e-consortia is to cut down on the customer's search effort and to provide a cornucopia of product offerings specific to the customer's needs.

> An e-consortium is an online entity positioned within a marketspace through which a group of organizations' individual strengths can be combined and leveraged to create future value.

Auction.com: An Auction Consortium

The auction arena on the Internet is extremely competitive, dominated by eBay, Amazon, and Yahoo! However, they are not alone in the space, and many organizations are busily attempting to create new market segments in the auction arena; in fact there are currently over 40 auction sites alone. The major problem most of these start-ups have is that they cannot differentiate themselves, and without differentiation viewers and sellers are impossible to attract. Their problem emanates from attempting to follow the first movers and copy their models, when what they need is a new business model. One such approach is the e-consortia. Consortia aim to allow organizations with individual access to data and customer "eyeballs" to truly leverage their position. The members of the consortium may also individually have existing strengths such as scale of economy through their physical presence, whether that is as an existing online organization, a clicks-and-mortar organization, or a traditional bricks-and-mortar organization. The aim of this business model is to combine their individual strengths to compete in cyberspace as one. This not only increases their reach but shares the costs. The e-consortia concept has a strong growth potential through Internet technologies, offering significant branding as well as market scale and scope opportunities to the members who unite by combining otherwise discrete markets.

An example of an e-consortium is Auction.com, a site initially with little public brand recognition, but with some very serious backers. Auction Universe, the company behind Auction.com, is part of Classified Ventures, Inc., an Internet services business formed and funded by eight leading media companies: Central Newspapers, Inc.; Gannett Co., Inc.; Knight-Ridder; The McClatchy Company; The New York Times Company; The Times Mirror Company; Tribune Company; and the Washington Post Company. With an expanding and lucrative auction market evolving on the Internet, the natural extension for these news giants is to link their classified advertisements from the local sources together into one large online auction site.

One scenario is that, upon agreeing to a reserve price potentially equal to the sale price of the item in the newspaper, a seller allows the item to be placed on the online auction. Through this action, the newspaper not only gets its guaranteed advertising revenue at the source for the print copy, but it also gets a commission on a bigger sale price at auction, which also makes the seller happy—a true win-win situation. However, the site has lacked the branding exposure that the top-tier sites have enjoyed; moreover, the liquidity of the sales floor is currently limited.

The future of e-consortia is vast; it represents a major step away from the one-to-one business-to-customer (B2C) experiences currently offered through individually branded Websites. However, there are several other new e-commerce category types emerging, such as the business-to-business (B2B), business-to-government (B2G), and government-to-business (G2B) e-commerce marketspace. Let's consider these in a little more detail.

B2C, B2B, B2G, and G2B

Business-to-Customer E-commerce

B2C can be considered an electronic-based marketplace through which a retail customer wishing to make a transaction interacts with an organization. Examples of pure online B2C-based organizations are Amazon.com, eBay, and Priceline.com. Traditional bricks-and-mortar organizations that have gone online and sell directly to the retail market are also in this B2C category and include Toys R Us, Wal-Mart, and Sony.

Business-to-Business E-commerce

The basis of this marketplace is the creation of transactions between commercial entities. This can be, in its most basic form, a business-to-consumer (B2C) transaction where a company purchases its computers one at a time from a manufacturer through the retail Website. However, this is clearly inefficient when the organization wishes to purchase hundreds, thousands, or even millions of components from multiple sources of supply. This is where the B2B "hub" or portal has filled the gap. According to Gartner Group, Inc., data, the worldwide B2B market for B2B services is projected to grow from $403 billion in 2000 to $7.29 trillion in 2004, and it projects that, by 2004, B2B e-commerce will represent 7% of the forecasted $105 trillion total global sales transactions.[23]

There are two types of B2B portals: the *vertical portal* and the *horizontal portal.* A vertical portal provides specialized services across several industries; a horizontal portal primarily provides a set of services across a single industry.

Vertical B2B Portals

A leading developer of vertical B2B portals is VerticalNet.com which created and operates a portfolio of *vertical trade communities* in a variety of industries including

- ☞ Advanced technologies
- ☞ Communications
- ☞ Environment
- ☞ Food and packing
- ☞ Food service/hospitality
- ☞ Healthcare/science
- ☞ Manufacturing and metals
- ☞ Process
- ☞ Service

Within the healthcare/science industry, for example, VerticalNet.com created a series of specialized communities such as

- ☞ *Biosearch.com*—an online community for biotechnology and life sciences
- ☞ *Drugdiscoveryonline.com*—a community for the pharmaceutical industry

---

23. "GartnerGroup Forecasts Worldwide Business-to-Business ECommerce to Reach $7.29 Trillion in 2004: E-Market Makers to be Key Driver of Business-to-Business Segment," San Jose, CA, January 26, 2000. www.gartner12.gartnerweb.com/public/static/aboutgg/pressrel/pr012600c.html

☞ *Nurses.com*—a community for the nursing community

☞ *Homehealthprovider.com*—a community for the professionals and executives associated with professions in the home health services segment

These sites aim at providing one-stop shopping for all services and information relating to a particular specialized domain or professional area.

Other vertical B2B organizations have focused more deeply in specific areas. One of these organizations is Commerx, which created PlasticsNet.com, the first B2B portal in that industry, thus gaining significant brand leadership as a first mover in the domain. It aims to provide "a neutral, secure marketplace that streamlines the procurement of plastics and services."[24] The PlasticsNet.com site provides a marketspace for buyers and suppliers in this community to come together, in addition to providing the industry with rich specific content.

Horizontal or Functional B2B Portals

The goal of a functional or horizontal B2B portal is to provide a basis of expertise that can be tapped into by organizations in multiple domains. An example of such a portal is Grainger.com. Grainger.com is a B2B horizontal portal that both distributes maintenance, repair, and operating (MRO) supplies to customers across multiple domains and provides resource centers relating product information and solutions to those customers.

B2B Does Not Necessarily Mean Born on the Net

William W. Grainger founded his company in Chicago in 1927. He wanted to provide an efficient solution to the need for a speedy and consistent supply of electric motors, a need not then being met by the motor manufacturers. *The MotorBook*, as the Grainger catalog was originally called, was an 8-page wholesale catalog that grew to $250,000 in sales within 6 years.

Today Grainger's has more than $3 billion in annual sales and is the nation's leading business-to-business distributor of maintenance, repair, and operating (MRO) supplies and related information.

Adapted from: www.grainger.com/about/index.htm

Horizontal portals allow those organizations with wide product offerings to come to the Internet and provide an electronic marketplace for their wares. The horizontal hubs primarily function as single owner-operators; however,

---

24. www.commerx.com/main.htm

there is no reason why multiple organizations could not collaborate as a horizontal portal. For example, a law center portal or a business services portal could combine the talents of many specialists at one location.

Business-to-Government E-commerce

As was the case with B2B, the B2G e-commerce can be subdivided into vertical markets and horizontal markets. Grainger, for example, has created within its portal a section specifically for the U.S. government and its agencies.[25] Having secured contracts with the General Services Administration and being a registered U.S. Government Javits-Wagner-O'Day (JWOD) program member, it is able to supply customers with goods as mandated under the appropriate regulatory framework.

The U.S. Federal Government's JWOD Program

The Javits-Wagner-O'Day (JWOD) Program creates employment and training opportunities for people who are blind or have other severe disabilities and, whenever possible, prepares them for competitive jobs. Under the JWOD Program, government employees are required to buy selected supplies and services from nonprofit agencies employing such persons. As a result, federal government customers obtain quality products and services at reasonable prices, while JWOD employees are able to lead more productive, independent lives.

Source: www.fss.gsa.gov/jwod.html

Vertical B2G portals also exist within the e-commerce environment which provide a specialized service to the government to fill a specialized need. This might include providing clerical services such as the processing of passports or fingerprints for the FBI and the INS or the fulfillment of a government contact supplying large volumes of information, goods, and expertise through the Internet channel.

Government-to-Business E-commerce

Clearly governments worldwide spend an enormous amount of money each year fulfilling requests for information from business in the form of reports,

---

25. www.grainger.com/gsa.htm

regulations, forms, and so on. The ability of governments to streamline the processes by providing documentation online and making the task of searching for documents easier will be an enormous boost to business and a cost reduction for the government. This is the focus of the G2B systems.

The U.S. government has established a portal through the Whitehouse.gov site known as the "Commonly Requested Federal Services" designed to provide Americans with one-stop access to federal services—online transactions, forms and publications available for downloading and printing, and information. Whitehouse.gov states: "Our long term goal is to offer the American people the ability to conduct all of their business with the Federal government electronically."[26] The portal facilitates access to major government institutions such as the Internal Revenue Service, Department of Labor, U.S. Office of Personnel Management, Department of Defense, and Department of Housing and Urban Development.

Interorganizational Systems: B2C, Consortia, B2B, B2G, G2B

The five different e-business models that developed above are all opportunities that can be pursued by an organization wishing to undertake commerce on the Internet. An organization born on the Internet can be positioned in any of these sectors and a business plan developed accordingly. Similarly there is no reason why an organization cannot transition or reposition itself to the Internet in any of these spaces and continue to flourish, as was demonstrated by Grainger, originally founded in 1927 as a catalog company.

The key is to determine the core competencies of your organization, determine the limitations in the new marketspace, and assess the mechanisms available to move forward. This may mean that the business will change radically, moving from a retail space to a governmental space or joining up with companies that were once competitors to create a consortium. Throughout the book we will discuss these issues and look at how a company can determine its technology, brand, service, and market strengths and then lay out strategic options in each of these areas.

---

26. www.White house.gov/WH/Services/info.html

Summary

Organizations that undertake e-commerce do so from one of two possible starting points:

☞ New online organizations—*born on the Net*—built on flexibility and agility

☞ Traditional established organizations *moving to the Internet* and repositioning themselves to take advantage of that marketspace

Several factors are key to determining an organization's potential for success:

☞ Does the organization possess first-mover advantage in the marketspace?

☞ Does the organization differentiate itself in the marketspace?

☞ Does the organization possess the ability to be flexible and agile in the electronic marketspace?

Having strength in at least two of these areas will give an organization the opportunity to compete in the online world. Its ability to compete is based upon its self-awareness and control over the four dimensions of its strategic vector:

1. Technology
2. Brand
3. Market
4. Service

A leadership position is achieved only when all four of these parameters are balanced. An organization that has great technology but low service quality will not be able to compete effectively against an organization whose brand is strong and which fulfills customer transactions with quality service supported and enabled through its technology.

These four areas form the basis for the creation of a unified strategy. However, in order for an organization to accomplish this and then to execute effectively over time, three other success factors need to be in place:

☞ Strong corporate leadership at the executive level

☞ A flexible infrastructure and information technology (IT) architecture

☞ A commitment to organizational learning

The ability of an organization to understand, cultivate, and develop these parameters is key to performance and consequently survival in the online world of e-commerce.

However, organizations have to determine the market they wish to serve and the mechanism through which they wish to service that market. Five types of mechanisms can be adopted:

- ☞ B2C (business to customer). The enterprise services the needs of the retail customer.
- ☞ B2B (business to business). An enterprise services the needs of other businesses. This is accomplished through either a *vertical portal* or a *horizontal portal.* Vertical portals offer a service or product to a single industry type, while horizontal portals offer a service across multiple industries.
- ☞ B2G (business to government). An enterprise services the needs of a government or its agencies.
- ☞ G2B (government to business). Governments interact with businesses (or citizens) through government portals.
- ☞ The e-consortium. A new vehicle through which multiple businesses come together to provide a leveraged service to either businesses or retail customers; i.e., leveraging the strengths of individual organizations and focusing them as a collective powerful force into the online arena.

The selection of an execution model is not an either/or proposition—an organization can service, for example, the B2B and B2G communities simultaneously, depending upon the nature of the organization. The limitations are, however, that the basic tenets hold: Does the organization possess first-mover advantage in the marketspace? Can it differentiate itself in the marketspace? Can it continue to be flexible and agile in the sectors?

The development and execution of a successful e-commerce strategy is a difficult intellectual and creative task, one that every executive will have to undertake. The building blocks for a successful conceptualization, formulation, and development of such a plan are discussed more fully in the remainder of the book.

Creating an Integrated E-commerce Strategy

Chapter 1 considered some of the issues that underlie e-commerce strategy formulation and noted that the strategy employed will vary depending upon

☞ The nature of the organization—*born on the net* or *move to the net*

☞ The nature of the product—*service based, manufacturing,* or *mixed*

☞ The online model the organization wishes to adopt—*B2C, B2B, and so forth*

In order to understand the process of e-commerce strategy better, a more systematic examination of the strategic factors involved has to be considered. To do this we'll use a model, which with modification can ultimately be utilized across the differing portal environments such as B2C and B2B.

Seven Dimensions of an E-commerce Strategy

The e-commerce strategy of over 40 leading U.S. and European organizations has been closely examined for this book. They represent a variety of industry sectors ranging from manufacturing to service; whose origins range from the most established and traditional of blue chip companies to born-on-the-net start-ups; with revenues ranging from $1 million to over $100 billion; in groups we could label *e-commerce leaders* to those we could label *laggards*. It became clear that the differentiation between those companies that have a successful e-commerce strategy and those that do not is a function of achieving balance among seven major factors (see Figure 2.1):

☞ Four *positional factors*

1. Technology
2. Service
3. Market
4. Brand

☞ Three *bonding factors*

1. Leadership
2. Infrastructure
3. Organizational learning

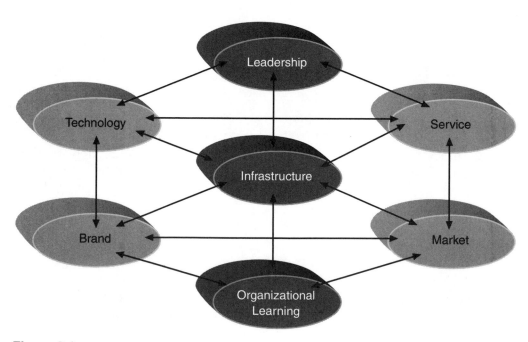

Figure 2.1
The Seven Dimensions of an E-commerce Strategy

It can be argued that the model in Figure 2.1 can be applied to all forms of organization in the traditional industrial and service sectors. This is in fact true, and it is an intentional component of the model's construction. The model is based upon the understanding that all organizations need to continuously address these seven issues, whether they are traditional organizations addressing an investment decision regarding the deployment of a new technology required to speed up a production line, a specialized financial services company on Wall Street determining its ability to operate in the electronic market, or a company born on the Internet that needs to assess its branding. Organizations will always be adjusting their strategies to meet the changing environment in which they operate, and the model aims at assisting executives in understanding the importance and weighting that need to be applied to each factor. However, the model is especially applicable to assisting the needs of e-commerce strategists and is applied to that domain throughout this book. The model is flexible enough that it can be used by giant traditional organizations in their e-strategy formulation processes as they move to the Net, just as it aims to meets the needs of start-up entrepreneurs looking at defining their marketspace and e-strategy from scratch. Furthermore, the nature of the model allows an organization to map its strategy onto any form of vendor-client relationship, whether that relationship is between two businesses, a business and a customer, or any other entity. The basic building blocks are consistent in their structure once the target relationship is determined. For example, should an organization be in a vertical B2G relationship, the dimensions of strategy formulation are no different from those of a B2B relationship. The decisions still involve branding, service levels, marketspace, and technology, but the balance and focus of their interactions change. For example, branding may be less of an issue in a B2G environment than in a B2B environment. However, global fulfillment and the ability to satisfy the agency's service levels may be more of an issue. Thus the aim is to present a flexible framework for e-strategists that facilitates their gaining an understanding of the interactions of the environment within which they are to operate and then developing a successful counterstrategy for their organizational entity.

First let's consider the bonding factors of leadership, infrastructure, and organizational learning. This will enable us to understand both their importance as foundations upon which an organization's e-commerce strategy is based and as a springboard from which all development emanates. This will pave the way to consideration of the four focal points around which a balanced strategy is created: technology, brand, market, and service. Each of these areas presents complex and intricate issues of its own, compounded through the need to achieve a balanced, integrated solution overall—a complete analysis is presented in subsequent chapters. Finally, in order to show how the strategy works in action, we step through a real-world case study of Royal Caribbean International Cruise Lines and its successful online e-commerce strategy through the lenses of this model.

The Bonds of an E-commerce Strategy

The foundations of a strong e-commerce strategy lie in the preparation of the ground before the functional issues are addressed. In this section we will consider three of those issues—leadership, infrastructure, and organizational learning (see Figure 2.2). As we have already seen, the creation of successful e-commerce can reap major rewards for an organization; failure can mean that even the most senior managers are vulnerable and frequently are replaced following an e-commerce strategy failure.

Clearly there is a strong interaction between these three components. For instance, when eBay had its outages, the leadership learned from the experience, upgraded the systems infrastructure, and moved on. Other organizations fail to learn from their experiences and consequently diminish or, like Levi's, are forced to leave the Internet space completely while they rethink their overall strategy.

Leadership

Previous research has shown that the primary drivers of change and the creators of strategic vision in an organization are the CEO and senior executives, a finding mirrored in this research. In every successful e-commerce project studied for this book, a strong project champion was present in the form of a

Figure 2.2
The Bonds of an
E-commerce
Strategy

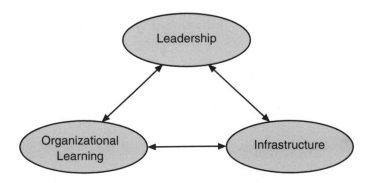

senior executive or someone in a position to demonstrate to a senior executive the potential added value such a project could bring to the organization.

☞ An example of such a leadership-technology meld can be found at Motorola Corporation. Bob Clinton, Director of the Internet Business Group, describes the discovery process:

> Originally we had started back in the summer of 1994 and at that time—this was even before we were aware of the Web—one of the things we were looking at was trying to find a communications vehicle so we could better communicate with our partners. These are channel partners, folks who would sell or resell our equipment. So we created a concept and we called it MOCA for Motorola On-Line Channel Access. Fortuitously, just about this time, around August 1994, going into September, a Motorola employee called me to say he had found a little thing called Mosaic, and we went back to his office and saw him all excited about it and trying to pull it up on the screen, and the thing kept crashing and he kept swearing at his computer. But he said when you finally get around to seeing it, it's really cool! We did see it. The graphics capabilities were pretty limited at the time—just a few icons—primarily text. But the whole concept of this as an available technology was amazing. We saw the opportunity with the Web, we started kicking it around, and I put together a business plan.[1]

This mimics the experience at many other organizations, including:

☞ Charles Schwab, who had a similar moment of Web enlightenment when a group of his researchers put together an experimental demo system for Web-based transactions. They demonstrated it to their chief information officer (CIO) and subsequently to Schwab himself, who subsequently refocused that organization to be a Web-based organization rather than following a traditional brokerage model (see case study, chapter 5).

☞ IBM's Louis Gerstner, who repositioned and transformed that organization based upon the e-business concept.

☞ Ford's Jacques Nasser, who has made e-business an integral part of Ford's strategy.

---

1. Phone interview with author, January 19, 1999.

The search for excellence in leadership within the e-commerce arena and the value corporations place on it can be seen by the rabid activity of the head-hunter community and the speed and volume at which senior executives of traditional organizations are leaving or being poached by dot-com operations. Perhaps the best example of this is the move by George Shaheen from Anderson Consulting to start-up Webvan.com, becoming its president and CEO. Shaheen had been Anderson's managing partner and CEO since the firm became an independent unit in 1989, building it into a $9 billion organization. However, the challenge of developing a very well-funded start-up—in addition to receiving 1.25 million shares of Webvan.com plus an option for 15 million more[2]—was too good an opportunity to turn down.

The market for intellectual capital in the form of experienced, proven, and successful leadership has never been more extreme. However, it is also a time for executives to expand their vision for their organizations and develop creative strategies that can be effectively executed. Failure to transition or demonstrate leadership will inevitably lead to a subsequent change in leadership.

The lessons for executives here are clear:

1. Keep an open mind with regard to all new technologies.
2. Don't get isolated from new and experimental technologies that are coming over the technology horizon.
3. Encourage a "skunks works"[3] (a quickly thrown together, in-house) research team thinking and philosophy.
4. Be ready to make the necessary amount of change in corporate strategy as indicated by the "seismic shock wave" of the technology.

---

2. *Fortune* 140, no. 8, October 25, 1999, p. 44.

3. "The Skunk Works was created to design and develop the P-80 Shooting Star, America's first production jet aircraft. Lockheed Martin Skunk Works is a research and development division that continues to serve as a wellspring of innovation for their entire organization and, indeed, the industry itself—one of the world's preeminent sources for advanced aerospace prototypes, technology research, and systems development. They aim to continue to follow in the footsteps of the first alliance of dedicated engineers formed and led by legendary innovator Clarence L. 'Kelly' Johnson. As in Kelly's era, we're also not big on titles or protocol—just getting the job done, regularly meeting schedules on time and under budget." Adapted from www.lmsw.external.lmco.com/company_overview.html

> **Webvan.com**
>
> Webvan is a full-service, online grocer and drugstore that provides free delivery, offering customers the most convenient and affordable way to shop. Customers simply place their order online 24 hours a day, 7 days a week, at www.webvan.com and select a 30-minute delivery window at the time most convenient for them. Orders are then hand-delivered to the customer's desired location on the same day or up to 7 days later.
>
> Source: www.webvan.com

Infrastructure

Once the need to develop e-commerce in some form had been identified, the single most important issue facing the executives and technologists charged with developing Internet-based projects is infrastructure. This spans the technology spectrum from a single Internet file server connected to a commercial Internet service provider (ISP) all the way to the information-intense online transaction processing of a company like UPS, the giant global parcel delivery company. UPS's site assisted customers in tracking 12.92 million packages a day during 1999, hitting a peak of 18.7 million packages in a single day during the busy holiday peak shipping season as customers increasingly embraced the Internet and retail e-commerce and tracked their parcels online. Online tracking activity at UPS's Website established a new all-time record of 3.3 million requests in a single day.[4] To handle the volume, UPS employed 90,000 additional workers, adding more than 3,000 additional trucks to a fleet of 149,000 tractor-trailers, vans, and delivery vehicles, as well as coordinating the activities of the world's tenth-largest airline composed of 229 aircraft.

UPS's infrastructure also includes a growing set of online partners and tools utilized by over 15,000 of its customers to improve its efficiency at both the B2C and B2B levels.

The infrastructure needs to be considered at several levels:

☞ strategic

☞ organizational

☞ physical

---

4. Press Release: UPS, "UPS's Record 4th Quarter Results Cap Year of Outstanding Financial Returns," Atlanta, January 31, 2000. www.ups.com/news/20000131results.html

At the *strategic level*, the focus is on determining the impact future technologies will have on the market and the organization.[5] The aim is to align future business planning initiatives with the new technology challenges. This issue is considered fully in chapter 4. The first level at which the implications of technology and strategic change become apparent is the *organizational*. At this level, the challenge is to align the work practices, process flow, and structure of the organization to execute the strategic goals effectively and efficiently. The execution occurs through the *physical layer*: the hardware and software of the computing environment, in conjunction with the telecommunications infrastructure. Keith Butler, Director of Internet Commerce at Office Depot.com comments on the balance required between the strategic, organizational, and physical levels, together with the role of executive sponsorship:

> the [online] initiative was triggered internally; it was a champion inside the company who knows the industry well enough and knows the opportunity of e-commerce and said, "Look at this…", and two things came into play. First of all, the infrastructure that we had in place could support a move to the Web very robustly. And second, the web itself had reached critical mass or mass enough that it represented a great opportunity to generate new revenue. It was really driven from the fundamental get-go internally. It was a corporate decision that this was the right thing to do.

However, not all organizations have the ability to be nimble in responding to these challenges. Frequently, in mature organizations the infrastructure has grown old and lethargic, unable to adequately cope with change when asked to, at least within the allowable cost and time parameters. Successful organizations and their CIO's have recognized this and worked toward a fluid and flexible architecture that allows for change, whether that change be of organic growth through corporate acquisition, or of streamlining through divestiture, or of a complete strategic turnaround due to the pressures of new technology.

It is clear that it is easier to create a brand-new value chain that is based upon a Web pipeline philosophy than it is to change an established value chain which has inertia built into its practices and processes. Butler of Office Depot indicates that an organization needs a solid infrastructure to succeed in deploying an Internet channel: "All of our delivery centers currently operate

---

5. "Gerstner on IBM and the Internet," *Business Week*, December 13, 1999, p. EB40.

under a common order processing system, common warehouse management system, common inventory system"—an eclectic approach to infrastructure may not have worked so well.

Again, several lessons for executives can be distilled:

1. Create a flexible infrastructure that can act as the "shock absorber" of change.
2. The factors that influence the infrastructure come from strategic, organizational, and physical levels.
3. Infrastructure creation requires open levels of communication at and across all levels of the organization.
4. Create a technology solution that is scalable, secure, and robust
5. Maintain awareness of all standards as they evolve and attempt to influence the development of standards where possible. Plan for their integration as soon as is feasible, so that actual integration will not occur in a pressurized environment.
6. Executives cannot divorce themselves from technological understanding: the Techno-CEO is the leadership model of the future.

Organizational Learning

The ability of established organizations to react, understand, and deploy an e-commerce solution is very dependent upon the ability of an organization to effectively leverage its organizational learning. Roy Stata, Chairman of Analogue Devices, Inc., has stated that "organizational learning occurs through shared insights, knowledge, and mental models... [and] builds on past knowledge and experience—that is, on memory."[6] Organizational learning, however, is not an isolated process; it is clearly linked to our earlier discussion on leadership. The learning that occurs in formulating and creating brand, technology, market, and service leadership positions as well as the interconnection between these focuses are just as important as if not more important than the individual elements themselves. Leadership with vision facilitates, encourages, and allows an environment to develop within the organization where institutional learning and memory thrive. A few factors drive this: senior executives place trust in their colleagues at all levels; they stimulate an environment of

---

6. Ray Stata, "Organizational Learning—The Key to Management Innovation," *Sloan Management Review*, Spring 1989.

intellectual curiosity; they facilitate new concepts and technologies even when a traditional return-on-investment metric may not be applicable.

Successful organizations have always been able to internalize the learning brought about by developing an understanding of their processes and functions. Henry Ford, for example, internalized process control, while American Airlines internalized passenger yield management. In doing this, these enterprises gained a dominant position in their respective fields. Therefore, it would not be unexpected, within the emerging e-commerce arena, to find organizations exhibiting similar leadership characteristics developed through superior organizational learning skills. The front-runners such as Priceline.com, Officedepot.com, and BMW.com all demonstrate great creative and visionary leadership, but they also differentiate themselves through their ability to execute that vision. Two of the keys behind the success of the leaders in e-commerce are their ability to understand the metrics that drive their e-commerce marketspace, and their ability to understand their own relationship with their customers. From these two issues, the leading organizations have determined how to respond to those metrics and then improve the processes, structure, and communication accordingly. Many organizations start this process through the use of easily accessible metrics; for example, Alamo Car-Rental measures the yield ratio between metrics such as click-throughs and reservations, building upon its strong organizational understanding of yield management.

Leading organizations clearly understand the importance of metrics. BMW's Carol M. Burrows constantly assesses the customer and retail feedback through BMW's site, which attracts over 1 million hits a day. BMW then builds this into retail connectivity. Burrows states, "We communicate with retailers all the time. They are very, very complimentary of our site and very pleased with the amount of individuals that come to our site and who then use our link to their local retailer, to whom we refer someone for a test drive and to get a close-up look of a car. We provide a kit for all of our retailers to help them get on-line and to do it in a way that we think is complimentary to the brand."[7] Not only is BMW measuring its hit rate; it has also created a mechanism to involve all dimensions of the organization in the creation of its site, including customer service, dealer network, and financial services, to provide reinforcement of the BMW brand. In doing so, BMW has aligned the e-commerce strategy with the organizational strategy as a whole.

---

7. Phone interview with author, September 1998.

Several key drivers with regard to organizational learning can be gleaned:

1. Create an environment that stimulates and fosters organizational learning. This is vital not only for the successful introduction of technology but for long-term organizational survival.

2. Organizational learning has to have a focus and that focus has to be driven from the strategic objectives of the organization as a whole, taken one at a time in the areas of brand, technology, service, and market and then combined to provide holistic learning.

3. Organizational learning creates an environment of positive change and continuous process refinement. Should this not be present, organizational inertia will cause the organization to "stall in flight."

Four Positional E-strategic Directions

In creating an e-commerce strategy, it is clearly necessary to align and integrate the four main areas of positional strategic focus: technology, brand, service, and market (see Figure 2.3). This is a challenging task that must be deeply considered at the outset of strategy formulation since both the dollar and opportunity costs of dramatic strategic change after execution can be high. This is not to say that change is not occurring; change in this arena is inevitable and continuous, with victory coming to those who can adapt fastest and be nimble in the face of change. The remainder of this chapter will introduce the

Figure 2.3
Integration of the
Four E-commerce
Leadership
Propositions

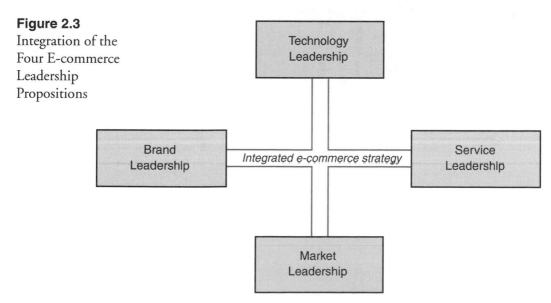

basic strategic issues in each of these leadership propositions and consider some of the key interactions between them.

Technology Leadership

We can find e-commerce strategies that are focused on leadership through technology in all industry sectors. Technology leadership involves the early adoption of an emerging technology to achieve a preemptive position. Many of the companies studied for this book followed this strategy or viewed technology leadership as an integral part of their overall leadership strategy, including UPS, Nortel, SUN Microsystems, Motorola, and Dow Jones.

At the World Economic Forum in Davos, Switzerland, Nortel Networks issued the statement on page 43 illustrating the technical and strategic challenges facing the company in an evolving Internet- and communications-driven marketplace.

B2G & B2B Technology Leadership

An example of B2G-mandated technology change is that originating from the regulatory conditions decreed by the U.S. Department of Energy, which, under the auspice of the Federal Energy Regulatory Commission and the Open Access Same Time Information System (OASIS), mandated that the Internet be used to buy and sell natural gas, as well as to make nominations for gas and pipeline capacity.

The utilities, which through other deregulation have been forced to relinquish monopoly power and become competitive, have been quick to recognize the potential that a technology leadership position offers in the B2B and B2C markets. With their ability to rapidly pass through the learning and experience curves, internalize their learning, and create new infrastructures, utilities such as Florida Power & Light (FPL) have rapidly moved to the front of the technology leadership arena. Utilities such as FPL aim through the use of technology to increase the strength of their customer relationship by offering more informational services and decreasing power costs, thus locking in market share for both residential (B2C) and corporate (B2B) consumers.

While their mandate is to reduce their customers' power consumption, they balance this with a strategy of increasing their market share. Through the deployment of Internet technologies they can achieve this at a lower cost than would have been possible even 5 years ago. The technology leverages the ability of the power utilities to monitor their customers' usage and offer them

January 30, 2000   Davos, Switzerland

Internet, eBusiness to Fuel Trillion Dollar Economic Growth, Nortel Networks Research Says Explosive Growth of Internet Economy Driving Demand for High-Performance Internet

Construction of the high-performance Internet is essential to support the massive increase in eBusiness and other investment fueling the growth of the Internet Economy, according to Nortel Networks' research unveiled at the Annual Meeting of the World Economic Forum.

Produced in conjunction with IDC, a leading global consulting firm, the research projects the Internet infrastructure segment of the Internet Economy is expected to more than quadruple to reach $1.5 trillion, larger even than spending on e-Business in 2003. This massive investment will be required to create a high-performance Internet with the reliability, quality, speed and economics that business and consumer demand.

The global Internet Economy is forecast to reach $2.8 trillion to become the world's third largest economy by 2003, larger than the gross domestic product of Germany, France or the United Kingdom.

The study also found that eBusiness is expected to grow by 86 percent annually to reach US$1.3 trillion. Europe will be the fastest-growing region for eBusiness over the period with annual growth of 118 percent. eBusiness growth will be driven by the decisions of thousands of businesses to shift billions of dollars of commerce from traditional methods such as EDI (electronic data interchange) to Web-based alternatives.

"This is further evidence of what Nortel Networks has been saying for years," said Ian Craig, executive vice-president and chief marketing officer, Nortel Networks. "The explosion in demand for bandwidth and the growing reliance of business and industry on the Web requires building a new, high-performance Internet as a matter of urgency. This is the task on which Nortel Networks is focused. We are leading the way with the Optical Internet, but the opportunity remains huge."

"Far from any bandwidth glut, there is a shortage of available bandwidth in both the US and the European market," Craig said. "Nortel Networks has been doubling the bandwidth and halving the cost of fiber optic networks every nine months as we improve the performance of the Optical Internet. The challenge facing us is to deliver an Internet with the reliability, quality, speed and economics that users need and demand."

Other key findings of the research include:

- Faster business-to-business growth expected, accounting for 87 percent of all eBusiness by 2003.
- Forecast continued bottleneck in the 'first mile,' with 87 percent of homes still relying on narrowband connections to the Web. Cable modem and DSL connections should continue to grow rapidly, but is expected to reach only a modest 7.7 percent and 4.4 percent of homes worldwide.

Source: www.nortelnetworks.com/corporate/news/newsreleases/2000a/
01_30_0000037_davos_ecommerce.html

suggestions on how to be more power efficient. This is a win-win strategy for both the utility and the customer, but it simultaneously changes the nature of competition within the industry. No longer is it based on the lowest-cost solution per kW-hour; it is based on a technology added value strategy that allows the utilities to get closer to the customer and create wider market coverage. The issues surrounding technology leadership strategies are discussed further in chapter 4.

Brand Leadership

The emergence of the Internet as a dynamic branding mechanism has done much to fuel the debate over how to most effectively utilize this benefit within the development of the organization's overall brand strategy. Potentially the most important of these debates focuses on the Internet's ability to influence, change, or reinforce corporate branding. The Internet is unique in modern times as it is a truly new conduit to the customer, and as such it has extensive ability to create a new corporate branding position, to reinforce the existing brand, or to enable the existing brand to be repositioned.

Louis Gerstner, Chairman & CEO: IBM

Branding—it is a very important issue and it will dominate business thinking I suspect for a decade or more.
   Source: IBM Executive Conference on Information Systems, Latin America, Miami, FL, September 1, 1998.

The development of an e-commerce branding strategy will clearly mean something different to a new entity than it will to an established organization. The *born-on-the-net* category is epitomized by Amazon.com, a company that only just commenced selling books on the Web in July 1995 but that had by 2000 sales of $1.64 billion (net sales for fiscal year 1999, as reported in its SEC filing)—a staggering growth rate of 169% over the net sales of $610 million for 1998. Amazon is not only the Internet's dominant bookseller; it is potentially the Internet's most dominant brand. To most North American Internet users, Amazon is a reflection of the Internet's e-commerce potential; to most executives, it is the *specter* on the horizon, and they do not want to be caught cold like the "café latte" high street booksellers. To the book-buying public, the added value is financially clear—everyday low-cost pricing. However, cost alone is not the only added value factor; convenience and service are the key. The customer feels connected to the company rather than disconnected by the technology. The secret of the branding at Amazon.com is also more than its efficient, quality customer service. It is based on the added value of mass customization. The customer is dealt with the way customers wish to be dealt with—as a valued and familiar client with whom a store worker has built up a long-term relationship. Thus, value comes from recognizing the customer's patterns of purchasing and through making subtle suggestions to the customer rather than using overt direct marketing techniques. The key to mass customization is getting close to the customer and providing the product on demand at a low cost while maintaining sufficient margins for the supplier.

> Brand reinforcement comes through reflecting the values of the physical product through the medium of the Internet. A brand reinforcement strategy does not necessarily imply the Internet is used to transact, merely to interact.

The goal of being a leader and developer of Internet sales may not be the goal of every organization. Many established organizations do not actually wish to develop a new sales channel at the current time and hence have determined that a *brand reinforcement* strategy is a suitable complement to their existing corporate strategy. The goal of this channel is to reinforce the organization in the eyes of the customer. In order to do this the organization has to utilize the added value of "information provision" to its viewers, providing information and building a quality relationship with the customer on a continuing basis through that information content. This is not a static information interchange relationship but a dynamic one in which the customer will expect change and continual value from the relationship or the linkage will be severed, potentially for a significant amount of time. An example of a leading brand reinforcement strategy can be found in the automotive area where BMW is continually stimulating its customers through subtle incremental changes to its site. BMW utilizes the technology to increase the involvement level of potential, current, and past customers. In the past the site has allowed customers to build their own dream car or, at the launch of the M series Z3 roadster, to listen to its engine. However, unlike Amazon, BMW would prefer the potential new owner to visit a traditional dealer subsequent to visiting the site. This is not because BMW is not capable of creating the technology to sell a vehicle via the Internet, but because the company feels that the interrelationship between customer and organization is best served by human reinforcement and bonding.

Even though this channel is not directly generating revenue, the *brand equity* (discussed in chapter 10) is developing tangible benefits to those that understand and execute effectively in this marketspace. An automobile manufacturer confirmed during the research for this book that there is a tangible return through retail feedback and retail connectivity and that the insights gained through the online channel are superior to those of traditional marketing channels. The issues surrounding branding are considered more fully in chapter 7.

The Service Payoff

An obsessive focus on all information surrounding the customer at all contact points is the most effective way to establish service leadership via the Internet. Service should not always be expected to translate immediately into purchases by customers because its value often consists simply of building relationships with, and gathering information about, potential customers and maintaining relationships with existing ones.

The value-adding effects of building virtual communities have been well documented by management consultants John Hagel and Arthur Armstrong in their 1997 book *Net Gain*.[8] Their communities are developing in parallel to the e-consortia relationship within the B2C and B2B environments. Over time, e-consortia will attract more and more customers (and potential new sellers to add to the consortia) through their service strength. This derives from the specialized nature of the individual organization's information being available under the umbrella of the consortia to service the needs of the customer from a data and information provision perspective.

Healtheon.com: an E-consortium

A fundamental feature of e-consortia is that the value increases exponentially even as they grow incrementally. Over time, the companies that nurture e-consortia can look forward to more customer transactions and greater revenue. One growth area in which communities and consortia will proliferate is healthcare. Currently there are many stand-alone Websites—e.g., WebMD and Dr.Koop.com. However e-consortia, of which Healtheon is a variant, look at becoming a dominant force in this arena. Healtheon's mission statement is "to leverage advanced Internet technology to connect all participants in healthcare, and enable them to communicate, exchange information and perform transactions which cut across the healthcare maze. This will simplify

---

8. John Hagel and Arthur G. Armstrong, *Net Gain: Expanding Markets Through Virtual Communities*, Harvard Business School Press, Cambridge, MA, 1997.

healthcare, reduce costs, enhance service and result in higher quality, and more accessible healthcare."[9] Healtheon is forming alliances with the necessary groups within a healthcare framework to ensure its consortium is effective, including preferred provider organizations (PPOs) and other partners in ancillary fields. The value here is in providing 24×7 access to information, prescription drugs, and so on, thus creating services that are not possible in the modern health management organization (HMO)-run physicians' surgeries where interaction is the most valuable service item but the provision of which has become too expensive and too rarefied.

UPS.com—A B2C, B2B, and B2G Enterprise

Other companies have taken less radical—but nevertheless profitable—approaches to service over the Internet. Consider UPS, the world's largest package distribution company, which transports more than 3 billion items a year. Through adoption of the Internet and Net technologies UPS has repositioned itself as a deliverer not just of packages but of information. UPS's Document Exchange service enables businesses to transmit documents cheaply and securely over the Internet, with the same benefits—such as package tracking and delivery confirmation—UPS offers with physical packages. The Internet also makes it easier for UPS to customize logistics for its customers—for example, by ensuring that parts from different countries arrive where needed at the same time.

The Internet allows organizations to offer innovative types of service variations to more and more customers. There are examples in all industries: utilities such as Entergy, serving the Louisiana, Texas, and Mississippi areas, and Florida Power & Light analyze their customers' bills and power usage; biotechnology companies such as Genentech support community activities; American Express provides tools for customers to carry out their own financial portfolio management; and companies across the board provide investor information to shareholders.

Furthermore, the Internet makes it possible for international companies to offer a level of service to all markets that was previously restricted to their home countries and major markets, a realization of a long-held dream. The development of service leadership strategies is discussed further in chapter 6.

---

9. www.healtheon.com/com/index.html

In Search of Market Growth

Nimble, creative, and agile corporations have achieved disproportionate market growth via the Internet through responding to changing market conditions with product offerings as well as through their approach to understanding the market within which they operate. One successful approach has been to combine marketing, service, and information systems groups to focus on issues as a cross-functional team. Some examples of organizations innovatively using the Internet to spur market growth follow.

☞ **Royal Caribbean International**, one of the world's largest cruise lines, evolved from a *Technology* leadership focus in 1997, through a process of brand enhancement, to a more recent *Market* focus, achieving significant market growth through online sales.

☞ By contrast, **American Express** first focused on brand reinforcement. As one marketing executive stated:

> The Internet is where the home run is—when you leverage what you are good at already and you use online systems in a way that cannot be duplicated. It reinforces what your products and services are, makes them better, and reinforces your brand and what it means.[10]

Building upon its early Internet learning experiences, American Express has subsequently moved into a *market growth mode*. Some examples include helping customers to trade stocks online; providing consulting services and expertise to customers; and assisting business to identify and implementat direct and indirect cost savings. In addition to its more traditional business areas, American Express is offering real-time air, hotel, and car reservations, as well as last-minute travel bargains.

☞ **Office Depot**, the U.S.-based office supply company, receives over 300,000 orders a day for its products through its straightforward, user-friendly Internet site. The company aims to retain customers by providing a convenient and efficient service. It's building market share by creating free services for office managers and small businesses and by providing real-time inventory checking, along with its traditional customer call centers.

☞ Car rental company **Alamo** is aggressively pursuing a strategy of being the first to facilitate wider market coverage and closer relationships with

---

10. Personal interview, September 1998.

customers. Naturally, this has influenced the speed at which it is developing its Internet activities. The company reports that the Internet is not only more profitable than traditional channels, but that it tends to receive a fairly constant amount of use. In Japan, Alamo's Internet revenue has grown significantly compared to revenue growth through traditional channels.

Companies with this level of success clearly see the new business model made possible by the Internet and are willing to commit to the hilt the financial, technical, and management resources needed. As an executive at the American Bankers Insurance Group remarked: "It's a bit like ATMs [automated teller machines]. Everybody was getting them and if you didn't you lost customers. But the Internet also reinforces organizations, adding new channels. It is a real transition in business, one of those points where huge differences can be shown and made."

The issues surrounding the development of market leadership strategies are discussed in more detail in chapter 5.

A Case Study: Royal Caribbean Cruises[11]

Royal Caribbean Cruises is the world's largest cruise-based leisure company, with revenues of $2.64 billion for 1998. It carries over 4.5 million passengers a year to Alaska, the Bahamas, Bermuda, Canada, the Caribbean, Europe, Hawaii, Mexico, New England, the Panama Canal, and Scandinavia.

Leadership and Organizational Learning

Since its inception in 1970, Royal Caribbean has tried to be an innovator in ship design and construction techniques, logistics, and reservation systems. Building upon this reputation, the company created its first Website in February 1996. The site was redesigned in 1997 to incorporate a stronger brand message and sales and marketing initiatives. The amount of information provided for—and obtained from—visitors was increased.

The relationship between technology and the strategy of the organization is acknowledged at the highest levels. According to Jack Williams, president of Royal Caribbean International: "Royal Caribbean recognised long ago the potential that the automation held for us as a company.... The past decade has been spent identifying how this new tool could be incorporated into every aspect of our

11. Based on personal interviews, conducted May 1999.

business to bring more information about our brand into the homes and offices of our customers and our travel partners worldwide." This vision of technology at the executive level is critical: it drives all sections of the organization toward a common goal through the medium of technology.

Some elements of the system are done out-of-house, however. As with other advertising media, the company employs an interactive agency to be creative on its behalf. According to the director of Royal Caribbean's Marketing Automation Group, this is so that the company can gain access to "the latest and greatest ideas" on the creative side while focusing its own energies on other areas of marketing. The organization uses a partnering model: it gains external expertise where necessary and carefully manages the relationship with its in-house information systems department.

Technology

Companies such as AOL, Amazon.com, and eBay that have mastered the technology of e-commerce ahead of their competitors have been able to create and dominate new markets. Established companies also see a technology focus as crucial to successful competitive positioning.

Royal Caribbean uses a variety of information systems to manage its shore- and ship-based operations—in other words, its business-to-business customers such as travel agents and its liners. With the former, the existing technology of its traditional booking channels—Sabre's Cruise Director, Galileo's Leisure Shopper, Worldspan's CruiseLine Source, and Amadeus Cruises—accounts for 30% of its bookings (the highest degree of automation in its industry). Royal Caribbean is aiming to increase this percentage by introducing CruiseMatch 2000 Online, a Web-based reservation system, through which agents can access its logos, interior and exterior ship photography, information on reduced rates, and downloadable advertisements. It is also planning to enable long-standing customers to book directly online.

Marketing

The Internet has two attributes that guarantee its success: Websites can be accessed by a global audience 24 hours a day, 365 days a year, and those sites can be made to appear personalized for individual users. Marketers can finally realize their dream of mass-customized, one-to-one marketing when they structure Websites effectively.

Royal Caribbean Cruises operates two cruise brands: Royal Caribbean International and Celebrity Cruises. By 2002 the combined fleet will consist of 16 vessels with a capacity of 21,700 berths. In addition to the many different countries the ships visit, the company offers a wide range of trip durations, from three-day cruises to epic voyages that take in several continents. This complexity of offerings necessitates a complex pricing structure.

Sales are traditionally made through travel agents. If Royal Caribbean were to bypass these agents by selling directly to customers online, it might provoke a hostile and perhaps even damaging reaction from the agents.

The company, however, sees an opportunity to colonize an underdeveloped marketplace. Research has shown that 93% of the public has not been on a cruise, and that only 31% of travelers use a travel agent; the company's internal studies show a high correlation between its existing customers and the fastest-growing segments of Internet users.

Its strategy is thus to exploit the power of information systems to inform this set of customers of its complex array of products and services. Customers can book directly through Royal Caribbean's telephone call center or use the online reservation request form to check availability. Internet-based online booking is the next step.

Service

As with the ability to create a perception of individualized marketing through the Internet, organizations can also service the needs of their customers on a global, 24-hour-a-day basis.

Success in the premium sector of the leisure industry depends heavily upon quality of service. So like many companies in this sector, Royal Caribbean aims to deliver a branded, high level of service whenever a customer comes into contact with the organization. This especially includes the customer's interaction with the Website; after all, the site is a direct channel to the retail customer.

Royal Caribbean's strategy consists in gently shepherding the customer toward the greater resources of professional travel agents (where this does not conflict with the segmentation strategy outlined above) while attempting to provide total customer support and satisfaction. E-commerce should be about total customer service as well as transactions. A Website is not simply a low-cost sales channel but a means of giving customers greater choice and detailed, relevant information.

Branding

Branding is a process that creates within a consumer's consciousness a heightened awareness and recognition of a trademark or product, creating a brand-image. The term "brand-image" was coined in the 1950s by David Ogilvy of the Ogilvy, Benson & Mather advertising agency. Ogilvy conceived of marketing strategy as the reinforcement of a product's brand to the point where the product is elevated above products of equal quality but of unknown brands.

The positioning of the Royal Caribbean brand as a "quality" brand is of vital importance to the organization. Jack Williams has said that the company's brand identity "needs to illustrate the quality product that we offer and needs to signify the international scope with which we operate our ships and sell our vacations."

Through its Website, the company aims to communicate this at all stages of its relationship with a customer: for the first-time cruiser, there is the visual "electronic experience" of the ship and cruise; for prior customers, there is a loyalty program;

and for stockholders, there is an online investor relations channel. The Website brings together many normally disparate points of contact. Thus a key task for Royal Caribbean—as for other companies that rely heavily on their brand associations—is to ensure that these are presented in a coherent way.

Developing a Winning E-strategy

Several keys to the successful development of an e-commerce strategy have been highlighted:

- Ensure the project is backed by a senior executive.
- Develop a strategy before developing a Web presence.
- Develop a strategy by focusing on technology, branding, marketing, and service.
- Develop an IT infrastructure capable of matching the strategic objectives.
- Identify and use knowledge in the organization.
- The strategy must add value for customers, and it must change as the requirements of those customers change.

It is possible for companies that were not "born on the Web" to create similar Internet-based channels to those that the newer competition has so far exploited. By focusing on the factors outlined above they stand a good chance of success; by monitoring their performance and responding to changes in their markets, they can sustain that success. The established fixed-asset company of today can be the nimble Internet company of tomorrow.

Summary

It became clear after researching the e-commerce strategies of more than 40 companies, over half of which had revenues in excess of a billion dollars, that, in order to be successful in the creation of an e-commerce strategy, the strategic positional focuses of technology, brand, service, and market leadership require careful consideration in order to achieve a balanced strategy. In order to support a balanced strategy, at least three further drivers, some quite traditional in nature, were required to bond the organizational strategy and the IT strategy together. Most important among them are:

☞ The necessity for a senior management champion, preferably the chief executive.

☞ The basis of a strong and flexible IT infrastructure upon which to deploy the organization's e-strategy.

☞ Active support by the organization's *content owners* (that is, groups and individuals that have a direct stake in the positional e-strategy mix—leaders in the corporation's technology, marketing, service, and branding groups).

☞ The ability to climb the learning curve quickly. The companies that make the best use of e-commerce are identifiable by the speed at which they developed online projects and the wealth of future online options that they considered.

☞ Belief that R&D for online activities is a strategic investment. The research for this book found that funding for net projects sparked no serious return-on-investment questions in leading online companies.

☞ Adoption of a sourcing option that reflects the mission-critical nature of the Internet. Often companies start with an in-house group thrown together quickly (often dubbed a "skunk works") or opts for complete outsourcing. Then as the importance of the Internet and the technology becomes recognized, other options are considered. This includes *partnering*—working with a set of specialist providers. Partnering differs from traditional outsourcing in the sense of the relationship being developed. Traditionally outsourcing has been a useful mechanism to more effectively use internal resources while maximizing the efficiency of vendors. Partnering on the Internet, however, is focused upon developing working relationships. This stems from the fact that the technologies being incorporated into corporations' e-commerce systems are new and continually being updated. The vendors are also often new and they wish to build relationships, place their software in successful companies, and go through learning curves with their customers. Corporations are also constantly adjusting their e-commerce sites and strategies, making a partnering relationship preferable to long-term outsourcing options.

The issues surrounding ownership, technology leadership, market, brand, service, and development of corporate e-commerce strategies are discussed more fully in subsequent chapters.

3

Ownership Issues

E-centric Structures + Content = Success

It is clear from examining the history of e-commerce strategy that many organizations have had excellent conceptual strategies that have derailed in their execution. One area where this has happened is online grocery delivery. Many organizations have attempted to go online in this space. After all, the demographics look wonderful—baby boomers with a taste for luxury are online but, due to their lifestyle, do not have the time to shop for groceries. Fine in theory, difficult in execution. The business models that have been applied to this problem are numerous and nearly all fraught with problems. Information Neighborhood, a start-up out of Tampa, Florida, initially had a strong relationship with Publix, the seventh-largest supermarket in volume in the United States. However, Information Neighborhood failed to recognize that the demographic profile of its target community lacked the Internet user base required to establish a profitable business. Not giving up, however, it moved its operation to New Jersey where the local supermarket chain with which it partnered failed to provide adequate marketing support, and Information Neighborhood folded.[1] Others such as NetGrocer at the outset did not appreciate the razor-thin margins of the food industry; it carried too large an overhead and was eventually forced to restructure its operations and make severe

---

1. Dale Buss, "Damaged Goods," *Business 2.0*, April 1999.

55

job cuts. Other business models had problems in the execution. For example, customers had to pay a delivery fee; online grocers were unable to service the complete list of requirements for the customer, in the sizes they required; there was a lack of secure refrigerated storage for deliveries; deliveries to apartment buildings were problematic.

The existing business models that worked for home delivery of other products such as bottled mineral water simply did not work for the online grocery business. The problem is not in conceptualizing a Net-based grocer's business. The problem is in the execution. In considering the failure to execute effectively, it becomes clear that the problem lies in bringing to bear Web-based experience on each of the value chain activities (see Table 3.1).

Table 3.1 Value Chain Activities

Primary Value Chain Activities	*Secondary Value Chain Activities*
Inbound logistics	Infrastructure
Manufacturing or production	Research and development
Outbound logistics	Procurement
Sales	Human resource management
Service	
Marketing	

Existing delivery businesses and grocers have had many decades if not centuries to pass through the learning curve that their online cousins have had to do in months. Other industries will also feel the same growing pains as they move online, converting static business models into dynamic ones, changing processes honed from decades of experience with a customer-base that changed slowly to flexible processes that have to change continually to accommodate the new customer requirements.

Content alone is not sufficient for success.

Successes come from a balanced business model that involves each business area content provider contributing to the overall business model.

In order to overcome this learning-curve ramp-up problem, several approaches can be adopted.

☞ One is the creation of new business models, such as the e-consortia model, discussed earlier in the book. In this environment the collective strengths of different organizations are leveraged to provide content and expertise to compete in the selected marketspace.

☞ Another approach is to outsource all operations and act as a content manager through contacts. This is efficient and enables organizations to maintain leading-edge technology focus through "hired guns." However, the limitations are clear—the company loses out in terms of its internalization of its learning experiences by passing that knowledge base to the outsourcer. Further, this approach in hiring talent from the leading-edge software houses can be very expensive. They themselves have problems recruiting sufficient talent, and thus even the leading software houses are unable to put their top talent to work on all their clients' requests simultaneously.

However, if it is not feasible to partner or belong to a consortium, then organizations need to consider their own internal dynamics and their online strengths with respect to the value chain activities. Maximizing the internal efficiency of an organization's e-commerce group is vital to its development. New systems of communication, control, development, and structure need to be not only considered but also adopted. The old structures and methods of working are not applicable to the online organization. This is a belief echoed by an executive in our study who, when asked to comment on the major problems and issues facing e-commerce strategists going forward, states:

> There are several issues. One for me would be the whole issue around the business model and that is do I try and transition or transform from the old to the new? Or do I start from afresh? This is based upon the problems associated with "cannibalism." Can I make the organization move at the speed I need to be able to move from where we have been to where we need to go as opposed to saying no, we need to start a whole new concept?
>
> The second issue is around culture, which is really about saying "those that have built the old find it very hard to tear it down and start anew"—I would refer to the Greeks, then the Romans and then the next empire came in. It takes a new kind of regime to see a different light, a different civilization if you will. In this case a different economy. A different business model. The question therefore is can the mindsets of the current business leaders change? After they have

built so much and of which they are proud, will they be willing to tear it down and start afresh or do we need new players in town?

The third issue is around time. Time to market, and what speed we are moving at and the biggest challenge will be can you get sustainable competitive advantage and change the customer value proposition in a timely way?

This and subsequent chapters will attempt to address these issues and provide detailed models to enable executives to change the organization and change it effectively. This change will be achieved through detailed consideration of the four positional dimensions of e-commerce strategy formulation—*technology, marketing, service,* and *brand*—in addition to the implications for the differing B2C, B2B, B2G, and e-consortia environments.

However, it is first necessary to consider some of the internal *organizational issues* that companies face—issues such as functional structure, control, leadership relationships, and content provision, issues that, if successfully managed, will facilitate and support the rapid ramping up of the learning processes necessary to turn conceptual strategies into successful operational endeavors.

The E-centric Management Structure

The research for this book identified that the one key issue of strategy execution often neglected by an organization is that of *content ownership*. Content may be king, but the best content comes from an acknowledgment that it is the total environment within the organization that contributes and supports that final Web page and its relationship with the customer.

> A *content owner* is any member of the organization who will either display information on the site or have his or her function affected by the site and its use (e.g., logistics, purchasing, service).

In order to facilitate the development of strong organizational content ownership, it is necessary to reconsider the structures adopted by organizations in their e-commerce environments. Unlike traditional organizational situations, in which horizontal command and control structures predominate (see the light boxes in Figure 3.1), e-commerce organizations require a much more adaptive structure in which the functional head of e-commerce (the VP of e-commerce

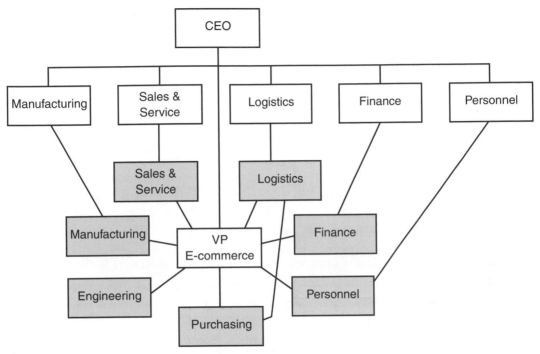

Figure 3.1
The E-centric Management Structure

in Figure 3.1) has to be central to the organizational structure (the darker boxes in Figure 3.1). This enables the communications overhead to be cut and the decision-making process to occur much more quickly than it would if the CEO had to see every item from every department before passing it back to department heads who would then communicate it to their peers. In this Web-centric organization, the head of e-commerce is well served by having close, rapid, and intimate contact with the four groups shown in Figure 3.2.

We will now consider the dynamics and properties of these relationships in more detail.

Senior Strategic Management Group

The overriding driver of a successful Internet strategy is the leadership demonstrated by senior levels of the organization. An executive charged with the creation and deployment of the American Internet strategy component for BMW, the luxury automobile manufacturer, states:

There is at the top of the company, from high senior management, an interest and awareness of it and a clear understanding of what it is and how it can benefit customers and BMW.

The executive charged with developing an Internet strategy for a leading hotel-leisure organization reinforces this.

I think that, for any organization to really have a meaningful presence on the Web, really you need the blessing from the top down.

Clearly, the role of the senior management is to provide the vision and the space for the creation of an Internet strategy. In those organizations where the Internet strategy is not successful, or has not been implemented at all, two major contributing factors can usually be found:

☞ Senior executives fail to see the relevance of the Internet to their industry.

☞ The organization is absorbed in another technical project, such as the rollout of an enterprise resource planning (ERP) or a Y2K project, to the exclusion of all others.

Even when an organization has an active vision for its Internet strategy, when a project champion leaves, that vision often withers on the vine. As one executive put it:

The Net was going pretty well—one of the smart things they did was they got the CEO to be champion so they were really on a roll; so when they wanted to do a launch, the CEO was there saying it was a wonderful thing. It was all going pretty well until he got fired, and then the project lost its momentum.

Figure 3.2
The Relationships
Structure of an
E-centric
Organization

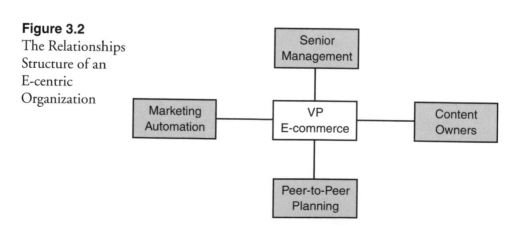

The financial demands from technology can also conflict with implementing a successful Internet strategy; thus the requirement to have a strong proponent at the executive level becomes even more pressing, with those organizations lacking a strong CEO-CIO relationship faring the worst.

However, there are many examples of strong visionary senior management leaders such as Gerstner at IBM, Golub at American Express, Charles Schwab, Kelly at UPS, and Idei at Sony. It is their ability to understand the role, function, and applicability of emerging technologies that separates them from their competitors. They also share a common characteristic in that they have created agile and nimble corporations that can respond quickly to change which, given their size and global reach, is remarkable. In terms of an e-commerce strategy, all have adopted flexible management styles and structures to facilitate the needs of this new channel; for them it is business as usual, that is, *coping with change.*

At the center of the charge for e-commerce in organizations that have adopted the e-centric management structure, we'll find the CIO or VP responsible for the function. The CIO is best served with an informal and open channel of control to the senior executive group but also with a wide degree of autonomy and authority to create and develop content. Content and services are based around the *value and investment criteria* defined by the executive steering group. These criteria will be in the form of brand, service, and market specifications, with a directive on technological leadership issues. Again it is necessary to stress that a balance across all of these is necessary for success. Use of technology to lower service costs at the expense of brand is clearly counterproductive. The CIO as depicted in Figure 3.2 has several groups that interact and share the initiative, the integration of which is facilitated by cross-functional groups that bring technical and managerial skills together.

Marketing-Automation-Strategy Group

The functional unit charged with integrating and deploying the Internet strategy has many names. It is often a subgroup of traditional units such as marketing or corporate communications, or it might be a specialist function that has been created especially for corporate e-commerce and technology issues. However, it has been recognized that there are limitations to this approach and that a more flexible solution is appropriate.

American Express created the Interactive Enterprise Development group, while Royal Caribbean Cruises created the Marketing Automation group.

Automobile manufacturer Land Rover formed the Marketing Communication Strategies group. All of these groups have the same primary responsibility—to ensure that their company's Internet presence reflects and extends to the customer the branding strategy as determined at the executive level. We will use the term *marketing-automation-strategy* (MAS) *group* to signify this function.

The MAS group develops a framework for the operational e-commerce strategy, which is then implemented at the level of the content owners. This is performed through the creation of *peer to peer planning groups*. Membership in the planning process will vary from organization to organization and with the intent of the planning objectives. An executive at a major financial institution describes an aspect of its institutional planning process:

> We can have 1,000 people in a centralized role working on this stuff; it would not be as fluid and it would not be tied into our core business. We need to have two different goals. One is to be separate enough so that it gets the attention it needs because it may not always hit the top of the business unit's priorities on a day-to-day basis, but yet it needs to be integrated enough so that, when you do something, it pays back and you don't want to have an us versus them.

This sentiment and approach is echoed by groups at other successful organizations, whereby the responsibility is passed out to the content owners, who better understand the business drivers in each area. The involvement of the content owners also reinforces the *responsibility ethic*; that is, if the content owners are asked to add value in their function by paying for it from their own budget, the efficiency of the return on investment promises to be much higher. The interaction of the content owners comes together in the cross-functional teams or *planning groups*. An executive at a major logistics organization identifies three of the business drivers in each content area of the organization:

☞ The Internet as a conduit of information to customers
☞ The need to get closer to the customer
☞ Information that surrounds or adds to a process

The planning group provides the central structure through which the core operational issues of e-commerce strategy are derived, policies such as:

☞ Security

☞ Content parameters

☞ Access parameters from a technical perspective (speeds, bandwidth requirements, etc.)

☞ Format issues

☞ Partner-relationship management

☞ Request for comments, proposal standards

These allow the content owners to work together through a standard modus operandi.

The scope of the planning process can vary considerably depending on the reach and responsibility of the group. International considerations are becoming more vital. Even basic questions—Which languages does the organization utilize? How do we best tune for cultural sensitivity?—require careful and thorough consideration from multiple aspects of the organization. Again, the execution is often more difficult than the concept; for example, can the technology used by a New York financial institution for its U.S.-based customers be replicated in its global markets? Careful consideration of both the technical and cultural issues is required before blindly deploying leading-edge technologies to global markets. One approach is to examine this issue through the three parameters of format, access, and content (as discussed in chapter 6), where the customers' content need is addressed in light of their ability to access bandwidth.

Many organizations have chosen to drive their planning through a marketing-driven focus; for example, the planning group at an automobile manufacturer is composed of members of an *Internet agency*, a *direct marketing agency*, and a *relationship marketing group*, with the head of planning coordinating the group as a whole.

A biotechnology company executive perhaps best identifies the requirement for a strong planning process:

> Everyone has adopted the Internet as a way of life; however, different groups wish to use the site for different objectives, which requires a cross-functional team to balance this out.

Content Owners

The content owners not only have responsibilities to their own functional unit but also to the overall strategic objectives of the organization, the balance between the two coming through the planning process as discussed above. An aim of the planning process is to keep the different content providers from going in different directions, as this would not reinforce the overall brand of the site, which is effectively the brand of the organization. This is a noticeable and significant issue with those organizations that do not have a methodology through which development is coordinated. One example is a large European manufacturing company. Its group headquarters was late in getting onto the Internet. However, its American division had already created a separate entity on the Internet to represent its interests. The Americans viewed the role of the Internet as a *sales and motivation* channel, while the corporate headquarters viewed the Internet as a channel to *educate and inform.* A separation in alignment had definitely occurred.

The process of getting content owners to concede what they have already done and convincing them to rework their sites and processes in order to align themselves with the head office can often be a very difficult task.

On the positive side, content ownership can create a stimulus of excitement and interest across many fronts. Another manufacturer states:

> There is a very clear understanding of the medium and enthusiasm for it. There is support from all areas within the company—that is how our site is going to grow, and we're going to add more aspects to it because other people in the organization are very anxious to be a part of it and to make our site the best it could be.

This view has created internal successes in addition to the external strategic benefits, including the fact that "it [the Internet] invoked a lot of discussion with all people who are involved."

Hence, for an automobile manufacturer's Internet site, for example, the designer of the antilock braking system would assist in the development of that aspect of the technical information content. Thus the site owners are interfacing with associated content owners as well as the marketing and communications groups, building commitment, teamwork, and organizational learning.

Thus, if we take the value chain and consider it in this context, we see the critical role performed by content owners in each activity. See Table 3.2 for the primary value chain and Table 3.3 for the secondary value chain. The integration of all these factors is the *hidden key* that successful organizations use to

Table 3.2 Primary Value Chain

Activity	Content examples	Examples of the value added
Inbound logistics	Furnishing shipment data to the enterprise	Facilitates inventory projections to manufacturing
Manufacturing or production	Product and industry information	Product content to customer
Outbound logistics	Shipping details	Tracking information
Sales	Pricing	Online pricing and bidding
Service	Customer service center	Online service provision
Marketing	Demographic profiling	Mass customization of product offerings to customer

Table 3.3 Secondary Value Chain

Activity	Content examples	Examples of the value added
Infrastructure	ERP systems and data	Structural implications can be modeled, e.g., warehousing
Research and development	Customer modeling	One-to-one customer modeling
Procurement	Purchasing models	Cost reduction and increased information content surrounding new mass customization purchasing models
Human resource management	Human capital	Retention of skilled employees

create value. It is not only Amazon's first-mover status that has enabled it to create its empire; it is the ability to create a strong virtual value chain and strong internal linkages that has enabled Amazon to change and adapt to the market. It has also enabled it to be able to adapt and change to accommodate the internal problems that were encountered in development. It is interesting to consider that Amazon may not be a bookstore at all under all the Hyper Text Markup Language (HTML) code and marketing gloss—that it really could be categorized as a logistics company that just happens to sell books. This is similar to Nike in the 1990s, which could have been considered a marketing company that happened to sell athletic shoes. It is the underlying core competencies that surround their value chain activity that are the true strengths of the leaders in e-commerce.

A key to success therefore is to understand and to establish a virtual value chain that adds content at each stage; the content must integrate to meet the overall value criteria goals of the company.

Content

Content may be king, but it is value chain that is the power behind the throne.

A book on e-commerce should be focused upon content. It should detail what content is necessary for success, what customers want in their content, and how that adds value to them. However, it is our belief that content is so specific to an organization and flows from the composition of that organization's value chain that we can give only general commentary. A rationale for this is that new organizations are less about specific content than they are about structure. The content of the site has to be derived from extensive industry- and organization-specific research and must be centered upon the environment in which the organization has selected to participate, together with the form that the organization wishes to adopt.

Stephen Case, chairman and CEO of AOL, in his conference call reporting second-quarter FY00 results, commented upon the merger with Time Warner:

> Make no mistake: This merger is not just about putting different forms of media together. It is about creating something new and powerful—a truly mass market interactive company, providing services on a global level that will become even more central to people's lives.[2]

AOL Time Warner is not just about content—true, they have an enormous capacity for content, and that is ultimately what the customer comes to them for—but rather the interesting aspect of this company is the exciting business model it has created to provide that content. For example, the hotel rooms of

---

2. AOL conference call transcript, January 19, 2000. www.corp.aol.com/conffy00q2.html

the world are already connected to Time Warner's CNN; the next step is to ensure that content is available in all spheres and all channels. The content can often be duplicated by rivals such as the BBC, News Corporation, or Knight-Ridder, but the value chain that delivers that information cannot. Thus reliance upon content alone provides no defense to attack from alternative sources. Content is strong only when derived from a strong and flexible business model such as that of AOL Time Warner, which can service the customer globally on the customer's terms.

Summary

The key to successful business on the Internet is not the formulation of a conceptual strategy but the execution of that strategy. To execute effectively, content ownership has to be exploited. The content owners must buy into the strategy and have the confidence of senior executives. Often the decisions the content owners make may have serious consequences to the organization and its strategy. Buy-in and open discussions are keys to success.

The central issues that surround content are in part about the structures that supply that content. The traditional command-and-control structures will need to be adapted to ensure flexibility and the ability to change quickly to meet market demands. One approach is the adoption of e-centric structures that place the CIO or VP for e-commerce at the center. This allows the four major ownership groups—the senior strategy group; a peer-to-peer planning group; a new cross-functional group, such as a marketing automation group that manages the operational deployment of the system; and the content owners—to interact in a more timely and informative manner. The information content owners need to buy in and commit to the project because it is their individual value chain contributions that ultimately add value and flexibility in times of change. Remembering that organizational inertia kills, all organizational members have to learn to think outside the box if they are to survive.

E-strategy Leadership Through a Technology Focus

In this chapter we examine the first of the four positional factors that organizations must consider when creating their e-commerce strategy. The technology component has to be in balance and harmony with the other positional factors—brand, market positioning, and service—to be truly effective. For some organizations, the entire strategy will be based on strength and leadership in this area; for others the technology will take an enabling role. Thus this chapter attempts to identify the drivers behind the creation of a successful e-commerce strategy powered by technology, and it discusses technology's interrelationship with branding, market development, and the customer service value chain.

The Role of the Executive Technology Champion

In examining the factors that lead to successful technology leadership positions, it became clear once again that the key facilitator in many leading organizations is the *executive champion*. Those executive champions, whose organizations were at the forefront of their industry in terms of the online experience, exhibited high comfort levels with technology and understood its role and its relationship to the other functional areas of the organization. From that perspective they became arbiters of their systems' successful deployment and integration into corporate strategy.

> The most successful executive champions exhibit the highest technology comfort levels.

When describing its Internet presence, one executive at a leading lodging-hotel organization states:

> The "driver" is purely that this organization remains first—in its industry, in the front of technology, therefore, first in terms of the Internet. As early as 1996 it was very important to the company to have a Web presence and a meaningful Web presence and that it be a very good site.

The managerial leaders of the e-commerce function also identify this as a leveraging facilitator of their success. A hotel executive comments, "I think that, for any organization to have a meaningful presence on the Web, really you need the blessing from the top down." An Internet executive with a logistics company says, "In an organization this big, if it doesn't come from the chairman it does not happen." Without this senior executive support, technical leadership projects generally fail, ultimately adding very little value to a customer and potentially turning a customer off for a significant period of time. This is true of not only the individual end customer but also the corporate customer. As a Silicon Valley technology executive remarked, "If I type in xyz.com and just see what is out there and if they don't have a Web site, to be honest I discount them."

The importance of the executives' understanding and appreciating the technology and its implications for the business cycle of the organization cannot be understated. Some executives refer to this as *competing in Internet time*, or as John Nigard, CIO of Lennar Corporation, puts it, "Every month on the Internet is like a year." Failure to understand this can be catastrophic. Later in this chapter we will discuss some of the problems associated with assuming that the customer will "wait for a better Website," as one CEO put it shortly before being let go.

The position of technology leader has two dimensions, the *internal* and the *external*. The manifestation of the internal role is in the form of the business's ability to utilize technology and systems to remain flexible and agile relative to the organization's external connections and relationships. These external relationships can be either business to retail consumer (B2C), such as Amazon.com, or business to business (B2B), such as in the formation of a vertical hub for a specific industry such as plastics (www.plasticsnet.com) or a horizontal hub where an organization applies its services across industries (www.grainger.com). The relationships can also be between governments and business or vice versa (B2G or G2B). We will examine the external relationship further in chapters 5 and 6 when we examine the technology associated with the market and service dimensions of e-commerce leadership.

> A B2B e-commerce organization is primarily focused upon providing information, data, and connectivity between organizations in a vertical or functional product or industry market. Vertical hubs focus primarily upon a specific industry—entertainment, steel, construction—while functional hubs focus upon providing the same functions such as logistics, procurement, and project management across multiple industries.

While much is made of technology change within the Internet sector, the most pressing issue for senior executives is not the specific hardware and software but the strategic issues that surround their deployment. Hence, the focus of this chapter will not be on the hardware and software technology implementation issues, for which there are many alternative sources of information elsewhere, and for which the dizzying speed of change precludes a detailed assessment of any lasting value. Instead we focus upon the internal and external dimensions of technology leadership as related to an organization's e-commerce strategy as revealed through the organizations in our case studies.

Internal Technology Leadership: The Seven S Framework

In chapter 2 we became familiar with the three bonding dimensions of Internet strategy—*leadership, infrastructure,* and *organizational learning*—which link the positional leadership areas of *technology, market, service,* and *brand* together. To fully appreciate the issues surrounding internal technology leadership, we will in this section attempt to show how these seven aspects of an e-commerce strategy combine with the internal operational strategy of an organization. To

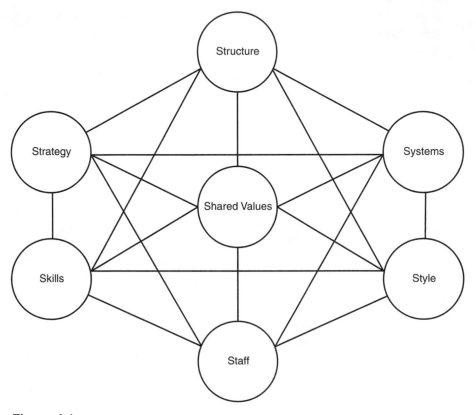

Figure 4.1
The McKinsey 7S Framework (Source: R. H. Waterman, T. J. Peters, and J. R. Phillips, "Structure Is Not Organization," *The McKinsey Quarterly,* Summer 1980, p. 7)

this end we utilize and draw upon an established strategy model from management consultants McKinsey & Company[1] known as the Seven S Framework (we will refer to it here as the McKinsey 7S model).

The essence of the McKinsey 7S model is that *a firm is the comprehensive sum of its parts,* and that the internal dynamics of an organization clearly determine that organization's ability to compete, the premise being that both the strategy

---

1. The 7S model was originally proposed by Richard T. Pascale and Anthony Athos in their book, *The Art of Japanese Management* (Simon & Schuster, New York, 1981) and subsequently refined by many, including Tom Peters and Bob Waterman of McKinsey, who refined the model through its application at McKinsey consulting engagements.

and the structure of the organization determine management's effectiveness. However, there is no rule or linear relationship among the structure, strategy, and organizational form, since clearly all organizations are different. Hence, the ability of an organization to develop and deliver an internal structure that facilitates competitive strength is both difficult to create and even more difficult to sustain.

The McKinsey 7S model attempts to create an awareness of the factors that, when utilized together, will assist in the formation of an organization that is greater than the sum of its parts. The hub and spoke unity of the seven factors can be seen in Figure 4.1. The factors themselves are defined in Table 4.1.

These factors form a strong basis for defining the basis for internal strategy formulation both in the traditional bricks-and-mortar world and, as we shall discuss in this chapter, within the online and clicks-and-mortar environments.

Table 4.1 A Glossary of the 7Ss[*]

Strategy (overall corporate)	Strategy can be defined as the determination of a course of action to be followed in order to achieve a desired goal, position, or vision.
Structure	An organization's structure is the interrelationship of processes and human capital in order to fulfill the enterprise's strategic objectives.
Systems	The organization's information systems and infrastructure.
Staff	Human resources management.
Style	Corporate style is a synthesis of the leadership philosophy of executive management, the internal corporate culture generated, and the orientation an organization adopts to its markets, customers, and competitors.
Skills	The unique or distinctive characteristics associated with an organization's human capital.
Shared Values	The concepts that an organization utilizes to drive toward a common goal through common objectives and a common value set.

[*]This table, from Richard Pascale and Antony Athos, is adapted to take account of the changes since their original definitions in 1981.

Strategy: The Alignment of Technology and Corporate Planning

The whole basis of technology strategy formulation is the ability of the organization's executive to achieve *alignment*, that is alignment between the technology strategy and the strategy of the enterprise as a whole. Key to achieving alignment is for the CIO to have as clear a vision as possible of the technology horizon and the implications of the new technologies coming over that horizon as is possible. Further, the CIO's vision of the new technologies and the associated changes they will bring must be aligned with, or preferably in advance of, the other executive members of the organization's strategy formulating body (see Figure 4.2). This gives the CIO time to plan ahead and bring to the boardroom carefully considered analysis made preemptively of change. As in the case of all technology issues and their potential impact upon the organization, the sensitivity of corporations to this *forward thinking* and advanced planning will be based upon traditional CIO-CEO issues such as:

☞ The degree to which the CIO is included in the strategic formulation process by the organization's senior executive

☞ The flexibility of budgetary constraints in times of special need

☞ Preexisting alignment of information technology and organizational strategy

☞ Special industry factors such as an impending threat of deregulation

Achieving acknowledgment at the highest levels of many staid organizations, with regard to the potential added value information technology can bring if positioned and used effectively, remains a difficult task for many CIOs. This presents a potentially huge problem for organizations that fail to accommodate this issue, especially in terms of organizational flexibility.

Figure 4.2
Strategy and
Technology
Horizons

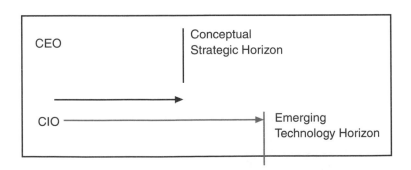

A second component to the alignment process is planning. The best-case scenario is for the CEO and CIO to have synergy and an aligned planning horizon. This derives from a shared sense of information technology values, strong communication dialogue, and a clear understanding of the leverage information technology provides when utilized in a timely and correct manner. However, this shared vision of the future has to be converted from the conceptual to the executable. This is the planning lead time. In many organizations that privately acknowledge that they cannot keep up with technology, the underlying reason behind this is that the lead time between the technology planning horizon and the deployment of systems necessary for, at a minimum, competitive parity is too small or nil.[2] In this situation executives are too busy being reactive, putting out fires, rather than being efficient and adding value by planning ahead and contemplating the bigger picture. In this situation the most important activity a CIO can undertake is to build the CIO-CEO relationship and develop an acknowledgment of the technology issues the organization faces at the highest levels of the organization.

In those organizations with *tech-strategy* alignment, the CIO's major concern is the *technology window*—a time period that consists of three parts (see Figure 4.3).

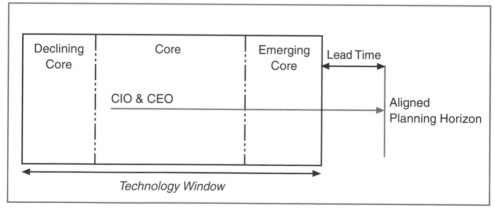

Figure 4.3
Technology Planning Horizons

---

2. At a CIO Forum (Miami, Fall 1999), 30 CIOs were asked, "Do you have sufficient 'lead time' to research emerging technologies, plan for their deployment, and execute to meet business needs?" All of them said no.

☞ Emerging core
☞ Core
☞ Declining core

Emerging core systems are systems involving the latest technological advancements, all of which are strategic to varying degrees of criticality. Top-ranked systems would be the *critical-to-survival systems*. For example, for a utility such as Florida Power & Light, the Open Access Same-Time Information System (OASIS) would be a top-ranked system because the Federal Energy Regulatory Commission has mandated that this system be used by all power utilities to buy, sell, and trade power transmission capacity. Also in this category would be systems that provide the organization with competitive strengths, such as:

☞ An improved logistics system that would provide a faster, more flexible delivery provision for a customer
☞ Security systems to prevent breaches by external entities
☞ Technologies that could be patented to provide long-term advantages

Emerging core systems may be subject to steep learning and experience curves, during which time the organization is attempting to execute the technology and adapt working practices to it. After the learning and experience curves have flattened out, a system moves on to become a *core* component of the organization's infrastructure and is used in a utilitarian manner.

In time, core systems that are not updated or amended will become *declining core* components. They will over time add less and less value to the company. Either the technology is too costly to support—the transaction costs are too high, even in terms of speed or efficiency of operation—or alternatively the organization changes its processes and the system cannot support the new systems being brought online effectively. Even if the technology is completely discounted, these are systems that need to be retired as part of a process of planned obsolescence.

The key to success in managing this technology window is the ability of the CIO and the organization to move from the learning and experience curve into the *lead time zone*, forward of the technology window (see Figure 4.3). This is, however, often very expensive in terms of time, resources, and skill sets and in some instances is not totally feasible, as was the case with Y2K and the EuroConversion issues. Clearly the technology window is a moving target, going forward each day, rolling new technologies onto the emerging core zone on the one side and rolling redundant technologies off the other.

A second key to managing this is the ability to perform financial decision making over this time line, the aim being to have:

$$\Sigma [\, W_{Inv.Core} \; ROI \,(Core), W_{Inv.Emerging} \; ROI \,(Emerging \; Core),$$
$$W_{Inv.Declining} \,(Declining \; Core)] \geq Required \; return \; on \; technology$$

where:

$$W_i = \frac{Investment \; amount \; in \; that \; technology \; space \; (core, \; emerging, \; or \; declining)}{Total \; technology \; investment}$$

Thus, W_i represents the weightings between investments in technology over the different stages in the applications life cycle, e.g., 30% in emerging core, 60% in core, and 10% in declining core. This provides a means of evolving an investment allocation model so that an organization can apportion its investments in a way that can drive future growth and earnings. Clearly the reality of deriving values for this equation are complex in reality, due to their intertwining, the ability to project and apportion earnings based upon individual technologies, the difficulty in deriving returns on intangibles, and so on.

> The alignment of IT strategy and organizational strategy is the key that unlocks a firm's ability to compete effectively and adapt to changing market forces.

The following sections consider the remaining six dimensions of the model in greater detail.

Structure: Characteristics of a Flexible, Agile E-organization

The second key issue organizations need to address in leveraging technology toward reaching a position of marketspace leadership is their ability to manage their internal structural dimension, generally characterized by a company's organization chart, i.e., functional, decentralized, etc. Organizations must ensure that their structural characteristics facilitate their ability to be flexible and agile enough to effectively and efficiently meet the needs of their market as it changes. In order to understand this better, let's consider two of the major parameters in this equation: the *nature of the product* and the *maturity of the organization.*

All firms wishing to compete in an electronic market space must have alignment between their organizational and technological strategies. However, refining this analysis we see that *youthful* and *start-up companies* have different strengths to mature than established organizations. Youthful companies in the manufacturing sector have attempted to create flat organizational structures with wide spans of control. They have streamlined their value chains and have tended to focus these advantages on providing mass customization at low cost. For example, Drugstore.com provides low-cost health, beauty, and wellness products through the convenience of home delivery and backed up by a staff of licensed pharmacists. Youthful service-based companies also frequently attempt to offer flexible solutions for customers; e.g., Priceline.com allows customers to negotiate prices with hotels, airlines, and car rental companies.

Mature enterprises generally have other strengths. In the manufacturing and production sector, successful firms are still competitive based upon their ability to regenerate themselves, to manage their "self-knowledge" effectively, and to ask themselves meta-knowledge questions such as *"What makes us effective?" "Who knows how to effectively optimize process X to maximize the output?" "Where is this data and information stored?" "How can this process be improved?"* and *"What are the constraints?"* This knowledge management task is a key to their success. In the mature service sector, organizations have built up decades of data and knowledge on customers and their requirements. These meta-data warehouses are mined to allow the organization to remain relevant to its marketplace.

> High degrees of self- or meta-knowledge are a characteristic of successful organizations that allows them to adapt and be flexible within dynamic marketplaces.

This is a shallow taxonomy of success factors; clearly there are many, and they are, as the McKinsey model points out, different in each case. However, in studying over 40 organizations in relation to this model, I noticed two interesting phenomena:

☞ ***The youth learn and the mature adapt.*** The first phenomenon identified was that youthful, flexible, service-based companies were attempting to create a complementary *market knowledge* strategy in order to capture organizational learning and grow effectively, while the mature market-knowledgeable organizations were attempting to shed management layers, leveraging the information technology to become more flexible. Further, a similar cross-directional movement phenomenon is also occurring in the manufacturing arena. Low-cost, youthful goods producers are also wishing to create knowledge management components to complement their organization, while mature, knowledge-rich companies are looking to leverage that knowledge through information technology to create lower-cost production mechanisms and compete effectively.

☞ ***The e-organization future will be a convergence of new operating models with experience.*** The second phenomenon identified was that those companies wishing to compete on the Internet in an e-commerce environment need to combine the factors of both youthful and mature organizations: flexibility, low operational costs, knowledge management, and market knowledge. These are the characteristics of tomorrow's e-organization (see Figure 4.4). This will be especially true once the "honeymoon" period in e-commerce has occurred and the first-move advantage has become less important. In this environment the start-up "darlings" of the late 1990s will have to compete head-to-head with the traditional powerhouse blue chip organizations that have become enabled for e-business, e.g., Merrill Lynch, IBM, Asda (UK Grocer), Wal-Mart, and News Corp.

Let us consider some of the companies in these sectors:

Youthful Service: **Charles Schwab,**[3,4] once a small discount brokerage but one with a passion for technology and its application, leveraged that technology to recreate itself as the number one online brokerage house. However, it is facing competition on two fronts:

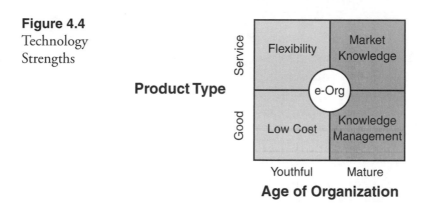

Figure 4.4
Technology Strengths

3. *The Charles Schwab Corporation in 1996*, Graduate School of Business, Stanford University Case: SM-35, August 1997.

4. www.schwab.com.

Future online competition: The drive for greater and greater efficiencies in this sector is matched only by the customers' desire for higher amounts of information and content at lower prices. Schwab will, in the near future, be forced to compete head-to-head against the awakening giants of Wall Street such as Morgan Stanley, Merrill Lynch, and Citicorp as they enact and develop a full-scale e-commerce strategy. The traditional companies in this sector may have lost some of the early battles of the war, but they are prepared for the duration and well armed with skills and financial resources. On the other flank will be the new start-up and youthful trading firms, offering creative new products and solutions to the brokerage market. Schwab will need to utilize its flexible organizational structure and develop self-knowledge to maintain agility in the market and focus and to not fall prey to lethargy, even if the biggest battle is with the traditional sector.

Youthful Manufacturing: **Dell Computers**, started as a flexible, low-cost producer, obtained superior market position by utilizing technology to create organizational self-awareness through knowledge management and data mining systems, levels of awareness that mature computer manufacturers failed to reach as they neglected these techniques and technologies.[5]

Future online competition: Competition in the manufacture of computer "boxes" for Dell as in the case of Schwab comes from two sectors: the traditional computer manufacturers such as IBM and Compaq who will be working to reestablish their market, and new organizations, who will probably not threaten Dell directly in the category of box manufacture, but who will challenge should a new technology paradigm shift occur. Such a shift may be the result of a move to high-bandwidth, multimegabit wireless systems. This would change the playing field significantly in the mind of the consumer and would allow IBM and others to reenter the "new" computing-device marketspace. It would also allow traditional companies in other sectors such as Motorola and Ericcsson to enter.

While this discussion has barely touched on the complexities that relate organizational structure with technology leadership, it is intended to serve as a general introduction to the dynamic nature of that important relationship, one that is different for each organization and each industry. This issue is one of the cornerstones of an e-commerce strategy and will be revisited as other topics are considered throughout the remainder of the book.

---

5. Michael Dell and Catherine Fredman, *Direct from Dell: Strategies That Revolutionized an Industry*, HarperBusiness, 1999.

Systems: The Nervous System Through Which the Organization Reacts to Its Environment

In developing an e-commerce strategy, one of the hidden strengths an organization can create is a flexible systems infrastructure. While it is always possible for competitors to copy or duplicate a company's product—e.g., Yahoo! duplicates the functionality of eBay's auction system—competitors will have difficulty in being able to continue to duplicate and match the production of new market offerings if their internal systems are less flexible.

While this book does not discuss individual specific technological applications, since they change daily, research identified three major dimensions of technology infrastructure:

- ☞ Enterprise resource planning systems
- ☞ Data warehousing
- ☞ Knowledge management

These systems provide the infrastructure base for the competitive strategies executed in our case studies. Together they also provide for flexibility and are worth examining in greater detail.

Enterprise Resource Planning Systems

The basis of an enterprise resource planning (ERP) system is simple—all organizational activities that involve information processing are stored and maintained in a database through one image; that is, the data is stored once and uniquely as a set of tables. One such table might represent an inventory relationship—a book name in relation to the number of each in stock; another table could relate the book name to the retail price of the book; while a third might relate the book name to the publisher. By creating such tables, all the information content of an organization can be represented and manipulated efficiently.

Having represented the data, the next step is to represent the processes. This is done through the changes that occur when a process is activated. For example, if a book were added to the selection offered by the bookstore, the "add book" process would be activated. In this process, the new book information, added by an employee, might be the name of the book (Book Name), its recommended retail price (Retail Price), and the publisher (Publisher). This would then cause the (Book Name, Retail Price) (Book Name, Publisher) tables to add the relevant data items. Additionally the "initial inventory management" process and its tables would be initiated. Since the stock level on a new book being added is zero, then this would be below the reorder level as represented in those tables (Book Name, Stock Level) (Book Name, Reorder Level) and would cause an "order initial purchase" process to occur and the accounts payable processes to be activated. The activation of processes would continue rippling through the system. This spreading activation creates an organic spreadsheet of the company to be contained in the ERP in real time.

The decision to move to an ERP system is a critical decision that should never be taken lightly. Two major issues influence the decision:

☞ What is the driver of potential added value that motivates this change?

☞ Does the corporation have a clear understanding of its key sources of competitive advantage?

These issues need clear answers and should be addressed at the board of directors level. If the key driver of potential added value is the promise of process flexibility, then is the move to an ERP system the way to go? To answer this we need to consider the second issue in more depth. The strategic processes that actually deliver the competitive strengths of the corporation may in fact be weakened by a move away from so-called "legacy" customized programs to the ERP process models. The ERP process models aspire to be the best practice models, but by nature a widely applicable system can only be generalist in nature; beyond its plug-and-play basic setup, customization will be expensive and potentially perilous. The FoxMeyers Corp., for example—once a thriving $5 billion wholesale drug distribution company with over 2,500 employees, replaced its Unisys mainframe system that handled 420,000 customer orders per day with a $65 million ERP system from SAP. According to Bart Brown Jr., the court-appointed trustee who represented FoxMeyer in a lawsuit against SAP and Anderson Consulting, the SAP R/3[6] ERP system could process only 10,000 orders per day—about 2.5% of the former capacity.[7] Clearly, the return on investment for the ERP was forecast to be positive based upon a lowered transaction cost delivered through the ERP. However, the second of our two issues—the process basis of competitive success—seems to have been

---

6. R/3 refers to revision 3 (or sometimes it is referred to as standing for real time); R/2 ran on a mainframe and revision 3 was a client-server version.

7. Lynda Radosevich, "Bankrupt Drug Company Sues SAP," InfoWorld Electric. it.idg.net/crd_sap_12014.html

underconsidered. The logistics processes built up over the years at the company were its strength, dedicated to its customer needs and tuned to its product mix and turnover variations. The Unisys systems were also crafted to model these processes. The ERP in its standard form should not have been expected to model the existing processes, and clearly the further the new systems had to be tuned from their standard industry model, the more downside risk becomes present.

CEOs and executive teams therefore face a series of challenges:

1. Companies need to cut costs across the value chain. This requires that they reengineer their processes, reducing the "friction" across transactions.

2. In order to remain competitive and to facilitate moves to meet and counter market and competitor moves, processes need to become more flexible. This again requires systems to add—as Ian Robertson, BMW's managing director, Africa, states—"flexibility without complexity."[8]

3. In order to improve their relationships with customers, organizations need to generate information and content that add value from the processes themselves.

Enterprise resource systems focus primarily upon solving the first of these issues, reducing friction by forcing companies to move toward standardizing the processes,[9] while flexibility is facilitated by the organization's ability to reconfigure its processes more quickly and efficiently than ever before. Having standard corporatewide processes facilitates this as organizations achieve a clearer understanding of the ramifications of process change.

The third issue—that of improving the customer relationship—is enabled by the organization's ability to generate data regarding its processes and to use that information to better inform its customers. For example, in response to a request over the Web from a customer who is inquiring as to the status of an order, an ERP system can be utilized to generate an answer, delivered by e-mail, such as "Your computer is currently being created and will exit the assembly line in 20 minutes proceeding to quality assurance."

---

8. Personal communication.

9. Processes don't all have to be configured the same in the ERP; accounting processes may differ from country to country. Also inventory management processes at different corporate sites may differ. However, rather than generate two ERP routines, organizations often prefer to standardize to one process.

The major concern for the ERP vendors is that there are two dimensions to a transaction—the *back office* (back end) and the *front office* (see Figure 4.5). Until the advent of the e-commerce marketspace, the focus was on the back-end transactional issues, reducing the friction of the internal value chain. This value chain was being fed data from internal data sources (e.g., loading bay, warehouses, manufacturing stations) or externally primarily from electronic data interchange (EDI) mechanisms. The EDI interorganizational communication through which computers interact, swapping payments, credits, invoices, returns, etc., has been occurring invisibly for many years and is the basis of the B2B relationships forming in the e-commerce space. The B2B hub has grown out of the need to streamline the process, further facilitating interaction between community members.

However, the demand to transact externally either B2B, B2G, or B2C is such that the vendors have to create secure, online, front-office systems. This facilitates

Figure 4.5
An Integrated
E-commerce
Systems
Architecture

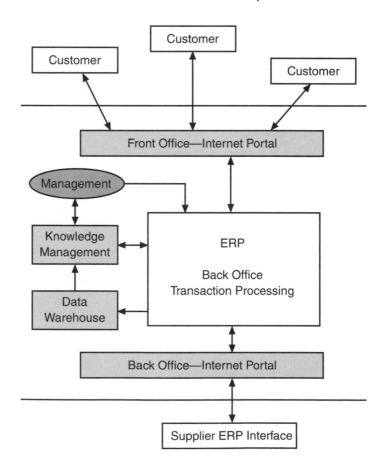

a direct customer channel to the ERP mechanism and gives the customer a feeling of interacting with a virtual organization, a one-to-one experience with that organization. In the case of a B2B hub or e-consortium, the aim is to provide one contact channel and one relationship management point through which the customer-organization experience is managed.

As the front-office capability is extended to meet the demands of customers and the changing environments through which they wish to interact—B2B or B2C—ERP vendors will have to create more process flexibility in their systems. This will be necessary to facilitate the internal flexibility requirements of organizations as they attempt to meet their customer requests for differentiated products and services. Again the challenge for organizations is to balance their internal flexibility with the market dynamics and the changes they require. We can summarize the ERP debate by looking at Figure 4.6. This shows two variables, *the efficiency requirement on the value chain* on the vertical axis and *the added value of information to customers* on the horizontal. As a company competes in the provision of a good or service, a commoditization of that good or service occurs. Thus, commencing from an original position at point X, three possible strategic directions can be taken.

1. An organization can, if it wishes, pursue the direction of being a minimal-cost producer (move to point A); it does this by increasing the efficiency of its value chain (e.g., the lowest of the deep-discount brokerages charges approximately $5—a low-transaction-cost strategy). This may be effectively achieved through successful deployment of an ERP.

    The implications of this strategy are usually realized at point C, the strategic inflection point, as Intel CEO Andy Grove terms it. At this

Figure 4.6
E-commerce
Information
Intensity Matrix

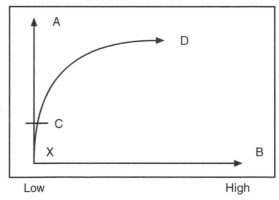

point the organization recognizes that a commoditization marketspace is one in which it does not wish to compete—it realizes that these marketspaces inevitably become saturated with players who continue to segment the market and engage in long battles for incremental increases in market share, living off of slim margins; ultimately corporate scale and financial backing prevail.

2. Once this realization has been made, the alternative path is to keep the existing product-transaction cost structure and move to provide an enhanced information-based product (point B), investing the transaction profits into product creation and for-fee services. Such a strategy was employed by the full-service brokerages. However, this is not acceptable in the long term, as competition is frequently a combination of the two variables—low-cost transactions with added information value.

3. The third strategy takes organizations to point D. To achieve this, an organization requires a two-part strategy: a successful improvement in its value chain efficiency leveraged using the ERP-based information, thus reducing costs; second, the provision of added-value services to the customer based on the information the ERP provides in conjunction with its integration to other systems.

The goal for the majority of e-commerce organizations is to reach and stay at point D. Charles Schwab utilizes and executes this strategy very successfully. The company moved from a traditional brokerage position to being the largest online brokerage, offering value-added research information on financial markets and trading at a discount to the full-service brokerages.

Data Warehousing

The creation by the ERP system of a full and detailed information trail for every transaction undertaken by an organization is clearly a wonderful starting point to attack the two dimensions of competitive positioning we identified earlier: cost efficiency and information effectiveness.

Cost Efficiency Focus: The data warehouse allows corporations to utilize historical data regarding their processes as data sets for analysis. The analysis may be within any function or level within the organizational structure.

The pyramid in Figure 4.7 represents the data warehouse in two dimensions. The horizontal axis represents the volume of data generated from the processes. It is from this historical data set that the person querying the data drills

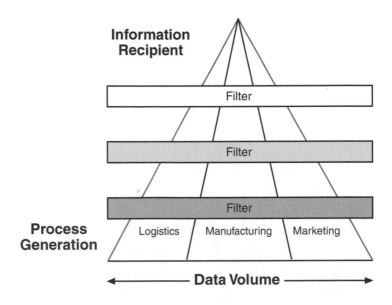

Figure 4.7
The Data
Warehousing
Pyramid

down, filtering the data to facilitate analysis. A data set will have many uses at different organizational levels. At the factory level the warehouse manager may wish to see the historical warehouse capacity requirements over a set of dates. This can then be used to predict future peak-time capacity demands to reduce costs. Divisional management may wish to consolidate the production from all the factories in that division to minimize duplication, while the executive level may wish to consolidate data to see if the organization is hitting its fiscal targets. An example of this top-level usage: A brokerage firm creates an executive information system through its data warehouse. This might be linked to a geographical database, which shows the performance of the brokerage's branch offices in a certain region against their management goals; these regions can then be compared to each other on a map. Alternatively the results for a single office may be displayed in a linear "traffic light" form, as shown in Figure 4.8. This allows the ERP to be leveraged to create a data source for the data warehouse, which in turn creates knowledge for the knowledge management systems. The Internet can also be leveraged to create a "Web warehouse"[10] which is the utilization of the Internet to allow access to the data warehouse.

Information Effectiveness: The second dimension of data warehousing is its use to further competitive intelligence. The aim is to focus data the organization has

10. R. D. Hackathon, *Web Farming for the Data Warehouse*, Morgan Kaufmann, San Francisco, 1999.

Brokerage Branch		Miami, Florida				Date: 2000, Week 17
New Customers	650	Target	500	Margin	150 (+32.5%)	◐
Trading Volume	6,789,256	Target	6,000,000	Margin	789,256 (+13%)	◯
Customer Retention	87.6%	Target	93%	Margin	−5.4 (−5.9%)	●

Figure 4.8
Executive Information System—Data Mining Analysis

gathered through its ERP and other systems with the aim of creating new business opportunities through knowledge management. This may be in marketing, where the data is used to identify direct marketing opportunities; in finance, to identify high-value customers who pay their bills in a timely manner; or in branding, where the need to study brand issues in a segmenting product space is increasingly important.

The ability to leverage information effectiveness is becoming more and more vital as the marketspaces in which organizations compete change ever more rapidly. Organizational survival comes increasingly from having a self-knowledge regarding the data the firm owns or has access to. This meta-knowledge may be a corporation's only lifeline when its traditional business environment morphs dramatically.

Data warehousing can be seen therefore as the basis of a knowledge repository that, when used effectively, enables cost reduction strategies to be identified, added-value services to be achieved at manageable cost, and the delivery of an improved data effectiveness within the organization. However, it is also the basis of the next dimension of an e-commerce organization infrastructure, that of knowledge management.

Knowledge Management

The third dimension of an organization's e-commerce infrastructure is that of knowledge management, an area that can be defined as "the formal management of an organization's knowledge resources."[11] Knowledge management

---

11. D. E. O'Leary, "Knowledge Management Systems: Converting and Connecting," *IEEE Intelligent Systems*, May/June 1998.

Baxter International

Baxter International is an example of corporate survival through successful information systems deployment. Baxter International is one of the largest U.S. manufacturers and distributors of medical supplies, its size resulting from the merger of Baxter Travenol, a major manufacturer of medical products, and American Hospital Supply Corporation, the largest distributor of medical products in the world, in 1985. However, when the healthcare industry was deregulated, Baxter's EDI-based ordering system, ASAP, could no longer guarantee a "lock in" on its hospital consumer base, a luxury it had enjoyed since the early 1960s. The government had in the mid-1980s mandated that all hospital EDI be performed under a standard protocol (X.12). As Baxter scrambled to replace its legacy EDI systems with an online X.12 and subsequently an Internet-based system, the true value of the previous 30 years of data became apparent.* The wake-up call for Baxter came during the 1980s when the government and the HMOs pushed for generic products to be utilized wherever possible. This signaled the potential commoditization of Baxter's products—a move toward a low-margin, high-volume marketplace. This signaled to Baxter that it was at an inflection point in its industry. It had two options: it could continue on its path and, if commoditization came about, compete on price; or alternatively it could change course and create information-based products. Baxter chose to do both, consolidating and streamlining its physical products business while creating a separate company, Allegiance, which provided added-value services to the health industry. These services included inventory and warehouse management, as well as physician-related services. This was spun off as a separate company in 1998.

*For further reading, see *Baxter International: On Call as Soon as Possible*, Harvard Case Study, 9-195-103 and J. Short and N. Verkatraman, "Beyond Business Process Redesign: Redefining Baxter's Business Network," *Sloan Management Review*, Fall 1992, pp. 7–21.

---

had been an area of academic study mainly since Vannevar Bush first defined the term *hypertext*. His 1945 *Atlantic Monthly* article described a vision of what we now recognize as the World Wide Web.

> Consider a future device for individual use, which is a sort of mechanized private file and library. It needs a name, and to coin one at random, "memex" will do. A memex is a device in which an individual stores all his books, records, and communications, and which is mechanized so that it may be consulted with exceeding speed and flexibility. It is an enlarged intimate supplement to his memory.

It consists of a desk, and while it can presumably be operated from a distance, it is primarily the piece of furniture at which he works. On the top are slanting translucent screens, on which material can be projected for convenient reading. There is a keyboard, and sets of buttons and levers. Otherwise it looks like an ordinary desk.[12]

Just as there are leaders and followers in other dimensions of e-commerce technology, the same is true in the knowledge management (KM) arena. Expenditures in KM have been explosive with spending of over $4.5 billion in the area by 2000.[13] However, as one might suspect, not all investment is adding value. The adage of "garbage in, garbage out" still applies; with some estimates of corporate databases containing up to a petabyte of information (a million billion bytes) the onus is thus upon the chief knowledge officer (CKO) to ensure that the knowledge management system produces a positive return on investment (ROI) for the organization. While ROI is difficult to measure directly, a scorecard approach can be taken. Questions like the following can be assessed:

☞ Does the KM system improve the organization-customer relationship?

☞ Does the KM system contribute to improved logistics management?

☞ Does the KM system reduce cycle time, time in development, production, and production changeover?

☞ Does the KM system improve R&D communications and effectiveness?

☞ Is the KM system effective in increasing organizational learning for all employees and levels?

These types of metrics can be developed for each organization and monitored over time, but it must be remembered that the KM system is effectively a living entity and its contribution to ROI should not "flatten off" over time.

In order to maximize their returns on this valuable asset base, organizations are creating new senior-level positions, usually titled with a variant of the term *chief knowledge officer,* or CKO. The relevance of this position has been growing as organizations realize the value of their internal knowledge base. Innovative CKOs are searching for tools and systems to help them create knowledge

---

12. Vannevar Bush, "As We May Think," *The Atlantic Monthly,* July 1945.

13. Wayne Applehans, Alder Globe, and Greg Laugero, *Managing Knowledge: A Practical Web-Based Approach,* Addison-Wesley, Reading, MA, 1999.

environments for their organizations. One approach is the *enterprise document management* (EDM) systems approach, in which an organization deploys an *automated metaphor* for an organizationwide filing system; this is the mechanism taken by IBM through Lotus Domino. This approach builds vertical silos of files and indexing mechanisms that are developed according to the individual organization and its structural needs. Domino and other EDM systems are based upon four basic knowledge-sharing relationships:

☞ Document to document
☞ Document to processes
☞ People to communities
☞ People to documents

Emerging in this domain is the second generation of EDMs—the concept of the *enterprise information portal* (EIP), a systems approach that is on a convergence path with the second-generation, browser-based ERP systems. ERP systems as we discussed earlier are currently aimed at processing back-end transactions. Second-generation systems are aimed at providing greater potential flexibility to the user through graphical-web-enabled, Windows-like interfaces, which are allowing developers to craft tools and applications for their functional areas such as logistics, accounting, and inventory management. Similarly, the second-generation EDMs or EIPs are aimed at providing greater flexibility to the CKO and his team by allowing users to view reports, information, and data through their Internet portal interfaces. Since the portals currently exist on most employees' machines, this offers an attractive solution for CIOs continually haunted by compatibility and legacy concerns.

There are three types of portals emerging—data, information, and collaborative—The IT & Media research organization estimates that the market for portal goods and services of this type will reach nearly $15 billion by the year 2002.[14]

☞ **Data portals,** where the stored data is *structured* in nature, containing historical data of the type usually associated with a data warehouse. This would include data like sales vouchers and inventory level data, for example. The primary use of this form of data is for the creation of reports.

---

14. S. L. Roberts-Witt, "Making Sense of Portal Pandemonium," *Knowledge Management,* July 1999, pp. 3–48.

The data portal is closely related to the second generation of ERP systems, where a portal or Windows-type front end allows users to create dynamic reports from structured relational databases.

☞ *Information portals,* where the stored data is unstructured data and stored in the form of text, e-mails, diagrams, and data objects such as voice and video streams. These portals are to assist in the navigation through and around these information-rich data items, ultimately to allow ad hoc queries and report generation.

☞ *Collaborative portals,* aimed at the distillation of information from heterogeneous data types or data from multiple sources, both structured and unstructured. The aim here is to provide group interactive functionality together with the ad hoc querying and reporting of information portals.

Clearly, the choice of portal is dependent upon the organization's technical maturity, its existing systems infrastructure, and its human resources. However, as the technology develops and the portal approach to knowledge management becomes integrated to the data warehouse and the ERP system, the organizational cost of implementation will decrease. This will enable younger organizations to leverage these technologies in conjunction with their nimble structures and processes. The competition through infrastructure will only intensify.

The creation, development, and integration of data and systems into a portal form is not easy, however, and there is considerable difficulty in automatically establishing information relationships between these often diverse information and data types. However the collective associated knowledge between them is a potentially rich source of corporate knowledge and one in which significant competitive advantage can be gained by those organizations willing to invest in this emerging core technology.

Staffing

Human Capital the Bedrock of an Organization

The bedrock of an organization is clearly its people. The old adage that 90% of the value of an organization disappears every evening in the elevator is more true today than at any time in the past. As organizations evolve toward becoming knowledge based, the value of an organization's intellectual assets cannot be overstated and is magnified by a drought in the supply of IT skills. The Information Technology Association of America (ITAA) estimates (1999) that about 190,000 information technology jobs in the U.S. are unfilled, while the

Labor Department projects that, between now and 2005, an average of 95,000 new computer scientists, systems analysts, and programmers will be needed every year. In 1998, however, only 24,553 U.S. students earned bachelor's degrees in computer or information sciences fields; according to ITAA this leaves a shortage of 346,000 programmers, systems analysts, and computer scientists in the United States alone (see Figure 4.9).[15] The scarcity of talent and the drive for change induced through the new technologies will be a significant potential problem for executives and one in which the human resources function will need to become increasingly creative.

Where Are All the CIOs?

The first problem facing e-commerce organizations and traditional organizations alike is where to find a CEO and CIO.

Born on the Net.com

As discussed earlier, the lure of a start-up, born-on-the-net organization is almost irresistible, and seasoned executives are being drawn to them like moths to a flame. Entire teams often leave a company together to join a start-up, or an entrepreneur "cherry-picks" as was described at Webvan.com—CEO George Shaheen moved from a prime consulting position to head the organization

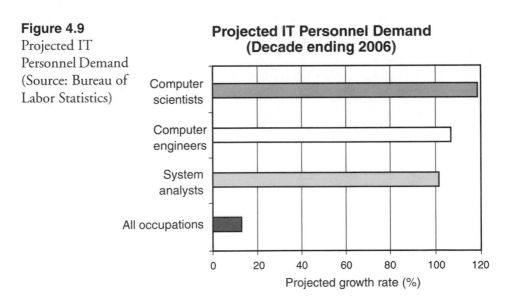

Figure 4.9
Projected IT Personnel Demand (Source: Bureau of Labor Statistics)

---

15. "IT Worker Availability, Skill Sets & Technologies," *ITAA Research Report*, San Francisco, 1999 (www.itaa.org).

together with Kevin R. Czinger, senior vice president, corporate operations and finance, who previously served as a managing director in the media and telecommunications group at Merrill Lynch & Co., and Peter Relan, the senior vice president, technology, who came from Oracle Corporation where he served as vice president of Internet server products in its application server division.[16] The list of CIOs who have left "traditional organizations" is growing every day—Mayland Webb left Gateway to go to eBay; Ken Harris left Nike to go to Gap's Internet initiative,[17] and the list will continue to grow.

> IT staffing rotation is often an indication of deeper organizational issues.

Traditional Organizations.com

For a traditional organization in the midst of a major change in information systems strategy, the pain of losing a CIO cannot be downplayed. These periods are when an organization is at its most vulnerable, needing strong, trusted vision and leadership together with firm and experienced project management skills in order to roll out the new systems on time and within budget.

One key issue for traditional organizations is building higher CIO and IT employee retention rates, because it is far more cost-effective to retain an employee than to recruit a replacement. Research revealed that "only 48% of employees are committed to staying with their current employers for the next one or two years." It identified that "the biggest reason people are weighing their options isn't money; it's the question of whether their current job offers opportunities for growth and development."[18] The High-Tech Retention Survey conducted by Linkage Inc., a Lexington, MA, consulting organization, examined 418 different organizations throughout the United States and identified the top five factors most strongly associated with retention:[19]

☞ Perceived value of the individual

☞ Opportunity for growth

☞ Trust

---

16. www01.webvan.com/default.asp

17. J. Mateyaschuk and R. Jaleshgari, "The New CIOs," *Information Week*, August 16, 1999.

18. Tom Field, "Half of all tech workers are ready to jump ship," *CIO Magazine*. www.cio.com/forums/staffing/edit/122199_staff.html

19. Linkage Inc., www.linkageinc.com/retention

☞ Communication

☞ Values of the organization

Strategies to Jump-Start a Flagging IT Recruitment Program

Research for this book identified two alternative paths to gain a CIO and develop a creative technology agenda.

☞ **Think outside the box.** CIOs for e-commerce do not have to be techies. The nature of the systems an organization wishes to develop should act as a strong indicator of the type of CIO it requires. The development of e-commerce systems is in many situations driven as much by the creative effort as by the technology. Thus a partnering mode of systems development is frequently utilized by organizations. This demands different skill sets that focus on both the creative aspects of deployment and the financial and technical. Thus, with the advent of the *marketing technology e-commerce groups* within companies, we are identifying many more marketing CIOs than before, supported by technologists, consultants, and vendors.

☞ **Outsource.** Develop a virtual e-commerce office strategy. Through the creation of a separate organizational entity, a firm can manage a series of contacts, which, when coordinated correctly through a set of relationship partners, can accommodate changes in the market and technologies, thereby reducing the associated internal learning and experience curve costs. This environment can be supported by minimal staff and enhanced through *nominated e-commerce groups* in the parent company when necessary.

The ability to attract and retain employees from the executive level on down within the technology fields is going to be a key lever of success. With the increasing speed of the Internet economy, a failure to develop this aspect of the business can be terminal for the business as a whole. It is always useful to bear in mind that the most imaginative business plan is useless if it fails to be executed, and the IT professionals need to be clearly acknowledged as valued team members who execute the strategic intent at the technical level.

Skills: Running Up a Down Escalator

Research for this book identified that a successful blend of two skill sets is vital to the development of a balanced e-commerce systems strategy.

☞ Technical skills

☞ Relationship management skills

These two skill sets form the pillars between which the information systems structure is supported, developed, and managed at the strategic, functional, project, and application levels (see Figure 4.10). Both skill sets necessitate adherence to the three Cs—**C**apture, **C**ultivate, and **C**reate employees and their skills—and are managed and coordinated through the executive team.

Relationship Management

E-commerce has revolutionized the customer relationship proposition[20] to the point where the customer has a direct interface to the mass customization production function. This is forcing organizations to develop new models for

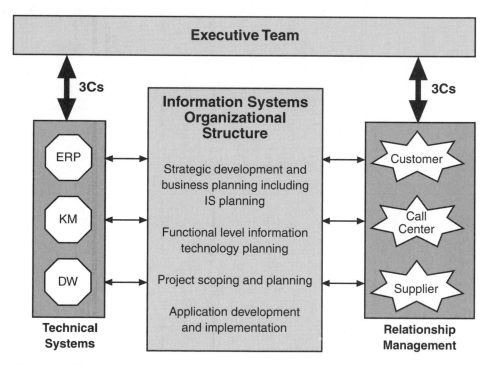

Figure 4.10
The Organizational Level HR Requirements

---

20. We can think of the supplier in this relationship as a customer to the extent that the organization wishes to maintain a positive relationship with that entity.

managing the HR needs for the employees who manage this delicate function. These models are based on drivers such as:

☞ **C**apture, **C**ultivate, and **C**reate straddle skill sets.

☞ Nurture employee flexibility and develop employees' creative skill sets.

☞ Build a dot-com mentality within the organization.

The ability to create crossover skills is vital, as the transformation of business ideas into technical solutions in a reduced time frame is the nature of e-business. The separation of the technology from relationship management staffing is no longer acceptable. An example of this new approach can be found in the technology/marketing-styled departments that have emerged to service the customer base of organizations such as American Express and Royal Caribbean Cruises.

In order to nurture this adaptivity and flexibility among employees, it is necessary to retain them. As discussed earlier, this is an ever more difficult task as the skill shortage encourages job-hopping for better pay and stock options. An approach successfully executed by organizations such as Office Depot and Toys R Us is to create a dot-com atmosphere within their own organizations. This may require setting up the e-commerce group in a remote location away from the traditional corporate center, such as in San Francisco, Cambridge, MA, or Silicon Valley, away from the day-to-day activity of the MIS shop. Without allowing this creative atmosphere and freedom of execution, retaining talent may be impossible. It may even be necessary to eventually spin the dot-com division off as a separate company as a tracking stock and with the stock option appeal of Silicon Valley start-ups.

Technical Systems

The skill sets surrounding the ERP, KM, and data warehousing (DW) environments are primarily technical in nature. However, the need for a reduced concept-to-cash cycle time requires developers to also have the ability to cross over easily into the customer relationship and management areas. In managing technical systems workers, the capture, cultivation, and creation of crossover skill sets require two sets of skills be enhanced:

☞ *Soft skills:* A difficult transition for many died-in-the-wool technologists to make is to understand that there is a customer or potential customer at the end of the system and that the applications are run for their happiness, not the technologists'. To this end "techno-MBA" manager skills need to be acquired by the technologists in order for them to understand the issues involved and the goals that the team is pursuing. Quite often this will result in a freeing of the mind and the production of interesting ideas during the course of brainstorming sessions—ideas that may never occur to techno converts who originated from the business side of the firm.

☞ *Hard skills:* This involves an appreciation of crossover technical skills, which entails knowing not only the ERP, KM, and DW environments, but also the technical systems associated with the Internet engines and interfaces themselves, such as networks, security, graphics packages, and database systems.

An organization must nurture employee flexibility if it is to avoid the "silo" effect of compartmentalized knowledge among its technical staff. This flexibility combined with a dot-com mentality allows the organization to keep its skill sets fresh and its employee base motivated while at the same time keeping employees financially and intellectually rewarded.

> Nurturing of employee flexibility is vital to avoid the "silo" effect of compartmentalized knowledge.

Management of the information systems group that links the soft and hard skill areas together in an e-commerce organization clearly has to demonstrate the traditional qualities through which CIOs need to add value. These six drivers are as vital for e-commerce as they have been for other technology developments in the past:[21]

1. The obsessive and continuous focus on the business imperative
2. Interpretation of external IT success stories
3. Establishment and maintenance of IT executive relationships
4. Establishment and communication of IT performance record
5. Concentration of the IT development effort
6. Achievement of a shared and challenging vision of the role of IT

However, in order to achieve a fluid and flexible systems function, three central tenets have to be reinforced.

---

21. D. Feeny and M. Earl, "Is Your CIO Adding Value?" *Sloan Management Review* 35(3), pp. 11–20.

1. **The CIO must be in a continuous and open dialogue with the CEO and other senior executives.** The speed of change within the competitive landscape requires that the CIO and IS management be not only aligned with the executive thought process, but often leading it.

2. **It's even more crucial for the management of an e-commerce organization to be multidisciplinary.** This is essential to reduce the communications overhead involved in managing the diverse aspects of e-commerce business operations. Not only must management have a strong technical understanding of systems and the "art of the possible" within the complexities of ERP, KM, and DW, but it must also have strength in marketing, planning, and operations in order to be able to execute the strategic vision.

3. **Finally, the CIO and management need to be great motivators to create an internal dot-com organization and to keep their corporate knowledge pool intact.**

Combined, these characteristics will provide an organization with a strong leadership and skill set upon which to draw as the market changes, as the technology changes, and as the organization *must* change to meet the demands arising from market and technology changes.

Style and Shared Values: The Magic That Raises the Ordinary .com to Become a Great .com

Richard Pascale and Antony Athos, in their original version of the 7Ss Model, define style as "characterization of how key managers behave in achieving the organization's goals; also the cultural style of the organization" and shared values as "the significant meanings or concepts that an organization utilizes to drive towards a common goal through common objectives and a common value set."[22] In their work they consider these as independent parameters. However, the research for this book into the drivers of success in e-commerce shows that it is becoming more and more difficult to separate the two, and thus they are considered codependent parameters in this discussion. In order to consider these issues further, consider Figure 4.11.

---

22. Reprinted with permission of Simon & Schuster, from *The Art of Japanese Management*, p. 81, by Richard Tanner Pascale and Anthony G. Athos. © 1981 by Richard Tanner Pascale and Anthony G. Athos.

Figure 4.11
The Dimensions
of an Agile
E-organization

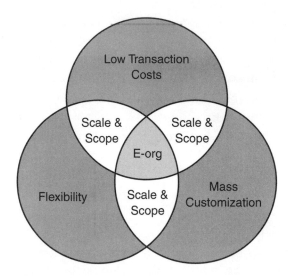

In the course of studying e-commerce strategies for this book, it became clear that the leading organizations were constantly striving for agility, whether they were in the service sector or the manufacturing sector, or through a B2C, B2B, or other environment. Key to achieving this were three initiatives:

1. The drive for flexibility in process
2. The drive to lower transaction costs
3. The drive to achieve mass customization for the customer

The aim is for executive management to achieve these three goals by working in a highly creative, flexible manner that rapidly delivers a customer-oriented solution to a changing marketplace.

Flexibility can take many forms. It may be in the composition of the management group; for example, as noted earlier, Royal Caribbean Cruise Lines created a new group to handle its e-commerce marketspace—the marketing-automation group. Alternatively, it may be in management's flexibility toward experimentation by members of the e-commerce group, whether that is in the area of new technical products or new marketing ideas such as live online video. It may go as far as creating a new organization with the dot-com mentality and relocating this company in the heart of the e-commerce world, as Toys R Us.com and OfficeDepot.com have done moving to Silicon Valley.

The drive to *low transaction costs* is the second key characteristic of an e-commerce organization. The very nature of competition on the Internet is to drive down the cost of transactions. The Internet is the ultimate equalizer of costs. Especially in a service sector, customers will expect the costs of frictionless processes to be passed on to them with very little margin or at zero margins. No aspect of e-business is exempt from this—even America Online (AOL), the Internet service provider (ISP), was forced to change its pure online organization business portal model through the acquisition of a content pipeline in the form of Time Warner, thus defraying the potential downside risk should a sizable competitor ultimately offer free Internet connection in the United States.

The third factor influencing the strategy of e-organizations is their ability to increase the value of the information surrounding the product. This is tied into the customer's need for *mass customization:* the delivery of customized products and services to individual customers or corporations in the case of B2B or B2G.

Summary

In order to achieve the status of an e-organization, *traditional established* organizations have to become more flexible, offering mass customized services online while being sensitive to pressures on margins. *Youthful organizations* need to be able to establish themselves in an increasingly competitive market while growing their own internal knowledge management to facilitate change, adaptability, and nimbleness to new market conditions. Should the organizations fail to maintain flexibility, not continue to lower costs, or apply their organizational knowledge—both internal and market, then they will fall outside the boundaries defining successful e-organizations and be unable to compete effectively. The understanding of this and the formulation of a strategy to execute this is clearly the role of the CEO and his team. Failure to comprehend this and execute accordingly is not acceptable and has led to the departure of many senior executives in recent years.

The Seven S Framework: Issues and Actions

The area of technology leadership involves much more than purely the hardware and software that compose an organization's physical infrastructure. We have, through this chapter, attempted to utilize the 7S model in a new way to provide a corporate framework through which executives can formulate an internal strategy for e-commerce. The major issues and areas for action can be summarized:

1. Strategy

Issue: Focus upon alignment and planning

Action Items:

- ☞ The CIO must have a clear vision of the technology horizon and be able to communicate the implications of these new technologies to the CEO and the business.
- ☞ Build a lead-time buffer for organizational learning between the technology horizon and the deployment of that technology.
- ☞ Create a roll-in, roll-out technology window; new technology becomes an emerging core technology, transitioning to core before finally declining and being discarded.

2. Structure

Issue: Focus upon becoming an e-organization

Action Items:

- ☞ Strive to balance organizational and technical strategies.
- ☞ Youthful companies must exploit the flexibility and low-cost structure to compete, aiming to capture self-knowledge and market knowledge to fend off existing organizations.
- ☞ Mature organizations must leverage their extensive self-knowledge and market knowledge in order to reduce their costs and recreate their processes in a more flexible manner.

3. Systems

Issue: Technology integration

Action Items:

- ☞ *ERP deployment:* Automation without change is detrimental; the ERP must be deployed with the aim of generating greater organizational self-knowledge, flexibility of process, and lowered operational costs.
- ☞ *Data warehouse:* Focus upon the two dimensions of data warehousing: *cost efficiency,* using the ERP data through the data warehouse to reduce

operational costs, and *information effectiveness* to generate competitive intelligence in the form of added-value information services.

☞ *Knowledge management:* The focus of the knowledge management system is to inform and add value, not to be a "look-up table." The creation of a metrics-based scorecard approach to the utility of the knowledge management system is vital.

4. Staffing

Issue: The role of the CIO

Action Items:

☞ Create a strategy for retaining and maintaining a strong pool of skills both at the executive level and at the technical level.

☞ Think outside the box for staffing solutions, and identify partners and consultants that could assist the process should internal skill sets be unavailable.

☞ Many issues surrounding staff development have traditional solutions that involve building trust, communications, and growth opportunities for the employee, as well as the organization understanding the value of the employee and the employee adopting the values of the corporation.

5. Skills

Issue: The role of the CIO

Action Items:

☞ The CIO must continue to add value through traditional routes, but adding to this list the ability to Capture, Cultivate, and Create an employee base with vision, technical skill, and creativity.

☞ Relationship management: This is a driver that requires heightened attention and focus by the entire organization. The relationship management system is the organization's early warning system of change in the marketplace and in customer needs.

☞ The heightened necessity to nurture employees and develop the organization's internal flexibility, creating a dot-com atmosphere of excitement, drive, openness, and creativity within the corporation.

☞ Technical skills: More than ever the CIO must develop crossover skills and the entrepreneurial atmosphere of the new dot-com organization to leverage an integrated ERP, KM, and DW technology position.

6 & 7. Style and Shared Values

Issues: Leadership

Action Items:

☞ Leadership has to come from the very highest reaches of the organization.

☞ Technology allows organizations to add value to customers through provision of information services.

☞ A technology strategy does not come solely from technology but is based upon leveraging the technology through marketing, service, and branding to deliver added value to the customer in the form of information.

☞ A technology leadership strategy must build value to the organization, delivering the information the organization requires in order to get closer to the customer and/or wider market coverage as determined in the overall strategic plan of the organization.

☞ The strategic technology plan must be aligned with the overall plan of the organization.

Developing a Market Focus: Sector Strategies in Segmenting Markets

Dominance of the Internet marketspace is the primary strategic goal for many of the newly formed e-commerce start-ups, many of which have operated only on the Internet. However, the importance of market leadership through the Internet channel has rapidly become an important strategy item for established organizations. They realize that they have to rise to the challenges posed by their virtual competitors in both cyberspace and in traditional marketspaces.

Internet market leadership strategies are, as we have discussed earlier in the book, based upon applying a mixture of service, pricing, technology, and branding strategies to a potential customer base. In order to consider this issue in more detail, we need to segment the marketspace spectrum, which ranges from the service industry to manufacturing, and consider the role of e-commerce and competition in each sector (see Figure 5.1).

Manufacturing

In a sector that includes automobiles, clothing, machine tools, and computers, products have normally been supplied to the retail customer through a series

Figure 5.1
The Marketspace Spectrum of E-commerce

of intermediaries, each of which provide a service in exchange for a fee. This sector is undergoing significant change—manufacturers are in the process of determining who their customers are and how that relationship is changing, as well as how their product is going to change and the impact e-commerce will have on their relationships with their suppliers.

The nature of the Internet in this area is also undergoing significant change; in a pure sense, the manufacturing and production sector is emerging as a separate business-to-business (B2B) process as described in chapter 4,[1] rather than the more established business-to-customer (B2C) process. In this section we will describe some of the issues facing a traditional manufacturing company using a case study based on the CA-Chemical Company whose customers are other businesses (B2B) but whose e-commerce also has a definite B2C dimension.

Case Study: CA-Chemical Company

In considering CA-Chemical as a case, we encounter a situation in which many of the rules for Internet e-commerce are not applicable. Founded in the 1970s by a venture capitalist and a biochemist, the company set forth on a mission "to be the

---

1. A B2B e-commerce organization is primarily focused on providing information, data, and connectivity between organizations in a vertical or functional product or industry market. Vertical hubs primarily focus on a specific industry, such as entertainment, steel, or construction. Functional hubs focus on providing the same functions, such as logistics, procurement, and project management, across multiple industries.

leading biotechnology company using recombinant DNA, achieving this while employing the highest standards of ethical behavior and standards of integrity to patients, employees, and the scientific community."

The organization is headquartered in Palo Alto, California, in the heart of Silicon Valley's research community. Early on it adopted computer networks to drive information flow within the organization. Being a creative, learning organization with a vision toward the future, the organization is a fertile ground for technology innovation. It registered its Website in 1995.

CA-Chemical, however, is not concerned with selling its products online—it is prevented by law to do so because all purchases that would be made from the company need a physician's prescription. Rather, CA-Chemical uses the Internet and the connectivity it brings in other areas, such as Community, Corporate Philosophy and Culture, Research, Clinical Development, and Manufacturing (see Figure 5.2), with each of these aspects having two dimensions—the internal and the external.

Community

The organization is very conscious of its standing in the community and the world. Through its Website it brings information to the public about its corporate responsibility programs. These include programs for indigent patients, the company's independent nonprofit foundations, and corporate support programs for patients and other researchers.

Research

The purpose of the company is clearly research and development. Being a knowledge-based organization, it cannot risk any form of information isolation, either internally or externally, and thus it utilizes the Internet as a connectivity conduit. The Internet facilitates access to a larger spectrum of information sources, whether these be structured research sites such as that of the National Center for Biotechnology Information[2] or informal news groups. However, the company has to be very careful in giving data to external entities, as security is a key issue. An executive comments:

> We want to be very careful about what an employee acting on behalf of the company says in an open forum, [as disclosure of information] can invalidate European patents. This [public disclosure] is not an issue in the U.S. As soon as we file a patent [in the United States], if the date of the patent in the filing predates any public disclosure, then we are covered... but we have to be very careful of the different international laws.

2. A U.S. organization sponsored by the National Institutes of Health that holds public databases, conducts research in computational biology, develops software tools for analyzing genome data, and disseminates biomedical information.

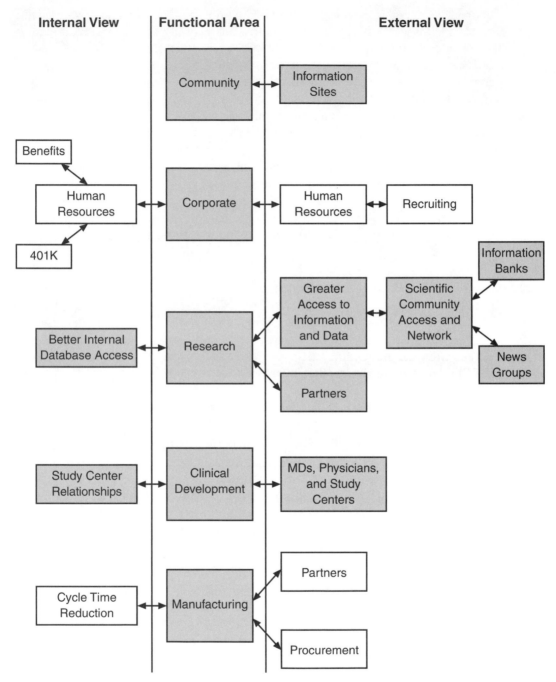

Figure 5.2
Internal and External Views of CA-Chemical's Internet Relationships

Internally, the company is highly networked and the aim of this connectivity is for better access to and distribution of information. Another way Internet connectivity benefits the company's research is that it facilitates collaborations with partner organizations. The partners can share data and resources more effectively, thus speeding up the cycle time of product development, a key component of success in this industry.

Clinical Development

The four phases of clinical development—preclinical testing and Phase I, II, and III trials—are often long, complex, and very expensive, involving many parties and information points. The ability to ease the information flow and meet requirements is greatly eased both internally and externally by the organization's utilization of a networked environment. Again the organization has a difficult set of information criteria to navigate. The development of drugs through the clinical trials is scrutinized by regulatory bodies such as the Food and Drug Administration (FDA), which monitors the highly involved Phase II placebo-controlled double-blind trials. The organization uses the information from its preclinical and Phase I trials to better design comprehensive Phase II trials so that the data collected can be more effectively analyzed prior to moving on to the very expensive Phase III trials. The organization has to be very careful about providing information to the public as it serves two masters. On the one hand, a Securities and Exchange Commission (SEC) ruling requires by law that investors have access to information on the company's future products. On the other hand, the FDA has the opposite requirement. As an executive at CA-Chemical comments:

> We are also under regulatory review of the FDA. The FDA says that we can't really talk about off-label uses or future uses of existing products or, in fact, future products because we can't sell those things until they are actually approved by the FDA, so we have this intriguing catch-22. SEC says you have to tell the people what you are doing because stockholders need to make informed judgment about whether to buy your stock or not. FDA says you cannot tell physicians or patients about future products.

A second external dimension of the research component is the organization's encouragement of external scientists to "get involved" with the company. The site facilitates this by providing information on where organizations can obtain access to research materials and how they can form collaborative relationships.

Manufacturing

The Internet is utilized in the manufacturing process, as in the other functional areas, to allow connectivity of data and information in B2B relationships. It allows manufacturing partners to furnish information to the company more quickly, increasing quality and reducing cycle time. The company allows their scientists to order products online, thus enhancing the procurement process.

Corporate

The ability to recruit highly talented scientists and employees is high on the list of priorities at the company because a research company lives and dies on its talent pool. The branding of the site is a key to the recruiting process—it has to reflect the dynamic, positive atmosphere within the company and encourage connectivity with the best talent available. The site, as we have already discussed, already does this through the relationships it encourages through collaborative research, some of which is by graduate students and scientists looking for future career opportunities. Internally the company offers its employees a series of Websites on the company's benefits plans.

As we stated at the beginning of the case, this organization is unusual: it cannot sell its products directly to the public; it is limited by one government agency in its ability to advertise its future products to potential customers; still another agency requires it to provide information to its investors. The company has however achieved significant competitive strength through its strategy of using the Internet to strengthen its core competency: the development of innovative products ahead of competitors. This is achieved by recognizing the information flow that facilitates this competency, by increasing how efficiently information is obtained, and by focusing the effective use of that information both internally and externally.

Mixed Goods and Service Organizations

A step away from the competitive dynamics of manufacturing is the arena of mixed goods and service, manufacture and provision.

Enterprises such as hotels, airlines, consumer electronics, and supermarkets that focus on a combination of goods and services are also considering their position relative to the Internet marketspace. In this sector the product is composed of a physical component, such as a hotel room or an item on the supermarket shelf, and a service component that ties the organization to the customer. To address these two components organizations have to internally structure themselves to create mass customization products in a reduced cycle time pattern, but also have to build their service relationship with the customer such that it can be leveraged to pull more customers through the sales channel or build customer loyalty.

The airlines were among the first organizations to recognize the power that information brought to their business. **American Airlines'** Saber reservation system dates back as far as 1953, and the ability it has given the company to understand and manipulate the yield of seats filled on each scheduled flight has been the key to American's success. Originally based upon SABRE, a proprietary reservation system and network, American went online in 1995, providing flight information and fares. American wisely moved into the Internet marketspace in order both to satisfy demand from the new Web channel and to continue its technology thrust competing against new entrants such as Airsaver.com, Fairfinder.com, Bestfares.com, and Travelocity.com.

The purveyors of food and other products at the retail level have been competing through personal customer service to establish brand and grow market share for many years. The low margin of approximately 1–2% in this business sector leaves very little room for error and continues to prove a creative challenge. However, **Tesco**, the UK's largest food retailer, has taken a predominant position by establishing an online store with home delivery. A Tesco executive discusses its strategy:

> The marketing strategy behind our Internet superstore is simple—
> we want to serve our customers wherever we can, including the
> Internet. Being the first online vendors of fresh grocery products in
> the world has given us great insight into this new market.[3]

The retailer is carefully rolling its e-commerce solution out across the UK, attempting to reinforce and reposition the brand as well as to gain first mover status. The irony of the home food delivery is that this was a very common occurrence in the UK from each of the commodity high street stores until the 1960s, when the supermarket-pressured margins changed the customer service relationship model and squeezed out many small vendors. Tesco's progress to the forefront of Internet shopping has not been completely without incident, but it is willing to pay the price necessary to lead the industry. The decision to create a system based upon a proprietary technology and a forecast of lower-than-actualized demand caused the organization to publicly recreate the site, which can undermine brand. However, due to the service's low area of availability, the changeover was not a major inconvenience for its users.

---

3. www.tesco.co.uk/indexn.html

In order to explore this sector further we will illustrate the power of creative market positioning, partnering, and technology deployment when coupled with a world class brand through the successful e-commerce initiative at one of the world's largest organizations—Sony Corporation.

Case Study: Sony

As would be expected from Sony, developers of the uniquely creative Walkman and countless other products, the development of its Internet presence was a highly evolved process. Since it commenced in 1994, Sony can be classified as an Internet early mover. The organization has already passed through several iterations of its Internet presence, both in terms of technology and in terms of philosophy.

Brand Leadership

The *organizational learning* associated with Sony's presence on the Internet since 1994 has been effective in all aspects of its e-commerce strategy. One of the most interesting issues centers around its efforts to formulate a branding strategy. Early on it became apparent to Sony that, with such a wide variety of products and offerings from its multiple divisions, a unified brand image was essential and far more valuable to the company than a fragmented set of e-commerce initiatives. An executive comments:

> It is always tough to bring people together, because the marketing, the sales people, etc.—they all have different ideas, especially in a large company. Everybody has a different angle and because everybody wants to focus upon their own bottom line. It was necessary to reaffirm focus and state: "Wait a minute—I know you all want to have your bottom line, but strategically as a Sony we want to have a bottom line which as a whole is better than all the individual parts."

This is apparent in the way Sony has brought together its movies, music, TV, electronics, and games empire through its Sony World gateway (www.sony.com) to reinforce its brand image.

Focusing on the electronics component, the branding strategy was complementary to an overall brand refocus. One dimension of the branding strategy at Sony Electronics is its *Sony Style* magazine sold at newsstands. An executive comments:

> I think we are the only company that produces a magazine of our product and sell it on the newsstand—it is as if we had a catalog and we sold our catalog. We called it *Sony Style*. It categorized all of the things that we did and what the product meant and where it was going. Plus it was a list of all the products that we sold and we said that, since we are doing that, let's electronically transfer it into an Internet medium.

Sony has since changed the format of its print version of *Sony Style* to a large-size format, but still acts to reinforce its brand jointly through the two media.

Technology Leadership

Sony is a brand synonymous with technology leadership, and the branding image is based on this projection. An executive at Sony explains the corporation's objective: "We want to be known as a technology company not a consumer company; we want to be known as a global entertainment company and when I say entertainment I'm not talking just movies and pictures but the whole conglomerate of hardware, software, and content."[4] Sony believes that this goal will be achieved through *content provision*. From a content perspective, Sony has a very extensive content base: Sony music and pictures, as well as Sony computer entertainment such as Sony PlayStation. Sony's future provision of content to a customer will become focused upon three main points: content, format, and access. The Sony executive continues:

> The content should be interesting, unique, and the content should be something that people don't usually get and Sony has a lot of content. Second, what is the format of the content itself? If people want to download the content, wouldn't it be nice if I can provide enough content.... Especially with re-writable CDs, people want to download it so it can run on a CD format. Especially if you're looking at research papers, and somebody says, "I know I have all this on the Internet," then I want to download it overnight. Especially with a cable modem, IDSN, and the different high-speed links, why don't I download it and put it on a CD ROM and have a library for myself? Especially for active information users such as researchers, business folks, you don't want to have to constantly keep going to the Internet and downloading the same information. However, how do we download information and in what format and how do I incrementally update this format? So, the format becomes a very important issue. People don't think about it, but format becomes very important because if you have to download something onto your CD now and you download 20 meg and then there is an addendum to that data/information that is, for example, another megabyte. You don't want to download all the 21 megabytes all over again. You are just wasting a lot of time. What I would like to do is take the same CD if possible and rewrite that with the extra 1 megabyte. The third issue is access. How do I provide access? Through home networks, not only through home networks, but outside; naturally we have to depend upon telecom companies, we have to depend upon cable companies, so we are going to have a relationship with all of these people.

---

4. Press Release: "The Station@sony.com Reaches Four Million Member Mark at Ever Increasing Pace," July 26, 1999, www.station.sony.com

The development of this *content-based technology leadership* strategy is also dependent upon other organizations developing along similar technology lines. McKinsey's John Hagel terms this the "web network effect,"[5] in that no organization alone can build an industry—it is simply too large a task. The aim is for an initiator to create a direction and a technology initiative and then go on and develop partnership relationships based upon it. This is the opposite of the experience Sony underwent with its Betamax video system, in which no web was created. VHS on the other hand created a web of partners, ranging from tape manufacturers and movie companies to clone machine manufacturers, each of which capitalized on a related business function. A Sony executive agrees. "There are some legal issues. But definitely we have got to have partners. I don't think that any company can do it 'on their own.' It is in the industry. Disney is having partners, Microsoft is having partners."

Central to this technology web is Sony's i-LINK, announced by Sony simultaneously in California and Tokyo in November 1998. An i-LINK (IEEE1394) link layer of large-scale integration (LSI) provides robust protection for digital content transmitted between digital electronics products at speeds of up to 200 megabytes per second (Mbps). Designed to meet the IEEE1394 digital interface standard, i-LINK will allow connection between a wide variety of digital electronics products. The chip can process audio-visual (AV) content transferred in Moving Pictures Experts Group (MPEG) data streams and other digital AV formats. It can also simultaneously transmit multiple isochronous signals and support functions that allow electronic programming guides and other applications to provide users with interactive network services. More important from the "Hagel-Web" perspective, i-LINK has been acknowledged by several important standards bodies: the Consumer Electronics Manufacturers' Association (CEMA) and the U.S.-based National Cable Television Association (NCTA) both identified the IEEE1394 interface as an important digital interface, which will promote compatibility between digital television receivers and digital set-top boxes. In addition, the i-LINK is compatible with the needs of the Copyright Protection Technical Working Group (CPTWG), an ad hoc cross-industry body organized to evaluate content protection technologies. The group includes Hitachi, Ltd.; Intel Corporation; Matsushita Electric Industrial Co., Ltd.; Sony Corporation; and Toshiba Corporation—its purpose is to address the concerns of the entertainment content industry, especially the Motion Picture Association of America (MPAA) which has requested two-way key exchange and multiple-level copy protection. The technology jointly developed by the five companies is known as the Digital Transmission Content Protection (DTCP) method. Under the DTCP method, AV and multimedia content would be classified as one of three levels of copy protection: copy prohibited, copy one generation, and copy free. *Copy-prohibited content* sent through the IEEE1394

---

5. John Hagel and Marc Singer, *Net Worth*, Harvard Business School Press, Cambridge, MA, 1999.

interface can be displayed but not recorded. Content designated as *copy one generation* can be recorded, but the resulting content would be designated copy prohibited. *Copy-free content* could be freely recorded by the user. This system provides flexibility for both content providers and consumers.

It is clear that i-LINK will create a central technology around which a "Internet web" will develop. However, Sony wishes to go further, not only to enable separate devices to interconnect but to have the Sony entertainment network be built right into the home of the future, taking Sony's vision of technology leadership right to the customer as the convergence of technology continues and as the battle for connectivity and access becomes more intense.

Market Leadership

The powerful global brand that the Sony name commands has historically been derived from its consumer electronics products: Walkman, Discman, Trinatron, etc. However, the electronics division also covers medical equipment as well as business and professional electronics, supplying entire TV studios, AV studios, imaging systems, and satellite systems, including mobile and wireless telecommunications. With this wide spectrum of product offerings, it is in the best interest of the organization to refocus the brand image in the public's consciousness, drawing together the electronics division with its movie and music businesses.

The natural linkage between all of these products and product grouping is the technology. As discussed above, the creation of a uniform interface between digital systems is a lever Sony can use in developing its market penetration. In conjunction with its powerful brand, Sony can create a powerful *desirability factor* that covers all aspects of a customer's technology needs—supplying the video or digital video disc (DVD) player, the sound system, and the viewing systems for a Sony movie downloaded from the company. The company can segment its marketplace and customers, such as supplying software upgrades to audio systems through the Internet as the consumer's profile changes, say, from student to working professional to audiophile, thus reducing the consumer's need to actually change the hardware upon which the technology upgrade is based. This locks in the customer and allows the organization to continuously build the customer relationship. The goal is for the organization to provide all the digital devices connecting a customer or group of customers through, for example, TV, computer, and telephone linkages. As an executive at Sony comments, "We want to be known as a technology company, not a consumer company; we want to be known as a global entertainment company, and when I say entertainment I am not talking just movies and pictures but the whole conglomerate of hardware, software, and content." An example of this convergence occurred on September 9, 1999, when Sony Electronics' Broadcast and Professional Company teamed with ResearchTV, a consortium of leading research institutions creating greater access to research information. They demonstrated the first-ever streaming of High Definition Television (HDTV) over the Internet, sending an HDTV video stream from Stanford University in Palo Alto to the University of Washington in Seattle over the new high-bandwidth Internet2 backbone.

The convergence of video and digital data is a global issue for Sony. Hermann-Josef Schanz,[6] marketing manager, videoconferencing, at Sony Deutschland GmbH, stresses:

> There is a clear trend towards video-assisted communication. The globalization of markets and the increasing international orientation of business relationships are making elevated demands on the speed and efficiency of communications. Furthermore, complex issues need images to explain the spoken word, typically in the form of graphics or illustrations. As an interactive medium, videoconferencing brings competitive advantages to decentralized companies that have a strong interest in communication.... The significance of cooperating with capable and expert partners is set to increase in the future. It constitutes an ideal means of realizing tailor-made solutions that comply exactly with the customer's individual needs. Sony contributes the potential harnessed by a global player, and its partners offer their expert knowledge of project implementation.

The initiative is not going to be just Internet related, but will also be oriented toward independent IP devices, software, and Internet capacity—for example, making telephones into IP devices that will be able to communicate in whatever way the customer's business or lifestyle needs require.

The direct accessibility of Sony products can be seen in other areas of its business. Sony created a separate division called Sony Online Entertainment (SOE) that produces and distributes online entertainment targeted to mainstream consumers and game enthusiasts. For example, SOE aims to reinforce its PlayStation product (www.playstation.com), successfully registering 4 million members since the site's launch in March 1997, a membership acquisition rate that is the fastest growing among all entertainment sites on the Internet. "The speed at which The Station continues to increase membership reflects the demand among mainstream consumers for quality online entertainment," said Lisa Simpson, president of SOE. "As The Station consistently reaches and surpasses expectations for growth, we continue to provide our members with new and innovative programming that has made The Station a success."[7] This also is a strong indication of a powerful demographics match between Sony and its online customer base.

Sony is also willing to create strong partnering bonds to create a market leadership position. In the music area, while it is possible to shop online at Sony.com

---

6. www.sony-europe.com/forum/march_19_25k.html

7. Press Release: Sony Online Entertainment, "The Station@Sony.com <mailto:Station@Sony.com> Reaches Four Million Member Mark at Ever-Increasing Pace," New York, July 26, 1999. www.station.com/press/4millionrel72699.html

and purchase CDs, minicassettes, vinyl, video, and DVDs. Sony also sells its music through Amazon, CDNow, other partners, and online retail sites.

This mix of market leadership strategies places Sony in a very strong position from a market coverage standpoint. Furthermore, this mix allows Sony, as a learning organization, to gather business intelligence and understand its channel effectiveness far more clearly than if the company stuck resolutely with one single strategy.

Service Leadership

The Sony brand leadership position has evolved through superior technology and quality assurance, backed up by a premier service strategy. The online Internet service dimension is no different.

An example of the effort Sony is putting into its service strategy through the Internet can be seen in its efforts to educate and inform videoconferencing resellers.[8] To this end Sony Electronics produced the Sony Video Information Network, a video-on-demand videoconferencing resource available via ISDN or the Internet (www.videoscape.net). The tool offers a videoconferencing overview, a marketing update, and sales and user training for the Contact videoconferencing system. "This project was constructed to offer our dealers a valuable, easy-to-use, interactive sales tool that can be updated instantly to provide up-to-the-minute information," said Glenn Adamo, vice president of videoconferencing for Sony's Broadcast and Professional Company. "With 24-hour-a-day accessibility, we believe the increased support will make the sales and use of our technology as seamless as possible."[9] Videoconferencing dealers must register for the service, but it is completely free to use. According to Adamo, the video is a tool for the dealers to use to provide product demonstrations to potential users. Dealers can also use the video for in-house training to help their representatives understand the videoconferencing industry. The project was facilitated by 2CONFER, a Sony and Videoscape.net distributor. "Videoscape.net has allowed Sony to automate training for the Contact videoconferencing system and leverage their resources in order to offer full support for the resellers," said Michael Perry, vice president of 2CONFER. "As a distributor, we helped to deliver the easy-to-access solution and bring it to life through writing and direction."[10]

2CONFER and Videoscape.net are two examples of Sony's Hagel-Web network where the organization grows its technology initiative by spreading activation

---

8. Press Release: Sony Electronics, "Sony Enlists videoscape.net and 2CONFER to Create Easy to Use Training Platform," www.videoscape.net/pr/sony_8_31_99_html

9. Ibid.

10. Ibid.

through partners. 2CONFER is a single-source meeting and conferencing solutions provider, specializing in video, audio, data, and networking applications, while Videoscape.net, founded in 1998, provides organizations with an easy and affordable way to leverage the power of live Webcasting-on-demand, video-on-demand, and *one-to-any* communication between content providers and their audience. Clearly Sony has the technical competence to create the 2CONFER and Videoscape.net systems on its own; however, the ripple effect of the technology, its support pool, and related companies can be more important in many situations than proprietary ownership of the technology.

The Sony case is an example of an organization that has a strong Internet strategy; Sony is repositioning and reinforcing its brand through a technology convergence strategy, focusing all its corporate initiatives toward a common digital medium through which all devices can communicate and interact. This will enable Sony to provide continuous upgradable solutions to its consumer base. The strategy is also based upon the type of Web strategy Hagel advocates. Sony is linking and partnering when it is suitable and appropriate, thus encouraging the growth and proliferation of technologies and services that complement its own products. Further, the company reinforces its B2B and B2C channels through Internet-based technologies. This is very effective; it produces workable configuration management solutions (each partner, vendor, customer, or reseller has access to the same data at the same time) that can be updated and maintained at low cost through an Internet site. The company also owns vast information content; this creates strong vertical integration and strong content attraction to its customer base.

Summary: Sony

Sony's leadership strategy stems from four key directives (see Figure 5.3):

- **Partnering.** It is essential for organizations to create strong relationships in their technology community. It is infeasible for a single organization to create, develop, and market all physical and informational products for a single technological area. Partnering allows organizations to create a Hagel-Web of product offerings in which niche market players position themselves to create complementary and added-value products around the strategy of the catalyst organization.
- **Convergent branding.** The need for organizations to create a single brand identity is essential. Multisegmented vertical organizations need to have a unifying brand in order to maximize their points of contact with the customer and leverage the sum of the parts to be greater than the whole.
- **Technology integration.** The necessity for products to be Internet compatible and to adhere to standards that facilitate cross-device communication is essential. Devices and products cannot be stand-alone, and customers do not wish to continually replace physical products with new ones. Hardware products have to be software reconfigurable.

- **Flexibility, change, and long-term desirability.** The organization being agile, nimble, and flexible is a prerequisite for technology integration. The organizational philosophy must be driven by the knowledge that, as technology is in a continuous state of flux, then this must be reflected within the company. This is achieved by continuously reevaluating the targets and goals of the organization's products and its partnering arrangements. This forward-facing focus, when combined with technology leadership, will create long-term product desirability and create customer loyalty—a difficult target to hit in general and within e-commerce in particular.

Figure 5.3
Sony Market
Leadership

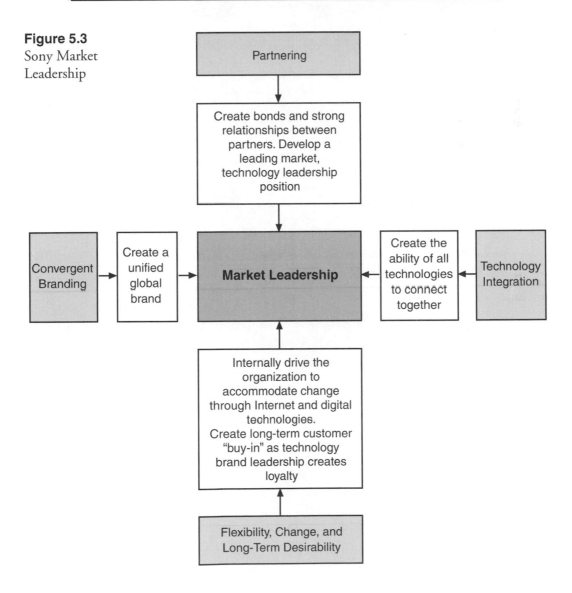

Case Study: USMedicalSystems (B2B)

It is clear that the sector of mixed goods and services has many variations and possibilities. Hence, we will consider a second case study, based on one of the world's largest manufacturers and distributors of medical equipment, which we will call USMedicalSystems. Sony and USMedicalSystems are to some degree very similar in that they both have a wide range of customers—Sony's ranges from retail to professional buyers, and USMedicalSystems sells a wide range of products to retail outlets and major hospital chains. In this case study we will consider some of the issues and decisions facing USMedicalSystems as a leader in the business-to-business channel.

Technical Focus

USMedicalSystems, one of the world's leading manufacturers of diagnostic imaging equipment, created an innovative e-commerce solution aligned to its corporate strategy. The basis of the company's success has been that it is part of a learning organization. The project being developed and funded internally has kept valuable development skills internal to the organization. The development group had the backing of the then CEO and knew it needed a strong technical solution that would match the quality level associated with its imaging products. This has led to the development of a sophisticated catalog engine that customizes itself to each customer's requirements as orders are placed—a definite advantage over the traditional online catalogs. The CEO of USMedicalSystems predicts that the healthcare industry will quickly embrace the e-commerce initiative for its value-added customer interaction, speed, and economy.

> The Internet has become a major influence upon the global healthcare community...The growth of electronic commerce promises to revolutionize the quality and productivity of medical care around the world. In healthcare, more so than in any other business, time and money are precious. Online purchasing is just one example of how we can help clinics and hospitals devote more of both to saving lives and making people well.

Marketing Focus

USMedicalSystems offers approximately 5,000 products that range in price and complexity from a box of earplugs costing a few dollars to a laser camera that can cost $100,000. The traditional sales channel for the majority of devices has been direct sales, with a sales person visiting the potential client on site. In the past the emphasis was on hospitals, hospital buying groups, and hospital networks, leaving sales representatives little time to visit small stand-alone imaging centers or individual doctors' offices. Hence the e-commerce solution goes a long way toward reaching a broader audience of potential customers. The site currently takes over 1,000 inquiries a day. The system has further revealed other benefits—

after-market sales are growing, and the site helps increase customer satisfaction with better after-sales service. The relationship between the company and the customer is enhanced through the dynamic e-catalog system which, for instance, facilitates the use of nationally negotiated discount levels to appropriate customers, no matter what the location of the order.

The technology is also being leveraged in creative ways. For example, the company has created a B2B portal in order to view and select quality, preowned diagnostic imaging equipment. The site is updated every 12 hours, giving customers instant access to equipment availability. Should required equipment not be available, a customer can post an advertisement on the site listing the specific items wanted. The site provides a customized response facility for the customers' requests, via e-mail or phone, within 3 hours in the United States or 24 hours around the globe.

Service Focus

At USMedicalSystems the ability to offer quality service to customers is high on its list of priorities. An executive describes the approach:

> The first area we are going to penetrate with this catalog is our remote services, where we have the ability to monitor our equipment from a central location. The application is really service focused and allows our people to take a look at the issues or problems that a customer is having with the unit in a hospital, say, in Boston, and we can actually download software, reboot the system, and help them with their image quality issues. Before we would dispatch a field engineer, this is a significant improvement. We can also, through the interactive media of our solution, monitor the number of procedures that are performed on a particular piece of equipment and anticipate when they are going to need replacements, for example, new table pads for the ultrasound machines.

The executive describes it as a mechanism to "intelligently sell" to USMedicalSystems customers with seamless, premium-quality service.

To facilitate the customer service function at the order level, all information relating to orders, including credit card information, is secured through password protection. Customers can receive their order history to use as a planning tool for future ordering, improving purchase efficiency. Customer service also includes a feature to notify the customer of special-offer pricing and service promotions that change regularly. The general manager of electronic commerce at USMedicalSystems affirms that the Internet is becoming a critical communication channel between the company and the healthcare industry, stating that "the Internet will not only be a conduit for transactions, but it will be a key source of information sharing…Our online offerings are helping to simplify and even streamline purchasing."

Brand Focus

USMedicalSystems describes itself as "having strategically positioned its sales, service, engineering, and manufacturing organizations worldwide to provide highly responsive local service to customers." The e-commerce solution it has chosen to develop and deploy enhances the brand focus in all of these dimensions. Building upon its U.S. experience, the company wishes to transfer that experience, further customizing the catalogs for its Asian and Latin American markets. The Internet is key for the organization as it is building brand equity through the reinforcement of customer relationships. The organization has won several awards for its e-commerce initiatives and, as an early mover in the field, is clearly well positioned to continue that reinforcement process.

Summary: USMedicalSystems

USMedicalSystems has achieved significant success with its online e-commerce B2B strategy, the four major dimensions of which can be visualized through Figure 5.4.

Service Leadership. Two of the drivers in this area are:

- The Internet gives the company greater opportunity to leverage the information surrounding its products and to supply that to the customer at remote locations.
- USMedicalSystems created a creative service dimension for the user community. This allowed the customers to communicate with each other through chat rooms and user groups, solving common problems and issues at decreased cost to the organization.

Market Leadership. The Internet plays two key roles for the company. At the macro level it assists in the unification of a global brand in a global market. At the micro level, the systems allow the organization to cover more marketspace in existing domains, filling in gaps where company representatives have no time or revenue justification to pursue.

Technology. Two objectives were established and achieved through this early-adopter Internet development effort.

- The technology of the Internet was used to complement the organization's products through service and distribution, wherever possible.
- The organization continues to focus on the major issues of the industry and to use technology to address them. These include responsiveness of the vendor and speed of delivery upon request from the customer.

Brand. The Internet channel and the technology were and continue to be used to reinforce the brand and expand the brand globally.

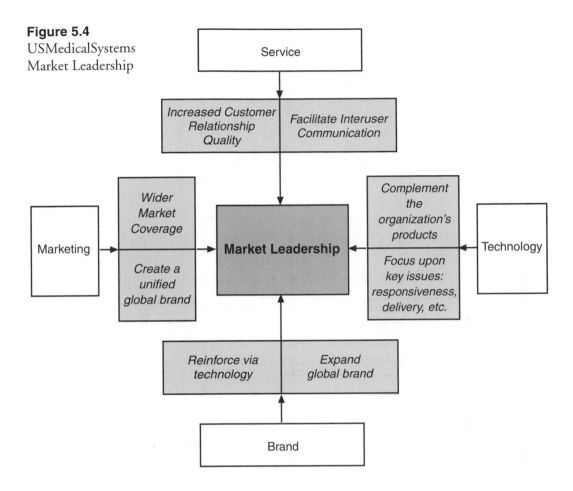

Figure 5.4
USMedicalSystems
Market Leadership

Service Organizations

Traditional service organizations have also had to decide on their new strategic direction in order to take or maintain a market leadership position. Organizations with traditional bricks-and-mortar-based organizational structures such as banks, mortgage brokers, and insurance companies are having to fend off the new, low-cost competition that has the ability to directly access customers in their homes, offices, or businesses over the Internet channel.

The ability to offer services at a low cost has been most apparent in the brokerage business where significant inroads into the customer base of traditional full-service brokerage houses have been made by competitors such as E*TRADE,

Ameritrade, and Datekonline which operate in only the Internet marketspace. Significantly it is often the most sophisticated trader that is lured away from the expensive full-service firms to the deep-discount brokerages, the very clients from whom the traditional brokerages make money due to their high-volume transactions combined with a low research overhead cost, since many of these clients often perform their own analyses of the markets. This development has spurred full-service firms to attempt a brand reposition strategy—one that allows clients to trade online at one fee, by telephone at a second fee level, and through a human broker at a third fee level. These organizations generally have not adopted a brand creation strategy because their brands are their strength and a dramatic change in the cost-to-service-level relationship could damage expectation levels across all channels. However, it remains to be seen if this strategy is sustainable with a sophisticated client base that is able to access information and data at a low cost from multiple alternative sources.

A similar situation exists in many of the service sectors where the customer has low switching costs and is searching for a one-time, low-cost solution, such as a mortgage. The sophisticated customer frequently makes a selection based purely on price, the lowest of which is easily provided by Internet marketspace providers with their low-overhead strategies. The vendors themselves often consider the product they sell to be a commodity that those customers who require heightened service levels will presently seek elsewhere. A potential alternative destination may be another Internet vendor found at an *aggregator* site—a site that groups together vendors from the same industry; aggregators position their sites at appropriate *high eye-traffic* Website locations.

The response to this from established organizations such as bricks-and-mortar mortgage lenders has been swift—they have established their own new Internet channels to compete and to offer further service products. This is clearly the definition of an active brand creation and reinforcement strategy.

The Internet has affected all organizations and it is the nimble that will survive. This is the case on Wall Street where Citigroup, the giant financial powerhouse, has acted to be a nimble player going forward. Its strategy is discussed within its 1999 annual report:

Innovation and the Internet

Citigroup has embraced the new technology of the Internet, which will dramatically change the financial-services industry. We have a long record of innovation in financial services; for example, our leadership in making ATMs a norm in banking has changed the way consumers access their money worldwide. Today, we are investing substantial management attention to take advantage of the convenience, efficiency, and reach afforded by advanced technology and the Internet, providing more services through these new channels and creating new services that could exist only in these new mediums. Examples are our award-winning online banking for consumers and, for business to business, our CitiCommerce.com, an Internet-based transaction processing service introduced in 1999, which automates electronic distribution, sourcing, end-to-end transaction processing, reconciliation, integration, and settlement systems. More than three million customers are already doing business with us online, and with numerous initiatives planned for 2000, we are positioned to be leaders in the electronic delivery of financial services to both consumers and corporations. As we create an Internet presence that leverages the entire business framework of Citigroup, we will be creating a truly distinctive, differentiated resource that will have great value to our customers wherever and whoever they may be.[11]

thus emphasizing the importance of formulating an effective strategy in the Internet marketspace. An executive at a large utility summed up the aim of market leadership strategy: "to reduce costs for the customer but not our margins and to add value to the customers by allowing them to do it for themselves." To illustrate this market segment, we will consider the e-commerce strategy associated with what may be the most creative brokerage house in the world—Charles Schwab.

Case Study: Charles Schwab & Co., Inc.

One of the great success stories in corporate America is that of Charles Schwab, the leading discount brokerage. Charles Schwab founded the company in San Francisco in 1971 as a traditional brokerage firm and showed his innovative thinking and penchant for risk by pioneering the discount brokerage strategy when the industry was deregulated in 1975.

Charles Schwab and his co-CEO David Pottruck had a vision of the brokerage business that stemmed from their ability to think outside the box, They created an organization that exhibits the product attributes customers wish for ahead of the

11. Annual Review: Citigroup, www.citi.com/citigroup/fin/sub/99ar

competition, whether it be in lower fee structure, better access through technology, increased information on the product, or better customer service channels.

Schwab's e-commerce strategy position exhibits all the dimensions of excellence we have outlined in this book. Key among these is **vision and leadership**. As we have discussed, the ability of an organization to harvest its creative resources and nurture talent is vital to the growth and success of any organization. This is especially true at Charles Schwab—it is part of the culture that goes back to the organization's earliest days. In 1982 the company created a handheld device that downloaded stock quotes through an FM receiver.[12] In 1986 Schwab created an "online" market data news reporting system the customer connected to via telephone. This background of innovation has created a dimension of **organizational learning** that fuels the organization's thirst for new technology and new ideas. The freedom to think and experiment around technology yielded its biggest payoff in 1995 when one of the "skunk works"[13] research groups in the organization's information systems department created an experimental system that created *middleware* between computer systems. The system allowed a personal computer to interact with the company's mainframe and to place basic trades through Mosaic, a then-new interface mechanism. CIO Dawn Lepore organized a demonstration for herself and Charles Schwab, who was "bowled over" by the technology and the opportunity it presented.

The leadership's next visionary stroke of genius came when Schwab created an independent internal IS group to look at this problem and to develop the prototype into a product. The project leaders reported directly to David Pottruck and thus had simultaneously authority and autonomy from existing systems projects, allowing it to operate and create in a more fluid and flexible manner.

The organizational impact of the **technology** and its potential system was enormous. The strategic implications had to be carefully weighed by Schwab, Pottruck, and their team. The technical, market, service, and brand leadership positions would have to come together simultaneously. The most basic of these issues is technology—make it work, make it secure, and make it reliable. Being first to market with such a system offered great rewards, but only if these three objectives could be demonstrated to the customers. Being first to market meant that, while the technical solution was not easy, the product would not have to enter the market with all the bells and whistles later entrants would have to produce. A key variable to this was demand. Schwab estimated that 25,000 customers might sign up for the service in the first year, a target met in the first two weeks. However, Schwab's internal systems development and organizational learning paid off,

---

12. E. Schonfeld, "Schwab Puts It All Online," *Fortune*, December 7, 1998.

13. See chapter 2. This term primarily refers to the fact that the system was created in a think-tank experimental atmosphere without the constraints of reporting, finance, and operational structure imposed upon traditional research and development groups.

in that the company first was nimble enough to get the system running commercially in 4 months from the time of inception.[14] it was also flexible enough to cope with the enormous growth that continued to follow, leading Schwab to become the largest of all online brokerages with 27.5% of the market in 1999—almost equal in size to the next three firms combined.[15]

Having initially developed the systems through a skunk works project, the organization adopted a *partnering* mode of development, an example of which is captured by the positivist solution to a potential system meltdown problem that CIO Lepore put into place with partner IBM (chapter 8 continues the case study with an examination of the IBM-Schwab partnership). In December 1998, following the volatile fall stock market "minicorrection," Alan Greenspan, chairman of the Federal Reserve, was preparing to address Congress. Lepore was worried that his words might launch a trading frenzy and bring the system down, and, as noted earlier, reliability and response are key to high customer satisfaction ratings. Normally, upgrading the Schwab systems to cope with a period of peak demand would require machines and service that normally would take 1–3 months to deliver. However, understanding the power of partnering, both IBM and Schwab did what was necessary. IBM put the system on a plane, flew it to the Schwab data center, and installed it[16]—a useful precautionary move as the site subsequently started to receive 76 million hits a day. Schwab has also used the partnering route in the dimension of systems ergonomics and systems interfaces. Its early interface was often criticized as difficult to navigate; thus, in June 1998, Schwab partnered with Razorfish.com, whose challenge was to solidify Charles Schwab's position as the leading online investing services provider.

They streamlined Schwab's 1000+ page marketing site to improve the rate of browser-to-customer conversion, as well as improve the usability of the online trading interface. The two organizations worked together to create a consistent user experience across Schwab's diverse product and service offerings which would reflect Schwab's online brand positioning. This partnership has had a dramatic effect on the quality of the site as ranked by gomez.com in its online brokerage rankings, with Schwab going from number 20 to number 2.[17]

Schwab continues to press forward with new technologies to improve its product and its customer relationships. In a move to develop greater call center effectiveness and efficiency, Schwab partnered with Nortel Networks to add Nortel's CallSPONSOR Customer Telephony Integration (CTI) solution to its own PBX/ADC exchanges, integrating voice and data domains. CallSPONSOR provides a

---

14. "Charles Schwab Corporation in 1996," Case Study SM-35, Graduate School of Business, Stanford University, August 1997.

15. "Fidelity.com Gets Serious," *Business Week*, July 19, 1999.

16. Ira Sager, "Big Blue at Your Service," *Business Week*, June 21, 1999.

17. www.gomez.com

full suite of CTI applications, including screen-pop, data-directed routing, virtual call center, event-based reporting, call blending, voice and screen recording, and Web-based call center management and reporting. Thomas Gunther, senior director for Banking and Brokerage Market Development at Periphonics, the Nortel subsidiary that develops CallSPONSOR, describes the synergy achieved:

> In today's converging financial services market, organizations are focusing on improving call center productivity and quality, to become more customer centric and proactive in the sales and service they deliver. By tightly integrating the CTI functionality of CallSPONSOR and the bundled solutions of PeriDirect in speech recognition or other media, we can further reduce operating costs while delivering an enhanced customer experience, to the delight of consumers and their financial companies. With CallSPONSOR, organizations can empower agents to handle calls faster and more efficiently by eliminating the need for callers to repeat information that has already been captured by the IVR system. Agents' talk time with callers will then be dramatically reduced. This increase in call center productivity will allow for banks, brokerage firms, and other financial organizations to introduce new revenue generating services without incurring additional staffing costs therefore improving bottom line results. Links to Customer Relationship Management and rules based AI engines can round out this solution to make the contact center a strategic sales and service organization, collaborating with customers in self service or assisted, via the media of their choice.[18]

Further, in an attempt to reduce the cost of replying to e-mails, while at the same time improving the speed and quality of its response, Schwab has partnered with Epipany.com which provides not only software to produce customized e-mail reponses but also systems to help Schwab better understand its customer base and its behavior. These systems have helped Schwab to know who its customers are by "aggregating widely distributed data from electronic commerce infrastructure, transactional applications, and legacy systems, as well as from third-party data sources."[19] They have helped Schwab to know the breakdown of its customer base by analyzing customer groups by demographics, profitability, length of sales cycle, cross-sell success rates, and other company-defined criteria.

Schwab also pushes technological issues at the legislative level; an example of this is the push for government legislation that would legalize digital signatures, which Charles Schwab feels would make online trading even more accessible to the public.[20]

---

18. Press Release: Nortel Networks, "Nortel Networks Adds Periphonics Call Sponsor CTI to its PeriDirect Suite of Interactive Financial Products," Bohemia, NY, December 21, 1999.

19. www.epiphany.com

20. "John Hancock, We Hardly Know Ye," *Business Week*, August 2, 1999.

The **market leadership** strategy that Schwab initially rolled out was heavily influenced by the problem of disintermediation—in this instance determining a mechanism for either separating or combining the Internet and bricks-and-mortar channels. As the first mover in this area, Schwab encountered the problem of how to separate channels without cannibalizing existing revenue streams or how to change a revenue distribution channel that includes agents or middlemen. Initially, the Internet channel, called e.Schwab, was separate and charged $39 for up to 1,000 shares being traded, while the bricks-and-mortar channel, Street-Smarts, cost $49.50. However, this *straddle* strategy confused and frustrated customers and brokers alike—customers who saw no separation would call brokers only to be told they could call a broker only once a month if they executed online. To overcome this, Schwab and Pottruck decided to unify the pricing strategy and charge $29.95 for all trades of 1,000 shares. This decision cut into the company's revenues by an estimated $125 million. However, as Schwab said, "This isn't that hard a decision, because we really have no choice. It's just a question of when, and it will be harder later."[21] Having stabilized the stock price, Schwab concentrated on growth, bringing Schwab's market share of online trading to 27.5% in 1999, representing client assets of $219 billion. The transition of trading from the high street branches to the Internet has also been swift; online trading represented about 54% of Schwab's volume in 1998, compared to 37% a year earlier. At year-end 1999, the company had grown to 3.3 million online accounts with $349 billion in assets, up another 50% and 100%, respectively, from year-end 1998.[22]

However, the novelty of online trading systems has worn off, and customers have become selective in their choice of an online broker. A report from Gomez Advisors Inc. indicates that the number of online trading companies has risen to 140;[23] within this group there is a wide spectrum of service and price levels.

The genius of Schwab's market leadership strategy is that it continued to understand its market and customer. There were two possible extreme strategies: low-cost no-research deep discounted trades with no information provided customers; and commission-based full research (see Figure 5.5). The middle position was clearly the solution, even if it was in somewhat undefined territory. Those customers who want very low-cost trades will always opt for a brokerage such as Brown & Company which offers $4.95 trades, and this area will only become more competitive with lower and lower trading costs becoming available. This segment will become a battle for market share in a segment of the market with very, very low margins.

21. See note 12 above.

22. Press Release: Charles Schwab, "Schwab Reports Record Quarterly and Full-Year Results 1999," San Francisco, CA, January 18, 2000.

23. "Where No-Frills Net Trades Are Sacred," *Business Week*, June 28, 1999.

Figure 5.5
Two Strategy
Extremes for
Brokerages

The traditional Schwab customer is a 47-year-old midlevel investor who wants to participate in the market but who is uncomfortable with the high fees of the full-service broker. Clearly, the full-service brokerages will ultimately be forced to compete in the online low-cost arena. Merrill Lynch, with its 5 million customers and 3.3% of U.S. financial household assets, has the potential to be a very powerful player in the market. However, the full-service brokerages' delay in entering the online market has given the initative to Schwab and the other online brands, creating a new set of rivals with which the full-service brokerages will have to compete. Schwab, for instance, took advantage of that period to further erode the full-service brokers' customer base. It also built strategic partnering relationships with research firms such as First Call and Hambrecht & Quist, through which it can provide a level of research information equal to any Wall Street firm. Schwab has also developed some creative systems that can add even more value to its customers, providing tools such as an *asset calculator* and an information base for many financial instruments and needs, including investment planning, small business retirement planning, estate planning, and stock research.

The fact that Schwab has been online since 1995 will become very valuable in the battle against the large, full-service brokerages. The organizational learning it has gained will, first, enable Schwab to understand its own customer costs better and, second, aided by its Epiphany systems, create layered service strategies for customers with different assets under management. This will allow Schwab to compete against such financial giants as Merrill Lynch, Morgan Stanley Dean Witter, and Citicorp. Merrill Lynch's strategy is to have two levels of service: Level I is to match Schwab with $29.95 trades; Level II is to charge 1% per year of equities under management, with a minimum charge of $1,500. Prudential has a similar strategy, charging clients fees based on the size of their accounts—clients with $100,000 pay 1.5% of their assets annually, while those whose accounts top $5 million will pay 0.5%, with each trade costing $24.95. Schwab's response to this has been to create a layered *service leadership* service—the *Schwab 500* service is for customers who make four trades a month and maintain a $50,000 account; *Schwab Select* is for those who make two trades a month and have $25,000 on account; there are no trading requirements for those with $500,000 in assets; and there is a variant of private banking for customers with assets over $1 million.

The key is to grow the customer relationship through these levels, Schwab equating **service leadership** with providing information and analysis for customers. It also pays its customer representatives salaries rather than commissions, and the bricks-and-mortar branch staff is paid incentive bonuses based on asset growth and the quality of the customer service being provided.

Schwab also sees its bricks-and-mortar part of the business as an asset to its customer relationship management, building technology linkages between the physical stores and the online dimension of the business, installing PCs in the 300 branches so that investors can trade online while on the premises—a clicks-and-mortar strategy. Daniel Leemon, the chief strategy officer of the company, states that "the branches are a comfortable place for investors to get started on the Web."[24]

The virtual nature of the online brokerage houses has allowed Schwab, in its market leadership strategy, to actively pursue providing services to a global customer base, thus leveraging the learning gained since 1995. Schwab has moved into the European financial sector by purchasing the British discount broker ShareLink and developing an online service.

The utilization of database technology as represented by the Epiphany system has allowed Schwab to create a new dimension to its business, that of comanaging IPOs. To maximize its flotation pricing and revenues, Schwab has created innovative data-mining techniques such as searching the database of the IPO company for customers who are also Schwab customers and then analyzing the match for suitable clients to whom the IPO could be offered. This use of technology to produce an information-based service leadership position produces greater customer loyalty and fuels Schwab's growth. Schwab *warm calls* customers who have shown an interest in opening an account but who have never acted on it. The company also contacts customers who have established cash positions or inactive accounts to service them with advice; it views the inactivity as potentially indicating a customer in need of financial planning assistance. Customers with higher assets under management also receive *warning indicator* advice from the Schwab team monitoring that account. The Schwab service leadership strategy is based on continually educating the customer to create a better-informed and more active investor rather than the passive-investor service policy epitomized by the full-service brokers. Part of this educational strategy is to move customers to the lower-cost Internet channel. In 1999 Schwab received the highest customer satisfaction ranking from online traders as rated by J. D. Power and Associates Online Trading Customer Satisfaction Study. "This study is a critical look at what matters to consumers, not what matters to industry professionals," said Gideon Sasson, Enterprise President of

---

24. "No Web Site Is an Island," *Business Week*, March 22, 1999.

Electronic Brokerage. "It validates what we have always thought is most important to investors: outstanding customer service."[25]

The J. D. Power study shows that *customer service* was rated the most important of the six factors considered together to comprise *overall customer satisfaction with an online investment firm*, these being:

Customer service—26%
Integrity/reputation—19%
Information/education—19%
Processing—17%
Portfolio management—12%
Fees/commissions—7%

The study found that Schwab showed

"considerable strength" in five of the six key factors, demonstrating high performance across a broad spectrum of the online trading experience. This strength includes Customer Service and Information/Education, which are two of the three most important satisfaction drivers because they serve as building blocks for a positive relationship with investors.[26]

In considering the market and service leadership positions to which Schwab has evolved, it is clear that successful **brand reinforcement** has also occurred. The strategy of established bricks-and-mortar retail sites (more than 300 branches as of spring 2000) has been spliced successfully with that of the online systems. Schwab has *redefined* branding in the discount brokerage arena, creating in effect an online, discounted, full-service brokerage with a growing information provision for increasingly sophisticated information-hungry customers.

Summary

In this chapter we have examined a series of companies, from CA-Chemical, which was unable to sell directly to the public, to Charles Schwab, which has revolutionized the brokerage business. From this we can distill the following rules of Internet strategy:

Market Leadership: Rules of Internet Strategy

☞ Determine the degree to which you will remove or offer alternatives to the layers of intermediaries that exist between the organization and the customer through the Internet channel.

---

25. J. D. Power and Associates, Online Trading Customer Satisfaction Study, 1999.
26. www.schwab.com/SchwabNOW/SNLibrary/SNLib098/SN098mainNewPage.html

E-Consortia: Charles Schwab & Company

Charles Schwab is also a member of an e-consortium that forms an after-hours trading environment. The consortium partners include:

- *Spear, Leeds & Kellogg*
- *Fidelity Investments* (its trading division is Fidelity Capital Markets)
- *Donaldson, Lufkin & Jenrette* (with its affiliates DLJdirect and Pershing)
- **The Charles Schwab Corporation** (its trading division is Schwab Capital Markets & Trading Group)

Additionally, the following have signed letters of intent to join the group:

- Bank of America, Credit Suisse First Boston, Inc.
- Fleet Securities Inc.
- Lehman Brothers Incorporated
- National Discount Brokers Group, Inc.
- PaineWebber Inc.
- TD Waterhouse Group, Inc.

The e-consortium is called **REDIBook** and is another electronic communication network (ECN) which in spring 2000 traded on average 70 million shares a day, for distribution of after-hours prices and orders (8:00 A.M. until 10:00 P.M.). REDIBook will consolidate pricing from other ECNs, including:

- Archipelago Holdings
- Island Trading
- MarketXT

as well as connect to other financial systems, including:

- The MacGregor Group's Predator and Merrin systems
- Thomson Financial's TradeRoute
- NYFIX
- EZE Castle
- LongView Group's LandMark system
- Charles River Development

In addition, over 120 institutions are connected via the Financial Information Exchange (FIX) and other links.

According to Larry Leibowitz, the acting CEO of REDIBook:

> These linkages will allow us to provide consolidated quotes and market access for our customers, ensuring that they will have the best prices and trading opportunities available. We feel that this is a big step towards improving our already significant extended-hours offering, and we will continue to work with other ECNs to provide and expand this service.

Source: Press Release, Charles Schwab, "REDIBook ECN Announces After-Hours Links, Buy-Side Connections," New York, February 3, 2000. www.prnews-wire.com/cgi-bin/stories.pl?ACCT=105&STORY=/www/story/02-03-2000/0001132041

☞ Disintermediation is not always positive. Play to your advantages—if you have a strong retail presence utilize it; it is a strength online rivals don't have immediate access to on their own.

☞ Regardless of product, you need a basic Internet presence and you need to offer value to the visitor. Even if that is merely traditional contact information, present it in such a way that the brand is reinforced.

☞ Carefully align your Internet strategy with your overall business strategy.

☞ Avoid frequent and abrupt changes of Internet strategy direction.

☞ Develop a cohesive strategy across all brands.

☞ Make your market leadership strategy consistent with the branding strategy in the eyes of the customer, not just in the eyes of the executives of the advertising agency and marketing groups.

☞ Develop a strategy before developing a Web presence.

☞ Develop an IT infrastructure to cope with and integrate the changes brought on by a Web presence before they occur. This may be a viable partnering growth opportunity with a technology vendor.

☞ Don't bring an e-commerce solution to the marketspace before it is ready or before the marketplace is ready for it.

☞ To get closer to the customer, you must add value for that customer and continue to add value as the requirements of that customer change over time.

☞ Derive flexibility and transaction capability from the technology infrastructure upon which the Web presence is based.

☞ The Web allows product-based companies to offer new information-based products through the low-cost, omnipotent distribution mechanism of the Internet.

☞ If the goal is mass customization, then incorporate the ingredients of speed, innovation, agility, and technology and leverage them through the Internet relationship with the customer.

☞ Low-cost commodity producers are not immune from the threat of information-added-value competition from within their industry as generated by large, traditional market competitors through the Internet.

Service Leadership— Adding Value to the Customer at Every Point of Contact

The Internet has brought about a radical explosion of new customer service opportunities previously only dreamt about by executives. As a consequence, corporations are spending significant amounts of time and effort determining how these new dimensions of service can be leveraged within their own organization in order to increase their competitive advantage as part of an e-commerce strategy. For pure Internet-based service organizations, this has come to mean fast, reliable service that is efficient to use and seamless in delivery. Customers expect the low cost of transactional services via the Internet to be matched by easy-to-use, ergonomic interfaces, backed up by an information-rich, premium, global, 24×7 level of service. For organizations moving to the Net, the race is on to replicate these online service levels, not only through the Internet channel but also through the company's traditional channels. This task is often simplified by separating the online and bricks-and-mortar components of the organization, allowing each to focus on its own goals, while conforming to consistent policy goals set by the parent organization.

Harrods—A world leader in customer service goes B2B

"Harrods Corporate Service is pleased to announce that it has developed a business-to-business e-commercial service. By using the latest on-line shopping technology and a team of dedicated Account Managers, Harrods Corporate Service is now able to offer you the ultimate in customer service with a product range from the world's most famous and prestigious store."
    Source: www.harrods.com/splash/index.htm

Bricks-and-Mortar to Clicks-and-Mortar Transition

OfficeDepot.com

Office Depot, the world's largest seller of office products, operating a total of 813 stores throughout the United States, Canada, France, and Japan, with sales of nearly $5 billion in 1999, successfully exemplifies the bricks-and-mortar to clicks-and-mortar transition. The company, headquartered in Delray Beach, FL, created a separate division called OfficeDepot.com and located it literally on the other side of the United States, in San Francisco's Mission District. Fueled by the company's mission statement to be "the most successful office products company in the world,"[1] Office Depot acknowledges that "Our success is driven by an uncompromising commitment to: **Superior Customer Satisfaction**: A companywide attitude that customer satisfaction is everything,"[2] a strategy that is clearly paying off, as its online channel has proven highly successful. The August 1999 Quarterly Report states:

> The introduction of the Office Depot public Internet site www.officedepot.com in January 1998 contributed to increased sales in our Business Services Group by offering our customers greater flexibility in their ordering choices. Sales from our public and business-to-business web sites increased to $70.2 million in the second quarter of 1999 and $120.5 million in the first half of 1999, compared with sales of $12.2 million and $18.1 million in the second quarter and first half of 1998, respectively.[3]

---

1. www.officedepot.com/corpinfo/mission.asp
2. Ibid.
3. Office Depot Inc., *Quarterly Report*, 2nd Quarter, August 10, 1999.

Office Depot's e-commerce strategy, based on providing the same high-quality service found in its stores, reinforces its brand, bringing a consistency of service, product offering, and quality to its customers from both channels. Keith Butler, vice president of Office Depot On Line, states: "The Internet is not a replacement strategy—it is an adjunct."[4] The online initiative is based on internal development and sponsorship by an executive champion within Office Depot. Butler comments on its initial strategy:

> It took the form of a dual strategy, e-commerce to provide more than an electronic brochure where customers could come to the site and buy products, the second [dimension] to provide another added-value proposition to them to come to the site that is not commercially based, so if there is information content, downloadable tools, forms and other reasons to come and associate with [us].

Hence, **service via free information provision** to the customer becomes an added-value proposition and a driver of customer acquisition and retention through the site. This information-based acquisition-retention value chain is recognized at OfficeDepot.com. Butler comments further:

> When I get a customer to buy, if I have customer service kick-in to help with the acquisition of that customer. Once they have bought from us and had a good experience, we are persuaded that the lifetime value of that customer is very high.

Customers will build an affinity with organizations through the Internet channel, but only if their service level expectations are reached. OfficeDepot.com meets these expectations in part based on the nature of the product offered and the effectiveness of the *information package* surrounding it. Stop adding or providing value to customers and risk losing them to alternative suppliers or to a traditional channel with its associated higher cost structure.

Just as the service dimension of the Internet channel is vital, the Internet serves the service parameter by allowing organizations to offer new and innovative variants of customer service to a wider range of customers in their attempts to grow their customer base and retain more of them in long-term relationships. Examples can be found in every industry—tracking of packages by the shippers, bill and power usage analyses by utilities, community activities by the chemical industry, mortgage calculation and planning by property

---

4. Interview with author, October 1998.

developers, provision of annual reports to shareholders by companies, and the list goes on. An interesting emerging development for multinational organizations is the potential ability to offer the level of service previously restricted to their home and major markets to all markets regardless of size or location. This will continue to grow as the Internet becomes more international in language and more culturally sensitive. In this chapter we will examine these **service value chain issues** within the Internet environment and discuss the strategic options in this area.

The Internet Service Value Chain—"Where the Rubber of E-commerce Meets the Road"

The Internet service value chain can be broken down into four parts: customer acquisition, purchase support, fulfillment support, and customer retention (see Figure 6.1).

The development and execution of a successful strategy in each of the Internet service value chain segments is vital for any organization wishing to operate all or part of its business online. Through examination of each facet and its linkages, organizations can determine their current strengths and weaknesses and develop a refined strategy going forward. This is applicable to born-on-the-Net organizations as well as move-to-the-Net organizations as the online service and logistical models for non-software-based services and products such as toys, books, and groceries still remain to be formally defined.

Figure 6.1
Internet Service
Value Chain

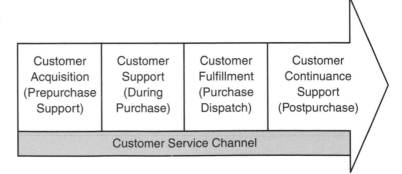

Customer Acquisition

The development of a customer service strategy is a direct reflection of a company's business plan and overall business strategy. The service strategy should reflect and reinforce the brand that the organization has created. BMW, for example, stresses technical excellence, innovation, and performance. As the company states, "It has always been the desire of BMW to create automobiles of unmistakable identity."[5] This brand position therefore has to be delivered and presented through BMW's Website and the service found at that site. An executive at BMW states:

> We launched the site in October of 1995 and it was really an awareness from the top, from senior management, that the Internet existed, that we are a company that prides ourselves in our technology leadership and we know that most of the people who own our cars, who appreciate them for their performance aspect and the technology, are early adapters. They are very comfortable with leading-edge technology and alternative media. So we knew that this was a very good way to communicate with them to maintain the benchmark that we have as far as leading-edge technology and brand awareness. It was a chance to not only speak to those people who know and appreciate BMW but to connect with people who didn't know us. We would have a voice. Our mission was to make sure that our site drove and felt like a BMW. It could never let down the expectation of anyone about what a BMW is.[6]

The reflection of BMW's brand and physical channel service levels through its Internet presence serves to act as a customer acquisition conduit. BMW does not sell its vehicles online because it feels that this would dilute the brand and detract from the personal relationship BMW forms with the customer through its distributors, a relationship that it wishes to develop.

> Content has to be consistent with the brand and attractive enough to create customer follow-through.

---

5. www.bmw.com/bmwe/enterprise/index_heritage.shtml
6. Interview with author, October 1998.

Another automobile manufacture, General Motors, has approached its customer acquisition strategy in a slightly different manner. GM has an extensive corporate Website that delivers several categories of information, all of which build the customer or shareholder relationship. The corporate site provides a **GM portal** for customers, routing them onward to more localized or specialized locations, a necessity when you manufacture 8.3 million vehicles a year and sell them in 190 countries.

Like its counterparts at BMW, GM strives, by providing information to potential customers, to reinforce its brand and move that potential customer into the second stage of the value chain, that of customer support during purchase. However, providing the "stickiness" required to achieve this is difficult; GM has two approaches. Its traditional solution has been to direct customers through the portal to specific auto brand sites such as Buick, Saturn, and Cadillac. This gives the customer a predictable introduction to GM's style of business, ultimately leading to a catalog of prices and products. However, GM also realized that it needed a more sophisticated channel for potential customers with an increasingly "Net-centric" view of purchasing, so it created GMBuyPower.com, a site designed to lure the more sophisticated customer inward.

The battleground for automobile sales and revenue through the Internet has also expanded into the B2B environment with the creation of portals for the fleet purchaser. Ford Motor Company has been developing its interface to this business line since 1997. They provide a spectrum of services for all fleet types, ranging from the specialty vehicles to alternative-fuel vehicles. These services include:

- ☞ Vehicle service
    - Quality fleet care
    - Quality fleet care components
    - Extended service plans
    - Quality fleet care reporting
- ☞ Dealer services
    - Preferred businesses
    - Professional fleet
    - Limo care
    - Alternative fuels (natural gas, electric)
- ☞ Financing
    - Ford Motor Credit

Ford's Website also services fleet account customers with personalized information programs, which include incentive notifications, Fleet-O-Grams, global capabilities, and order printer materials, among others. The B2B relationship is also extended to facilitate B2G in an effort to provide "complete fleet management services."[7]

Site Adhesion—The Three Dimensions: Content, Format, and Access

In order to improve the stickiness of a site, at all stages of the customer's interaction an organization will once again need to base its strategy on the three key drivers: content, format, and access.

Content

A customer accesses a Website for the content of that site. Initially a customer will want quickly assumable information and data, as well as the ability to navigate easily to gain a clear understanding of the site's progression to more detailed information. The key to this is to match a user's psychological, demographic, and technological sophistication profile with that of the site's initial and subsequent impact.

GM BuyPower, for example, opens up in an ergonomically pleasing manner, taking styling cues from its vehicle, using dashboard controls and a mirror to develop the interaction. It is simple and clear in its functionality. It caters to the curious viewer through sections such as "About GM BuyPower," "Dealer's best price," "Find your new vehicle," "Finance tools," and "Your personal page." These sections provide basic tools to determine vehicle types and costs and encourage customers to go see their local dealers. However, a more personal relationship is encouraged and facilitated through the low-key messaging system that allows queries to be sent as e-mails to GM or via a customer service center toll free number. The more advanced customer browser can use the "create your own page" facility to save information of interest on GM products.

There must be a balance between information provision to the customer and information collection by the organization on visitors. GM's privacy statement, shown on page 144, reflects its concern over this issue.

As illustrated by the GM BuyPower site, the goal in the early stages of customer-site interaction is to use content to move the customer toward the "sell," which is executed in the second stage.

---

7. Source: www.fleet.ford.com/get_started/prospective_customers.asp

---

GM BUYPOWER PRIVACY STATEMENT

You take online privacy seriously. You don't want your personal information to fall into the wrong hands. Neither does General Motors. We are committed to respecting your privacy and sustaining your trust in General Motors and our products and services.

GM BuyPower will never sell your information to any other company.

When you visit GM BuyPower, information about your visit (how you navigate the site) may be collected and stored on an anonymous, aggregate basis. This information is used to measure site activity and to develop ideas for improving GM BuyPower. The information collected may include the time and length of your visit, the pages you look at on our sites, and the site you visited just before coming to ours. We may also record the name of your Internet Service Provider.

During your online visit we will collect the necessary data to perform an inventory search at the dealer, as well as save data on our server in a personal file you can re-access when you come back to visit us again. The goal is to save you time and provide you with an effective way to simplify the shopping process.

The Dealer Contact Center within this site is designed to facilitate direct online communications between you and a dealer or the GM BuyPower Center. You are asked to provide a minimum amount of information, such as your name, e-mail address and, on certain message forms, a telephone number for confirmation of a specific request. This personal information is stored to enable follow-up communications. It may also be used for marketing research and other marketing purposes, and may be shared with other companies in the General Motors family and our business partners.

General Motors reserves the right to alter our privacy principles as business needs require. Any alterations to these principles will be posted on the GM BuyPower site in a timely manner.

COPYRIGHT AND TRADEMARK INFORMATION
Copyright ©1997,1998, 1999 General Motors Corporation.

OfficeDepot.com has created an interesting strategy for building relationships with customers that locks them into a lifelong relationship—it offers *A Resource Guide for Small Businesses*.[8] Office Depot offers a *Small Business Handbook* for starting and running a small business and gives advice on creating a business plan. The early developmental stage in a company's life is a perfect time to build a relationship with it and grow the office supply business, while offering basic consulting advice for free. This will encourage the customer to return for

---

8. www.officedepot.com

updates, with the hope that the business will grow into a large, self-sustaining corporation, at which time its relationship with Office Depot could be very strong indeed.

Format

The format of an organization's initial site is important with respect to the customer's technical sophistication. Vendors need to create a balance between information provision and information delivery speed. The selection of data format is crucial, as initially the goal is to create viewer interest and engage the viewer in a continued interaction. Thus many organizations minimize the sophistication of the interaction, using low-bandwidth solutions in an ergonomically positive environment to furnish "user bait" with the hope of hooking the user for continued interaction and ultimately a sale.

Access

Online data access depends on the bandwidth requirement. The clear rule in the initial interaction phase is to use as minimal a bandwidth as is feasible to facilitate as wide an audience as possible.

Metrics—Defining Internet Units of Measurement to Enable Effective Management

The e-commerce world has, since inception, been attempting to measure parameters associated with the Web and Websites in order to assess two things:

☞ Advertising—how many people saw our banner ad?

☞ Visitation—how many people came to our site?

For advertising, the metrics measured and their interpretation depend on the position of the measurer. The advertising perspective is that *hits* can give the advertiser the most accurate interpretation of the customer-to-site usage ratio, but this has come under increasing scrutiny as the technology and systems associated with Web interfaces and networks become well understood by the advertisers. There is a problem with using hits as a measuring tool. What advertisers want to measure includes the number of unique visitations to a site, as well as multiple other parameters such as duration of each visit. Hit calculation is often based on a frame of text or image file, whereas a single page may be made up of many of these, hence distorting the hit count. An alternative is to use a metric calculation, which uses the whole page as a metric. The problem with this is that a page is cached into the memory of a "reader" or

Web browser. This counts as one hit. But if the user then swaps between tasks and pages, this page may actually be read many times, which should count as multiple hits, not just one. Another problem is the user who utilizes a "bot" or self-propelled search engine to find some information. This search agent will visit sites on the owner's behalf, but will not actually report anything about the sites visited back to the owner, thus throwing off the hit count.

In software metrics theory, this problem is the separation of direct and indirect metrics or measurements:

☞ **Direct measurement** of an attribute is measurement that does not depend on the measurement of any other attribute.[9]

☞ **Indirect measurement** of an attribute is measurement that involves the measurement of one or more other attributes.[10]

Some examples of indirect metrics include

☞ Number of hits per page
☞ Number of successful hits per page
☞ Number of hits for total site
☞ Number of hits per page per session per individual user
☞ Average user session time in seconds
☞ Most accessed segments
☞ Top paths through site
☞ Views of banners
☞ Hits by user groups
☞ Total hits
☞ Cached hits
☞ Successful hits
☞ Failed hits

Examples of direct metrics include

☞ Number of individual authenticated user sessions
☞ Authenticated user sessions by location

---

9. Norman Fenton, *Software Metrics: A Rigorous Approach*, Chapman & Hall, London, 1991.
10. Ibid.

☞ Authenticated user profiles by region

☞ Top "entry" and "exit" pages by authenticated users

☞ Most downloaded files

☞ Advertising "captures"

☞ Most active authenticated organizations accessing site

☞ Most active countries, states, cities, and regions by authenticated users

☞ Organizational breakdown of site access by authenticated users

☞ Maximal, minimal, average number of authenticated users per period

☞ Most used browsers

☞ Spiders or bot activity

☞ Most used platforms

☞ Successful forms submitted

☞ Failed forms submitted

☞ Server error log (404 errors, etc.)

☞ Top referencing sites

Many organizations are using the indirect metrics as advertised by the vendors of packages and software tools, and this will significantly hinder the ability of executives at these firms to track directly the impact of their dollars being spent on their Websites. However, having some of these metrics, even as partial views of the activity occurring on a site, is better than nothing. Organizations in the online customer acquisition phase have attempted to refine some of the indirect metrics to their needs, understanding their limitations. These include

☞ **Click-through captures.** How many users click through to the next stage in the customer acquisition process?

☞ **Time spent.** How long did a viewer stay at the site, and which items, pages, or route did the viewer select to navigate through the site?

☞ **Time spent searching.** Did the viewer use the "site map" or "search" feature, and if so for what and for how long?

☞ **Time spent before click-through.** How long did a viewer linger in the opening stages of the interaction and where?

☞ **E-mails and toll free calls.** How many e-mails or call center calls did this section generate and on what issues?

☞ **Registered Users.** If the site has a registration facility in the opening stages, what is the registration rate? (How many registered?)

By assessing these metrics, in conjunction with data from other sources such as the direct sales and marketing channels, an organization can estimate the content, format, and accessibility of the online site. While not perfect, it does provide a useful set of parameters from which to judge the site's effectiveness to retain eyeballs and potential future customers.

Customer Purchase Support—A Helping Hand to Smooth the Transaction Process

The customer, having been enticed to the point of making a purchase, has to be supported in that activity. The philosophy adopted in the customer acquisition stage now has to be adapted to focus the customer toward a completed transaction. To do this we consider the role information content and format play in this process.

Content & Format. The service drivers in this portion of the Internet service value chain are focused on two issues:

- ☞ Facilitating the customer in making a trade
- ☞ Providing an environment that the customer will relate to an efficient, informative, and productive activity

Keith Butler and his group at OfficeDepot.com clearly understand this. Their approach exemplifies this content-driven service model. They have purposely developed a low-key approach to the site, limiting the "bells and whistles" to speed up access and maximize their user base, most of which is using low-bandwidth connections. Their site gives customers the ability to order supplies quickly and efficiently and provides the service to support it. A service focal point is their "Account Center" which helps both new and existing customers to establish or modify an account with Office Depot. The Account Center allows patrons to create customized shopping lists, order by item number, or search the database for an item, all of which reduces their reorder time. Office Depot has a commanding brand presence in the United States, but it wishes to reinforce its delivery of, and commitment to, service excellence through the leverage of third-party credentials. This is in the form of endorsements and rating certificates from MasterCard, VeriSign, and Bizrate. MasterCard has a banner that, when clicked upon, states that "Office Depot is an authorized participant in MasterCard's Shop Smart! Program and provides today's best available means to safeguard your transactions. See something you like? Use your MasterCard! Coming soon from MasterCard is SET Secure Electronic-Transaction™, a new and innovative system for securing electronic transactions."[11] Click on VeriSign and the company informs the customer that "Authentic sites use a VeriSign Secure Server Digital ID to offer proof of identity, to enable secure communications and to encrypt transactions with site visitors through their web browser connections."[12] Bizrate provides the customer with an independent "customer certified report card"[13] that rates the organization, based on customer survey feedback, in terms of ease of ordering, product selection, product information, price, quality of Website, on-time delivery, product representation, customer support, and privacy policies as well as shipping and handling. Bizrate also provides services-at-a-glance reporting of a company's ability to support different ordering, delivery, and payment methods; return policies; and special features a company might offer, such as the ability of Office Depot to ensure that a customer's information is kept confidential. All of these factors work to ensure heightened customer confidence in the site and the organization.

Customer service metrics can also be usefully determined to assist in the customer relationship-management component of the organization's value chain in order to establish a customer satisfaction index (CSI). CSI is based on metrics such as:

☞ Degree of search effort required to locate a sale item
☞ Number of accounts accessed but inactive
☞ Number of visitors to informational site features in comparison to sales volume growth
☞ Number of site browsers versus buyers
☞ Complaints and online queries

This provides the organization with the ability to benchmark its customer service directly to its sales volume. Failure at any part of this Internet service value chain can potentially cause the loss of a customer or severely strain the relationship.

---

11. www.officedepot.com
12. Ibid.
13. Ibid.

Customer Fulfillment—Timely Delivery: A Key to Successful Service

The service dynamic of the sale, of course, has to be carried through customer fulfillment, when a purchased item is dispatched and delivered. This component of the purchase cycle has separate dimensions depending on the nature of the marketspace in which the online organization operates and its heritage.

A pure online organization that sells and delivers nonsoftware services faces a major challenge when determining its fulfillment strategy. Several options are available, each of which has its own positive and negative aspects. One route is to use a third-party commercial carrier such as Fed Ex or UPS, which can facilitate e-commerce fulfillment through the provision of express mail delivery and logistics services.[14] Alternatively, organizations may wish to develop their own delivery networks from scratch. This is an approach adopted by Pinkdot.com and Webvan.com, which have successfully deployed their own in-house logistics solutions to deliver groceries.

The three types of organizations—pure online, clicks-and-mortar, and bricks-and-mortar—greatly vary in the costs associated with the creation of a national or even regional sales and distribution channel from "ground zero" because the business models are clearly different. Let's consider the grocery business further: The online grocers are aiming to create centralized super-hub-warehouses and utilize economies of scale to drive margins and to use their online data collection to drive the business intelligence. The offline grocery organizations are running the "shop keeper" model that has been in existence for thousands of years; they buy from a wholesaler and build vendor-client relationships one at a time. However, it may be the clicks-and-mortar organizations that are building the winning model based upon the business intelligence data and systems they have built over the last three decades. These systems facilitate the creation of micro strategies for individual customers based on their behavior patterns in the physical store or the home. The clicks-and-mortar organizations can change their patterns of behavior based upon a view of the whole customer profile, together with their ability to roll out infrastructure faster than the other two models. Combined with pre-existing

---

14. The logistics company's systems through which delivery is tracked are in themselves examples of B2B information systems.

economies of scale and strong branding, these enable them to build high barriers to entry in this highly competitive market.

An example of a clicks-and-mortar organization is Tesco, the UK's largest supermarket chain. Tesco developed an extensive Website, TescoDirect.com, having initially refined and prototyped it through 100 of its stores; it managed to attract 250,000 registered users and generated revenues of over $200 million. Developing this strategy further, Tesco is rolling the operation out in 200 more stores. To deliver the service to homes, it has created 7,000 new positions, with each store employing two truck drivers and a team of specialist shoppers to fill the orders, based upon estimates of 2,000 customers per store.[15] Other online competitors in the UK include Iceland, which delivers frozen food, and Waitrose, a division of the John Lewis Partnership.

The three different business models also cater to (or attempt to overcome) different customer expectations and preferences in different product categories. For example, we can purchase a Ford over the Internet, but we cannot purchase a BMW directly over the Internet; customers don't expect to read the whole book before purchasing, but still wish to browse a chapter or two as they would in a store; publishers do not wish to allow the e-businesses to offer digital books even though they could easily do so, holding the majority of new manuscripts in a digital format for print production purposes. These issues translate into the necessity to have many different fulfillment solutions. The return of the item is a strong component of customer fulfillment and demands a significant amount of focused effort on the part of the organization if the customer relationship is to be maintained at a satisfactory level. This stems in part from the fact that the return of an item often requires greater amounts of participation and negative bias from the customer. For example, not all customers have equal access to a local store or branch; thus, in their eyes, the store is not a clicks-and-mortar store, but a pure online organization. Hence the smooth facilitation of this activity can act to enhance the service dynamic in the eyes of the customer and must be included in the overall service strategy.

> A key to success is to keep the customer in the loop. This requires that the customer have easy access to the logistics information surrounding her purchase.

---

15. John Willman, "Store Group Trebles Online Outlets," *Financial Times*, January 20, 2000.

Metrics in this sector of the value chain are focused upon issues such as

☞ **Delivery satisfaction.** Number of on-time deliveries.

☞ **Service upgrades.** Does an upgrade in delivery service correlate to an increase in customer business?

☞ **Shipping preferences.** What are the popular options? Can these be offered in a better way?

☞ **Returns.** Voice versus online call center for queries on returns; store returns versus online service center returns.

☞ **Service requests.** Store, e-mail, call center, other.

These shipping and dispatching metrics can be used not only to monitor current product offerings but also to identify the needs and the further opportunities in the market, which might include the provision of worldwide logistics and materials handling for customers or the need to offer special services for clients such as providing customs and taxation expertise to accompany shipments or advising on third-party logistics. In identifying these opportunities, the organization is moving into the fourth dimension of the Internet service value chain—the customer continuance and support dimension.

Customer Continuance and Support—Maintaining That Customer Relationship Between Purchases

The final link in the service value chain is continued development of the customer-organization relationship, thus facilitating further purchases and increasing the lifetime value of the customer. The postpurchase support primarily builds on the service information provided through the previous three stages.

Developing our Office Depot case study further, we see that the products sold are primarily commodities, and therefore price is important. However, if prices are equal across all suppliers, then often service quality will dictate the winner. In the office supply business the customer, whether retail B2C or commercial B2B, wants service that facilitates a quick turnaround from order to delivery; the ability to customize order lists; and the ability to develop a corporate account, along with information that helps the office manager run that function more efficiently. It is this last dimension that is the *hidden service dimension* that the Web provides. This is illustrated at OfficeDepot.com—the company freely provides generic business forms; partners with other vendors such as Stamps.com to provide postage; provides easy-to-follow educational segments on improving product usage and office efficiency, e.g., selecting the right paper for your office needs, improving security in the office. The organization even provides online software tools such as planners and schedulers for the office. This will all ultimately bind the customer closer to the supplier, simultaneously improving that relationship to a mutual benefit. One of the levers that facilitates the organization's continued relationship with the customer is the customer service center which can be utilized to maintain the appropriate level of contact at the appropriate points of contact.

The Customer Service Channel

Central to a service leadership strategy is the ability of the organization to be simpatico with the needs of the customer across all aspects of the organization, particularly those aspects in direct contact with the customer. In order to control this customer-organization relationship, it is vital that the corporation's customer service strategy is carefully appraised in relation to its Internet strategy. In this area, three strategies are emerging: the transference strategy, the e-mail strategy, and the virtual call center strategy.

Transference Strategy

This is the most common strategy and involves the creation of a portion of the Internet Website that can be used for solving customer queries through Frequently Asked Questions (FAQ) and documentation. The goal is to reduce the load on the human operator in the toll free number system and move the cost of basic interactions to a low-cost channel. This is a low-risk strategy since customers usually will not be offended by being given online information because the information can be processed at their own pace.

The approach through which FAQ customer service is approached can vary between the extreme of not having any toll free number or call center number on the Website and having Web-focused service representatives. The former aims at discouraging and separating the traffic; the latter aims at utilizing call center representatives to be Web-centric, depending upon call volume, and capable of switching functionality as needed.

E-mail Strategy

E-mail strategy is a variance of the transfer strategy in that the customer is encouraged to interact directly with the organization through e-mail. This has the strength of creating and building a closer relationship with the customer; the weakness, however, is the associated overhead. Most organizations pursuing this strategy are directing the e-mails through their e-mail portal to the department that has the responsibility for it. The downside risk on this is large—several large and notable companies have become overwhelmed and forced to shut down this conduit to the company, alienating customers whose e-mails go unanswered even though the site may guarantee 72-hour turnaround response. Hence it can be seen that a successful service strategy has to be developed as an aspect of the corporate strategy as a whole.

Virtual Call Center Strategy

This is an emerging advanced service concept based on the traditional business-customer relationship. However, the customer is now given greater access to data and information that previously was accessible only internally to the business organization itself. One major aircraft engine manufacturer has adopted this strategy in its B2B virtual call center. After consolidating the data gathered from its customers in order to understand individual usage patterns and metrics, it allows customers to view the data in an anonymous format, thus enriching not only the B2B relationship of the manufacturer but also enhancing its customers' collective relationships as they interact through bulletin boards and "engine maintenance information points." Similarly in another B2B service center a telecommunications provider allows its customers to enter its problem management system and see all the problems that occurred with the equipment at various companies and locations, again anonymously. This type of service provision complements the goals of these companies. The telecommunications provider aims to provide excellence in terms of speed, innovation, agility, and technology for its customers, and this service strategy reinforces this objective. It also allows a certain amount of the load to be deferred to the customer and frees the organization to focus on the truly difficult and challenging problems a customer may have requiring extra effort on the part of the organization.

Summary

In developing a service leadership strategy, five components of the Internet service value chain have to be considered.

Customer Acquisition

Develop an online channel that will reflect the corporation's brand. Deliver service levels that are consistent with the other channels the organization possesses. The first few moments of contact with the customer are vital to developing that relationship further, and three dimensions of that encounter need to be considered: **content**, **format**, and **access**. Content has to be consistent with the brand and attractive enough to create customer follow-through, delivering a balance between a variety of new information and predictability of resource. The format and access of the information initially has to be at a low enough bandwidth so that it does not discourage new viewers and speeds user involvement. Metrics such as click-throughs can be developed to monitor the customer acquisition rate.

Customer Purchase Support

The content and format of the information provided to customers has to be carefully designed to accommodate the customer relationship that is desired. Commercial retail customers will value information that reduces the browse-purchase time; the general public values information supporting their purchasing style; etc. Customer support may include cross-brand partnering with items such as airline frequent flier miles, payment options such as cash on delivery (COD), check or credit, and privacy assurances. Metrics such as *customer sale completion rate* can be created to monitor this component of the Internet service value chain.

Customer Fulfillment

The purchase, dispatch, and return dimension of the organization's strategy will depend on the logistics solution adopted, whether that is to deliver its own products, to partner with a logistics agent, to outsource, or a mix of all these. The key to success here is to keep the customer in the loop—this requires that the customer have easy access to the logistics information surrounding his purchase.

Customer Continuance and Support

Service quality is one of the keys to customer retention. Developing an ongoing relationship involves adding value to the customer on an ongoing basis. The continued provision of data and information as a service to the customer after purchase is a highly desirable facet of the relationship. It keeps customers coming back to check on the latest developments and issues that may improve their ability to perform their own operations.

Customer Service Channel

The fifth dimension of the customer service value chain is the internal management of the organization's customer service channel. This is the creation of a strategy for physically handling the customer dialogue.

Three options can be considered:

☞ *Transference*, where the customer is moved away from the traditional call-center model to a low-cost channel such as the Internet

☞ The *e-mail* strategy, where e-mail is used as the primary communication channel between customer and organization

☞ The *virtual call center* strategy, where a customer data access point is created allowing self-directed data searches of the company's database as well as the facilitation of customer group chat rooms

Developing a customer service value chain that combines these dimensions into an effective strategy that touches the customer at all points in her or his relationship with the organization is a difficult and taxing issue, but one that needs to be conquered if the company is to build market share through customer acquisition.

Service Leadership: Rules of Internet Strategy

☞ Established strategies of customer service still apply.

☞ Internet service strength is derived from providing added information to the customer on the customer's terms.

☞ Internet customer service aims to build an affinity relationship.

☞ The Internet provides a low-cost, high-quality service channel opportunity with a global reach.

☞ A call center strategy must be defined.

☞ The e-mail interface channel must be defined and planned for.

☞ A strategy for the virtual call center must be defined well in advance of its potential implementation.

7

E-branding— The Emergence of New Global Brands

> Everything has been thought of before, but the problem is to think of it again.
>   Johann W. von Goethe

The emergence of the Internet as a vehicle through which organizations can transact has been remarkable. The creation of a truly new sales channel occurs so rarely that, when it does, the impact of the new channel upon staid industries, where many companies may have become complacent in a status quo environment, can be extremely radical. The key to organizational survival is, of course, to be aware of change and to be flexible enough to react to change in all aspects of the organization's value chain. The ultimate goal is to ensure that the customers, at all times, receive added value from the product, goods, or services from the company with which they are engaging, at all points of contact and at service levels that surpass their expectations.

> Progress is a nice word. But change is its motivator and change has its enemies.
>   Robert F. Kennedy

So far in this book we have examined three positional dimensions upon which successful e-commerce strategies are based: *technology, market,* and *service* leadership. However, any of these three leadership traits alone is not sufficient for success—an **obsessive focus on one or more of these traits to the exclusion of the others can lead to disastrous brand positioning**. For example, there is a temptation for organizations to focus on their technology and service levels—Do we have the correct hardware, software, and bandwidth? Does it interact with our infrastructure correctly? Is our service level adequate? What is the cost basis of this service level? Alternatively, organizations become obsessive with the mass-customization, one-to-one marketing dimension of this channel, focusing their marketing vision through the data mining. In order to understand the importance and relative position of these online issues, we must see them in a larger context, that of the organization's overall strategy, one of the key pillars of which is a corporation's brand and its branding strategy—an issue that IBM's CEO Louis Gerstner thinks "will dominate business thinking, for a decade or more."[1]

In this chapter we propose that key to the creation of a successful e-commerce strategy is the careful crafting of a balanced branding strategy, of which we identified four major variants: brand creator, brand follower, brand reinforcement, and brand repositioning.

Figure 7.1
Internet Branding
Strategies

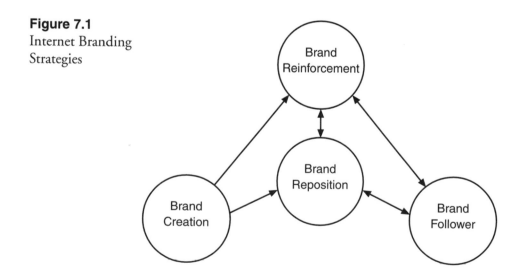

1. IBM Executive Conference on Information Systems, Latin America, Miami, FL, September 1, 1998.

Brand Creation: First to Market Wins and Wins Big

For new start-ups and for corporations moving to the Internet as a business channel, the formulation of an online brand is vital. In creating a brand, the organization has to be completely cognizant of its entire strategy, going forward as far as possible into the future in order to prevent dramatic repositioning of the brand image later on.

Successful brand creation strategies are obvious—Amazon.com, eBay.com, Priceline.com, and so on. These companies not only created a new brand, but successfully executed their business model. But what separates the winners from the losers in this online marketspace?

Amazon.com

A company founded in 1995 which has grown to be the Internet's most dominant bookseller, Amazon.com epitomizes the successful born-on-the-Net category organization. The added value to the customer is financially clear, a low-cost alternative. However, cost alone is not the only added-value factor. Convenience and service are the key. The customer feels connected to the company, rather than disconnected by the technology. The branding at Amazon not only emanates from its high-quality customer service, but also is based on the added value of mass customization. The customer is dealt with in the way that she wishes to be dealt with—as a valued and familiar customer, as if by a store representative with whom the customer has built up a long-term relationship. Thus, the customer's patterns of purchasing are recognized and subtle suggestions are used rather than overt direct marketing techniques. The key to mass customization is becoming close to the customer and providing the product on demand at a low cost, yet maintaining sufficient margins for the supplier.

Developing a Brand Creator Position

We must consider that a great brand name is nothing without a great business plan and the ability to execute it. Every day organizations are coming to the Internet in search of a market, hoping to create high brand dominance through an Internet added-value strategy, to challenge, if not displace, existing market leaders. Traditional organizations are pondering whether to create a dot-com position based on their existing brands or a completely new entity.

Brand creator strategies are based upon the following points:

☞ The organization must develop an exceptional business plan that offers value in a new and unique way to the customer. In essence, it must be first to the market with a new online concept. Differentiation is key. If the business plan does not differentiate, then the organization cannot be a brand creator.

☞ The organization must be able to rapidly execute the business plan, from conceptualization to either cash flow or brand recognition. Brand recognition can be equated to brand equity (a topic considered in more detail in chapter 10) and thus related to future earnings and corporate valuation.

☞ The organization must have a high degree of visibility and a prominent Internet URL address (a universal resource locator address is the address used to find a site on the Internet). Some examples are travelocity.com, eTrade.com, eToys.com, and wines.com. Increasingly creative solutions are going to be required, such as in the healthcare industry where "dot MD" has been utilized by companies such as Manage.MD.

☞ In the e-commerce environment, a rapid consolidation of cybermarketspaces is continuing to occur. The time between start-up and established brand has been very rapid in this space. The organizations already there have created high barriers to entry.

The runners-up positions in this arena are full of recognized brand names that failed to understand these points. This is the case with Amazon, which beat bricks-and-mortar giants such as Borders, Dillion's, and Barnes & Noble to the punch, all of which now have to accept and focus on brand follower strategies.

Brand Follower: A Last-Mover Disadvantage or Recoverable Position?

The brand follower position is one in which many new start-up companies and many more established organizations find themselves—those organizations that have either missed the first-mover advantage *brand creator* position or companies that have Internet sites that add little value for the customer.

This is evident in copycat sites that mimic the first, second, or even third mover in an industry but have little intrinsic value of their own.

> **A window on the psychology of brand recognition**
> Question: Who was second to Mark Spitz in the 1972 Olympics?

However, all is not lost for those companies that come to the Internet marketspace in an area where an online category killer already exists or where multiple high-profile brand names are already competing for market share. The long-term loyalty of online customers to the current top-tier Internet brands is, as yet, unproven. This is one rationale for the occurrence of product and market diversification by the online brand leaders. For example, Amazon has moved into selling videos, CDs, toys, and games. In order to consolidate its position as the number one destination for all niche-market shopping, it has introduced **zShops**, which specialize in the sale of merchandise from specialty retailers, small businesses, and individuals.

Follower organizations either have to rely on massive spending campaigns to brand their site in the mind of the public or they have to turn to technology to give them an edge. With the advent of intelligent agents (programs that can go and search the Internet for solutions as commanded by their master), Web shoppers can go to a site and look at a product offering—say a digital camera. They can then send the intelligent agent to locate the lowest-cost sales site for that camera, or they can get a list of 10 sites in ascending order of cost so that a choice can be made based on secondary factors such as service or clicks-and-mortar versus online. In this way, the brand follower can therefore effectively neutralize or weaken the brand leadership strategy of first movers. However, this strategy relies on two premises: first, that other online sites facilitate linkage to or openness to these agents (some organizations block them—e.g., insurance companies) and, second, that the end customer is comfortable with the technology and this aspect of the shopping experience.

Without the agent technologies, organizations employing the brand follower strategy must rely on gaining heightened visibility or, in the case of move-to-the-Net organizations, conversion of existing market share to the Internet channel to achieve success. To illustrate this, we need only ask a friend or colleague: "Name the fourth bookseller on the Internet. Now name four auction sites." People tend to run out of ideas after three. If they survive, as brands mature they themselves propagate a third branding strategy, that of reinforcement (as discussed in the next section). This was done by the online toy vendor eToys.com, which had significantly lower visibility as a brand follower organization prior to the purchase of the eToys.com site name, a feat it achieved through the acquisition of its nearest rival.

Brand Reinforcement—The Development of a Continuous Brand Model Across Media

A key to a successful business positioning is to achieve the position of brand leader—universal recognition of name and product. This is a unifying goal for organizations both in the online, e-commerce arena and in the arena of traditional business practice. Brands such as Visa, Coke, Levi, and Ford are known globally, as are such brands as Manchester United Football Club, the New York Yankees, the BBC, and CNN. The goal of executives in all dimensions of business is to ensure that their brand achieves universal recognition and that the brand carries across all channels, media, and languages, including the Internet.

Fending Off Brand Dilution: To Be Seen Online but Not to Sell Online

The goal of being a leader and developer of Internet sales may not be the goal of every organization, but ultimately every organization wants to ensure that its brand is reinforced online. Many established organizations not currently wishing to develop a new sales channel will determine instead that a brand reinforcement strategy is a suitable complement to their existing corporate strategy. The goal of this brand reinforcement channel therefore is to reinforce the organization in the eyes of the customer.

In order to achieve this, organizations have to provide their customers or viewers with current, relevant information, building the quality of their relationships with customers on a continuing basis (see building brand equity in chapter 10). This, as discussed earlier, is an aspect of the customer service value chain. The service value chain is composed of five parts:

1. Customer acquisition
2. Customer support during purchase

3. Customer fulfillment
4. Customer continuance
5. Customer service channel

Some organizations wish to focus on some of these dimensions to the exclusion of others. BMW, for example, certainly has the resources to sell online; however, the goal is to build the relationship with the customer, reinforcing BMW's brand image in such a way as to keep the customer informed and educated about the product. The customer then brings that awareness with him or her to the dealership to make the transaction. This is not a static information-interchange relationship; it is a dynamic one in which the customer will expect change and continuous value from the relationship or the link will be severed, potentially for a significant amount of time.

Tiffany.com

We can find numerous examples of the use of a brand reinforcement strategy in many niche markets. One of these is Tiffany & Company, the high-end jewelers. Tiffany did not immediately sell directly to the retail customer; instead it used its Website to present purchase and gift ideas from its classic lines and help potential customers locate stores. However, the company changed its sales strategy in November of 1999 when it relaunched its site to sell 228 items. "Our primary objective is to communicate a broad view of Tiffany by providing more complete information about our products, as well as our unique design heritage," said James E. Quinn, vice chairman of Tiffany & Company. "The expanded site will provide a customer with a menu to experience many aspects of Tiffany: superior design, a legacy of trust, a position of authority, and an uncompromised source of value."[2] However, the number of items sold is a fraction of the range the company sells at its stores and lacks the brand names and the items at the high-end fashion areas such as watches and engagement rings. Therefore executives at the company need to ask: Has this damaged my brand? If we don't sell the premium lines, what are we in fact selling? And what does that represent to our customer base, either existing or potential?

Another example, **Lennar Corporation**, one of the largest home builders in the United States, also does not sell directly, but allows potential customers

---

2. Press Release: Tiffany & Company, "Tiffany & Co. to Relaunch Its Web Site," New York, November 16, 1999.

to interact with the company at its site, allowing potential customers to look at floor plans, layouts, and visual tours of its model homes as well as examine inventories and pricing. This helps Lennar to bond with the customer and build the brand relationship, enticing customers to visit the construction site with the vision already embedded in their minds of a potential home.

Other reinforcement strategies come from the creation of added-value propositions for the customer through partnering. One type of partnering is selective partnering such as Casio's partnership with Microsoft, using Microsoft's Windows CE operating system in its palm-sized PCs, thus competing more effectively against the brand recognition leader, PalmPilot. Alternatively, the e-consortium approach can be taken to combine the strength of the individual brands to a focal point. An example of an established and very successful consortium is Visa, or the Visa International Service Association as it is more formally known. It creates credit card services for its member organizations. In fact, the consortium is jointly owned by more than 21,000 member financial institutions around the globe, whose mission is to "enhance the competitiveness and profitability of its members."[3]

More mature organizations such as those in the construction, automobile, and utility industries are not immune to the late-mover, brand follower mentality—inertia at these organizations can be immense. Further the initial B2C e-commerce phenomenon had little relevance to them. An automobile manufacturer explained the company's late arrival to the Internet:

> We did see the potential, but what we wanted to do was create a whole structure that encompassed all the brands...we were not going to go down the route of developing any Internet sites unless it was part of our strategy.

The automobile manufacturer subsequently moved online successfully in the B2C environment, reinforcing its traditional product branding strategy and developing an effective B2B portal to facilitate its supplier relationships.

Even though this aspect of brand is not directly generating revenue, it is developing tangible brand equity benefits to those that understand and execute effectively in this marketspace.

---

3. www.visa.com/av/who/main.html

Brand Reposition: Core Brand Values Combined with a Modern Customer Experience

The need to reposition a brand is often felt by organizations that have at some point in their history been left behind by a new technology, trend, or idea. The Swiss watch industry was unprepared for the battery-powered quartz watch, which it dismissed as a fad. Harley-Davidson Motorcycle Company almost went out of business due to pressures from machines with cheaper, smaller engines together with the inherently poor reliability of its own brand. The Wall Street brokerages, which originally dismissed the online trading market as too small to be involved with, have all subsequently repositioned themselves in recent years with varying degrees of success.

Organizations that have an established market and product often define themselves through these channels so tightly that it is nearly impossible to rapidly change to meet new market conditions. They are carried on by the inertia long after the opportunity to capitalize on a new strategic channel has occurred. This is compounded in the case of the Internet and e-commerce by the customer's wish to not only have access to low pricing but also to have as much information as possible regarding the product, together with other options such as purchasing, delivery, and format of product—e.g., MP3 music or CD. This is a model quite alien to traditional organizations whose products, sales, and distribution channels have been geared to the bricks-and-mortar mode of operations for decades if not centuries.

One strategy to avoid this trap is to pursue *brand repositioning*. This requires careful consideration and planning, because a "muddled" strategy can be worse than no Internet strategy at all. Repositioning may be radical or gradual, depending on the organization and its branding needs. At the most basic level, the company is looking to use the Internet and e-commerce as a process of complementing their bricks-and-mortar strategy. This was the case at Toys R Us in 1999. However, the repositioning did not quite match expectations, leaving some customers unhappy and eliciting negative comments from some members of the financial press. Thus, even slight repositioning strategies require very careful planning and coordination if they are to achieve their objective.

Other companies are more radical and completely reposition themselves online, as was the case with Egghead, which started life as Egghead, Inc., a traditional software reseller incorporated in Washington in 1984. By 1992,

> **Motley Fool—Fool on the Hill** **Dec 27, 1999**
>
> ### FOOL ON THE HILL: An Investment Opinion,
> ### Toys "R" Us: The e-Grinch Who Stole Christmas
>
> **By Yi-Hsin Chang** **December 27, 1999**
>
> Like The Grinch, Toys "R" Us has slithered down my chimney and swiped gifts from under the tree. I was notified on Monday that my December 6 online order would not be filled by Christmas, this after being guaranteed on December 18 that everything would arrive on time. In return for my trouble, the toy giant has offered me $100 in "Geoffrey Dollars" to use at any brick-and-mortar location. The gift certificate does not begin to make up for the aggravation and stress this has caused me in the days before Christmas. By the way, of the 10 companies I did e-shopping with this season, only Toys "R" Us has let me down.
> Source: www.fool.com. © 1999, The Motley Fool. All rights reserved.

Egghead, Inc., had over 200 retail store locations and had begun a direct mail division as well as a corporate, government, and educational sales division. On May 13, 1996, Egghead, Inc., sold the corporate, government, and educational sales division for $45.0 million and in February 1997 closed 70 retail stores in response to continuing retail store losses, recording a related $24.0 million restructuring and asset impairment charge. In August of 1997, Egghead, Inc., acquired Surplus Software, Inc. ("Surplus Direct"), which owned and operated two Websites and a direct mail division specializing in excess, closeout, and refurbished computer-related merchandise. The repositioning was complete by February of 1998, when the company changed its name from Egghead, Inc., to Egghead.com, Inc., closing its remaining retail stores and shifting its primary business emphasis to electronic commerce.

The transition has not been without difficulty, and the financial pain continues as the company continues to establish its brand and turn its business model to profitability. The company described the situation in its August 1999 10-Q:[4]

> Anticipated Losses. We have incurred substantial losses in the operation and closure of our former retail store network and in the operation of our online store. As of July 3, 1999, we had a retained deficit of $119.8 million. We have not achieved profitability as an

---

4. Egghead com, Inc., *Sec 10-Q Quarterly Report.*

electronic commerce company and expect to continue to incur substantial net losses for the foreseeable future. **We plan to continue to enhance our brand name** [emphasis added] through marketing and advertising programs, offer additional categories of merchandise for sale on our online store and improve and enhance our technology, infrastructure and systems. These initiatives will likely result in operating expenses that are higher than current operating expenses. We will need to generate significantly higher revenues to achieve profitability and maintain profitability if it is achieved. Although our net sales from electronic commerce have grown in recent quarters, such growth rates may not be sustainable. Because of these and other factors, we believe that period-to-period comparisons of our historical results of operations are not good indicators of our future performance.

It describes its success in boosting sales through effective branding:

Net Sales. Total net sales for the first quarter of fiscal 2000 increased 37.4% to $40.6 million as compared with $29.5 million for the first quarter of fiscal 1999. **The increase in net sales was primarily attributable to an increase in the online customer base, significant investments in marketing programs designed to promote and maintain brand awareness** [emphasis added], an increase in the number of daily and weekly online auctions, and an increase in the categories and amount of merchandise offered. Our customer accounts increased to approximately 1.1 million as of July 3, 1999 from approximately 530,000 as of June 27, 1998.

Also described were some of the perils of online retail sales; even though the company has increased sales, the margins are increasingly thin as competitors strive to gain market share and often discount products below cost.

Gross Margin. Gross margin consists of net sales minus cost of sales. Cost of sales includes initial margin (net sales minus cost of products sold), obsolete inventory charges and net shipping (shipping reimbursements less shipping costs). Gross margin from net sales was $2.9 million, or 7.1% of sales, for the first quarter of fiscal 2000, a reduction from gross margin of 10.4% of sales for the comparable prior year period. Gross margin in the current quarter was negatively affected by responses to some **competitors selling**

current version goods below or marginally above their acquisition cost [emphasis added]. Although we have not adopted this pricing strategy, we have responded to these competitive pressures by reducing the selling prices on certain products. This reduction in selling prices had a material adverse impact on our first quarter fiscal 2000 gross margins when compared to our historical online gross margins. This reduction in selling prices was partially offset by an increase in advertising revenue for the quarter. Management has initiated, and will continue to initiate, actions in an attempt to offset the reduction in gross margins; however, there can be no assurance that we will be able to maintain gross margins or that this reduction in selling prices will not negatively affect our gross margins in the second quarter of fiscal 2000.

Organizations that move through brand repositioning to create a new model successfully can be found in many market segments, including travel, where airlines and car-rental companies have created new channels to complement their existing ones, attempting to add value to the customer through reduced cost and convenience, but also offering a source of information for the discerning consumer. An example of this is American Airlines (aa.com) which in 1999 spent $3 million redesigning its Website[5]—the first major redesign since its inception in 1995. The organization wanted to position itself effectively in the travel bookings space to remain competitive against new start-up Internet competition such as Trip.com, Excite.com, and Priceline.com, which are themselves redefining segments of the travel market. The traditional organizations in this sector cannot risk alienating their existing customer base or distribution systems, and hence they cannot always jump directly to the brand creation category, instead relying on the creation of or repositioning of online brands such as aa.com.

Thus the rules for brand repositioning come from finding and pursuing an Internet strategy that will be beneficial to the business as a whole, understanding the cost considerations and ensuring that the organization learns as it moves to that new marketspace. This is clearly the case in the financial arena where traditional brokerages such as Merrill Lynch and Morgan Stanley Dean

---

5. Sari Kalin, "American Airlines' $3 Million Makeover," *CIO Magazine*, February 1, 1999. www.cio.com/archive/webbusiness/020199_design.html

Witter (MSDW) have had to create strategies to fend off competition in the Internet arena. MSDW initially provided investment research and information to its customers but did not give them the full ability to trade, invest, or interact with financial services online. This reinforced their existing brand and ensured that alignment between the channels occurred smoothly at the outset. Having done this, MSDW invested to bring its Discover brokerage to the forefront as an alternative low-cost brand to their premium MSDW brokerage. However, the Discover brand is not a global brand and as such does not appeal to the brand sensitivities of the upscale MSDW customer base; so the company rebranded again, creating Morgan Stanley Dean Witter On Line from Discover Brokerage Direct.

It's easy to see that the exercise of creating, reinforcing, or recreating a brand can be a major undertaking and one that can never be taken lightly, even for established organizations. The competition in the online market is highly competitive and very unforgiving; margins are razor thin and customer expectations are high. These factors, combined with the factor that loyalty is marginal and a competitor only a click away makes the need to establish a premium brand the first time a highly essential component of an organization's business planning process.

Summary

The four branding strategies introduced in this chapter are of a macro nature and need to be tied into the three other dimensions of an Internet strategy introduced earlier in the book:

- ☞ **Technology.** How are we attempting to leverage the technology, with what consequence on our brand?
- ☞ **Market.** What is our market segmentation strategy? How can we define brands across these?
- ☞ **Service.** What level of service will we deliver through this channel—full service, low-cost service? How will this impact our brand?

The development of an online branding strategy is a complex operation and one that clearly needs to be tied into the organization's strategy as a whole, based on the other three factors.

Brand Leadership: Rules of Internet Strategy

☞ In new organizations, creation of a brand has to be a primary strategic objective.

☞ Branding strength comes from being first mover in combination with high visibility and the added value derived from the information surrounding the product.

☞ Brand reinforcement is a continuous task. The aim is to use the brand reinforcement process to maintain an organization's relationship with the customer. This is achieved by continuously adding value to the customer through the site.

☞ Brand reinforcement adds significant value to organizations that can inform consumers, but not sell directly, such as drug manufacturers.

☞ Brand positioning can be considered using the *Internet service value chain* model, adding brand definition and value at each point on that chain.

☞ Added value for the customer comes from continuous and innovative change of the information surrounding the product and the organization.

☞ Utilize a mass customization approach in order to move closer to the customer and add value to the customer but not at the expense of the brand.

☞ The Internet allows low-cost global branding to occur, hence wider market coverage; however, the cultural sensitivities of the global brand must not be lost through the technology.

☞ Brand followers need to reposition as quickly and effectively as possible.

☞ Established organizations that have not established a branding strategy based upon the Internet need to develop one rapidly and align their overall strategy accordingly.

☞ Brand repositioning can be an expensive and difficult process. The establishment of a strong and vibrant brand at the commencement of online activity is vital.

Formulating an Internet Rollout Strategy

After extensive research into the e-commerce strategies employed at over 40 organizations, it became clear that, in e-commerce, as in all aspects of IT and strategy, strategic positioning meant little if it could not be implemented. As such the development and hosting of an organization's Internet presence forms a critical component in the level of success experienced.

The rollout of an e-commerce implementation is composed of two dimensions:

☞ **Site development.** The point where the rubber meets the road acting as the focal point where strategic goals, ownership issues, and technology all converge to produce a working system.

☞ **Website hosting.** Selection of, and deployment to, a location or organization where the system hardware and software will be physically located, maintained, and managed.

From our discussions and personal interviews with executives at the companies in our case studies, three basic development practices emerged:

1. **Internal development.** Corporations create their e-commerce systems within the boundaries of their organizations.

169

2. **External development.** The system's development is largely outsourced to third parties to obtain the desired results.

3. **Selective sourcing or partnering.** External vendors are brought on-site to assist in the development process.

together with four hosting options:

1. **Dedicated hosting.** The company outsources its requirements to a Web hosting company except that the system is located on a dedicated server.

2. **Shared hosting.** An organization outsources the storage, maintenance, and monitoring of its system to a Web hosting company. Its system is located on a shared server.

3. **Internal hosting.** A company stores, maintains, and monitors its own systems at its own internal data center.

4. **Colocation.** A company stores, maintains, and monitors its own information and systems, but utilizes the services of a Web hosting company to store the server.

Each approach has its own strengths and weaknesses, so the mechanism selected by an organization will depend on the strategic goals the organization is pursuing within its e-commerce agenda. Let's consider them in more detail.

Development Options—Where to Develop an E-commerce System (Internal, External, or Partnering)

The case study organizations researched for this book developed their Internet and e-commerce systems in a variety of ways. Key among the drivers that influenced their decisions were issues such as:

☞ Maturity of the organization
☞ Access to internal skills among the technology group
☞ Necessity to create and develop proprietary technologies
☞ Flexibility of the content owners to drive, control, and harness change
☞ Requirement to be online and compete in the virtual marketspace
☞ Requirement to lead the market in terms of service and brand

Figure 8.1 shows some of the major pathways through this development landscape.

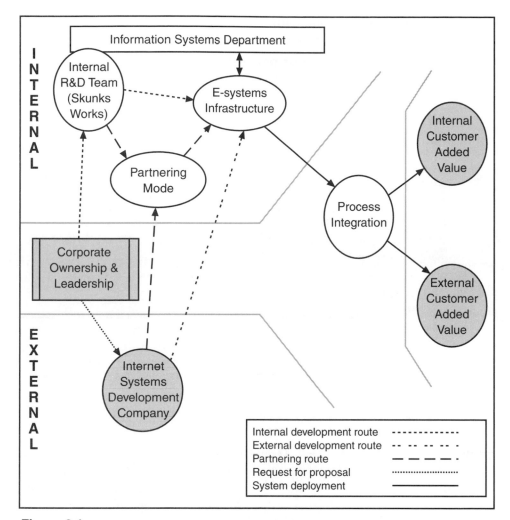

Figure 8.1
Dimensions of Corporate Internet Development

The Internal Development Route

The internal development route was the only choice for early movers to the Internet marketspace in 1994 and 1995. The technology was as yet unproven; there were few vendors and few tools to employ in developing the process. The marketspace was also extremely receptive and forgiving because the customers' expectations were low and any content was gladly accepted by them.

The early movers to the e-commerce arena were driven and motivated by one of two factors: the desire to be first into a marketspace, or the need to match peer organizations moving online. Those first movers who acted upon a sound business plan have reaped high rewards and prospered, as have more traditional organizations that have not been left for dead. Not all organizations that ventured online have been successful, so it is worth considering some of the keys to success for those that managed to make their mark in this rapidly changing marketspace.

The primary driver of successful internal development was found to lie in having a credible **project champion**, usually an executive officer or CIO, who oversaw the Internet development group. Even more successful were those that had a high-level project sponsor who also created space and facilitated the necessary budget and resources to get the project off the ground, while protecting the project from detractors at all times. Typically the best project champions provided and sustained both the vision and the motivation for the project, having the political influence needed to keep it moving forward. Such projects were often dubbed *skunks works* by their developers.

Case Focus: *A first-mover project champion focus* can be found at Charles Schwab and Company. Upon being demonstrated a basic hookup of the company's traditional trading system with a Mosaic Interface, the co-CEOs created, protected, and nurtured a new stand-alone Internet development group in order to acquire, learn, and adapt the technology to their needs. Ultimately, recreating their company based on Internet technologies has turned Schwab into the largest online brokerage company in the world.

Early movers in the area used the skunks works teams to focus initially, promoting *organizational learning* and, as they gained experience with the new medium, developed skills both in the assessment of potential associated development costs and the impact the technology would have on the marketplace as it unfolded. This was a vital component because it triggered acknowledgment that this technology was real and would become pervasive. As stated by an executive representing Dow Jones Interactive Publishing when discussing the initial products created by their organization:

> What they did was jump-start parts of the organization to understand the Web was real, and it needed the appropriate level of attention.

This tied in with the organization's ability to determine which technologies were worth pursuing early on and which were not. The executive continued:

> If we had taken a customer survey at the time, there would not have been anyone interested in the Web. It was a huge leap of faith, and

it was the correct leap of faith. So that was just an early effort in trying to understand the technology and possibly develop a product. We ended up not putting out a Web product at the time, but that was OK because we did eventually release The Wall Street Journal Interactive Edition and Dow Jones Interactive.

Many of the skunks works projects were funded from R&D budgets at low costs, initially. Florida Power & Light also took this approach in 1995; an executive states:

We knew that we had to have a vanity page, the static stuff out there, but we knew that we needed to understand from an IT perspective "how do you make it more active?"

Having reached this point, the leading organizations realized that, in addition to the creative development performed in the skunks works, two other issues needed to be considered: The *infrastructure* upon which the system was to be based and the mechanism for performing *process integration.*

The **IT infrastructure** was identified as the key to technological and organizational flexibility by many of the CIOs and executives at organizations in our study who have experienced successful e-commerce rollouts. An organization's Internet presence could easily turn out to be a static one without much of an impact. Successful organizations with dynamic Internet presence attributed their success to the careful creation of the organization's systems infrastructure. A successful infrastructure can be defined as *one facilitating the implementation of value-added services through different organizational business drivers, delivering a positive or potentially positive return on investment.* Since each organization has different objectives and goals for its systems, a useful route to determining the corporation's needs is through an objective scorecarding mechanism. Such an approach is outlined in chapter 9 and is intended to assist executives and technologists to come together and deliver the strategic systems objective through a solid technological underpinning.

The creation of a strong yet flexible infrastructure was a precursor for the second element of the development, that of process integration. For both new and traditional organizations coming to the Net, the key to their ultimate success is their ability to understand the processes necessary to facilitate their business objectives and integrate them into a unified, flexible, and effective value chain.

You Can't Manage What You Can't Measure[1]

A driver related to process integration is the ability of the organization to measure the business value from this process integration. Several approaches to dealing with this important process were identified in our research; an executive at a publishing organization summarizes the current situation for many of the respondent organizations:

> Presenting the value to people who say "what am I getting out of this technology investment?"—it's not easy, it's still pretty hard, but we are able to do that a little more effectively. We are still looking at different ways of trying to prove to corporations that there is a strong ROI; some aspects are so intangible that it usually comes down to big dollar success stories, productivity gains, and measuring that. In some levels we can do it—it is easy to do—and in others we are still searching for ways to describe that to customers so that they make it as integral as e-mail.

Again, in an attempt to help executives with this task, we have provided a scorecard approach (in chapter 9) to help them determine the specific value drivers for an individual organization and its e-commerce strategy, as well as the success levels they have reached in their attempt. Ultimately, the true measure of development effectiveness is how the *customer* perceives the effectiveness of the strategy and development, whether that customer is internal or external to the organization. Again these metrics have to be considered in advance, built into the organization's scorecard methodology and then monitored during system delivery, with the strategy being adjusted according to the feedback.

The External Development Route—Outsourcing as an Approach to Systems Creation

An alternative approach to internal systems development is that of the external development route, or "pay and display"[2] (see Figure 8.1), where an organization uses an external vendor to outsource some or all of the creation and

---

1. Adapted from a quote by Peter Drucker, *The Practice of Management*, NY, Harper & Brothers, 1954.

2. Termed "pay and display" due to the fact that often the company pays an external entity to develop the system and then to host that system displaying the contents.

development process. The decision to develop the system internally or to turn to the outside for collaboration or assistance in our study was found to be based on a clear understanding of three prerequisite organizational factors:

☞ **Leadership.** How does the executive management view the Internet development? Is there a project sponsor and champion?

☞ **Function of the system.** What is the intent of the system? To obtain technology leadership? Build brand? Create leadership in service or marketing? Has the corporate leadership defined this clearly and does it understand the entire consequence and intent of the endeavor?

☞ **Infrastructure.** What is the state of play with respect to the organization's internal technology and systems? Is the organization's systems technology infrastructure capable of supporting a "bulletproof" e-commerce system?

Based on these prerequisites, the following two factors need to be considered in detail:

☞ **Speed.** How quickly does the system have to be in place?

☞ **Expertise.** What skill sets are available within the organization?

The basic decision process can be considered through Figure 8.2.

Earlier in the book we considered the major issues surrounding the first steps toward the creation of a successful e-commerce development process, including ensuring participation of a project champion from the highest levels of the organization and clearly defining the functional intent of the e-commerce strategy. Once the e-commerce functionality has been defined in relation to the organization's total strategy, it can then consider the sourcing option for the system. To do this, it must look at several factors, the most important of which is matching the process, organizational, and systems structures. In creating the infrastructure (discussed in chapter 4), the organization must take into account the technical and functional considerations; for example:

☞ Do our current processes allow for single-unit production levels (mass customization)?

☞ Do we capture our organizational learning in knowledge management systems?

☞ Do we understand our customer? Can we capture this understanding from historical data that is captured in our data warehouse?

☞ How flexible is our ERP system? Can we interface this with our e-commerce direct sales engine? Also in combination with our logistics engine?

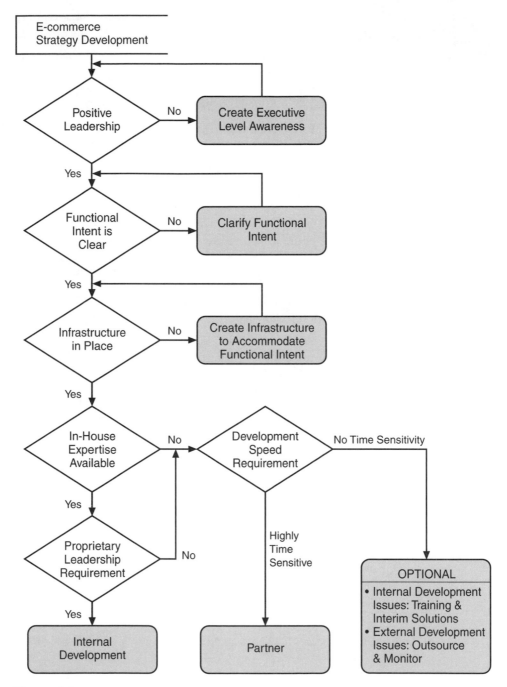

Figure 8.2
Determinants of Internet Development Sourcing Options

The consideration of these infrastructure issues may lead the organization to delay the deployment of an internal e-commerce system due to an inadequate or ineffective existing infrastructure.[3] This will itself need to be resolved prior to continuing internally and may require an outsourcing, partnering, or consulting process to be undertaken in order to resolve the situation.

Once organizations have formulated an Internet strategy through a planning process, research showed that the decision of which development route to follow was critically determined by two factors, namely:

☞ The availability of in-house expertise

☞ The urgency requirement—the speed at which the organization wished to move online (see Figure 8.2)

The greatest choices come to those companies which have the best preparation.

For traditional organizations moving to the Internet, the issues of in-house expertise and urgency also have to be taken into account. If in-house expertise is available, this is often the direct result of skunks works initiatives where the organization has a history and philosophy of disseminating information and hence the learning curve of change is inexpensive to the organization. Thus, in the case where the organization has internal skills, it is usually in a strong position to proceed with a new initiative, but most central to its success is its ability to determine its true strategic e-commerce intent.

The greatest choices therefore come to those companies which have the best preparation. For new companies, this is a significant advantage—they create their own new infrastructure to best suit their e-commerce strategy. However, even though these new organizations have heightened organizational flexibility and process integration, they may lack other strategic strengths such as access to detailed historical customer knowledge. These are the fundamental issues discussed earlier in describing the required attributes of the e-organization (chapter 4): flexibility, low production costs, strong market knowledge, and knowledge-management skills.

---

3. Chapter 9 includes a framework to help establish effectiveness of brand, technology, marketing, and service.

Proprietary Technology—A Barrier to Entry

In the case of where an organization wishes to create a proprietary technology product through the Internet, then the only route is to specify that internally, possibly allowing its production under contract externally. An example of this technology is the 1-Click customer-data-interface engine developed by Amazon, which Amazon sees as a key to its successful customer relationship management. Amazon sees any infringement on this technology as a serious threat and deals with it seriously, as shown in the following press release.

Amazon.com Sues BarnesandNoble.com for Patent Infringement

**Suit Alleges Competitor Copied Innovative
1-Click® Technology that Makes Online Shopping Hassle-Free**

SEATTLE—(BUSINESS WIRE)–Oct. 21, 1999–Leading online retailer Amazon.com (NASDAQ: AMZN) has filed suit against barnesandnoble.com, saying it has illegally copied Amazon.com's innovative, patented 1-Click® technology that makes online shopping as easy as a click of the mouse button.

The suit, filed late Thursday in U.S. District Court in Seattle, alleges patent infringement and seeks an immediate and permanent court-ordered halt to the defendant's copycat feature. It also asks for an unspecified amount of damages.

First made available to Amazon.com customers in September 1997, the 1-Click® feature allows customers to shop conveniently without multiple steps or re-entering their shipping and billing information every time they buy.

"Being a pioneer and innovating for customers is always hard," said Jeff Bezos, Amazon.com founder and CEO. "We spent thousands of hours to develop our 1-Click process, and the reason we have a patent system in this country is to encourage people to take these kinds of risks and make these kinds of investments for customers."

The 1-Click® feature securely stores billing and shipping information so that returning customers need only click their mouse once to buy a selected item, rather than re-entering the same information over and over again for each purchase. In recognition of the innovative and unique nature of the 1-Click® technology, the U.S. Patent Office awarded Patent No. 5,960,411 to Amazon.com on September 28, 1999.

Some of the issues surrounding internal development can be summarized as follows:

☞ Internal Development Advantages

— Development potential for proprietary technologies

        — Internalization of organizational learning

        — Understanding of the organization's internal processes and integration issues

        — Understanding of internal IT infrastructure

☞ Internal Development Disadvantages

        — Opportunity cost of mistakes

        — First mover expense

        — Scarce IT skills resources inhibiting development

        — Not knowing if the business side will commit necessary resources

Organizations with in-house expertise but with no desire or need to create proprietary technologies have a wide series of options they can utilize. They can still develop the mainstream core systems internally using their own hardware and software skills or develop them in conjunction with packages and tools. Organizations that follow this approach do so to maintain organizational effectiveness, preparedness, and future flexibility but without having to become a research-based organization. However, the key determinant of an organization's course of action is the time pressure to come to the Internet marketspace and to maintain the level of presence required.

A further option—to route some or all development to a third party—is driven by several motives, including time and internal-skills sensitivity.

Outsourcing and Partnering

At the extreme of outsourcing is the total outsourcing option. This is favored by organizations that need to bring their e-commerce visions online rapidly. They tap into existing expertise and a variety of external services offered. Vendors can provide a "soup-to-nuts" service—from assisting in the specification of the systems requirements to deploying and hosting of the site at their Web farms. This is favored by many organizations, both large and small, familiar and unfamiliar with the Internet and what its potential can be. At the most basic level, organizations wishing for a minimal yet effective presence can utilize vendors successfully in this way. Using the jewelers Tiffany & Company as an example, Tiffany is not pressured in its marketspace to be at the leading edge of Internet commerce from a sales perspective; rather the company perceives the Internet as a complementary vehicle to its primary advertising channel.[4] In reinforcing its brand through the site, Tiffany however will need to ensure that its site maintains the correct level of sophistication, matching its advertising as delivered through other channels. In order to achieve this, the company may wish to take the opportunity to outsource to specialists its complete development operation, including the brand-sensitive graphic design work, market analysis, customer-relationship management, and site maintenance. The goal for a site such as Tiffany's site is to balance ownership with pragmatism, aiming to generate the return on investment through traditional channels but focus the online customer to the corporation's core strengths. The weaknesses to this approach stem from the lowered growth of technical and channel learning. Some of the issues surrounding outsourced development can be summarized as follows:

☞ Advantages of total outsourcing

— Taps into existing expertise
— Gives access to a wide variety of external services
— Quickly gets up to speed
— Allows an organization to come to the market quicker

☞ Disadvantages of total outsourcing

— The internal learning processes associated with the adoption of new technologies are not immediately facilitated or reinforced.
— The process builds the vendor's experience base rather than the client's.
— The outsourcee may lack the skills to manage the project.
— The lack of experience in outsourcing emerging technology projects may lead to extensive cost overruns.
— May interrupt continuous management and close vendor-customer communications channel needed to ensure the technological alignment of the project with its strategic intent.
— The cost/overhead from coordinating content owners are significant.

The key strategic strengths acquired through the outsourcing approach have been desired by other organizations whose e-commerce strategy is not to sell

---

4. Press Release: Tiffany & Company, "Click Here for More Information, Tiffany & Co. to Relaunch Its Web Site," New York, November 16, 1999.

online but to use the medium to reinforce their brand. BMW for example is a classic example of brand reinforcement through the Internet. However, due to the higher technical demands of its customer, its product, and its customer relationship, BMW has a more extensive site and a higher level of sophistication requirement to deliver to its customer. An executive at BMW states:

> We wanted to design a site that said to those people who are BMW enthusiasts, BMW really knows who I am. So there is an intimate relationship there. We wanted to make it as personalized and individualized as possible; we wanted to make sure that it added value to the ownership relationship of having a BMW. We wanted to make sure that it navigated and felt like a BMW.

By focusing on the customer and developing its site requirements from that customer relationship, BMW understood the necessity to have a strong internal understanding of the development requirement, as commented upon by the executive:

> There is a very clear understanding of the medium and enthusiasm for it and there is support from all areas within the company and that is how our site is going to grow and we're going to add more aspects to it because other people within the organization are very anxious to be a part of it and to make our site as best as it could possibly be.

But BMW also understood the necessity to cherry-pick, the best tools, techniques, knowledge, and expertise available to build a world-class destination site—for example, partnering with the advertising agency partners and interactive marketing specialists to ensure full integration of the site with their other initiatives.

Partnering allows companies to quickly tap into a wide variety of existing areas of expertise to bring a superior presence to their site than would otherwise be possible, while at the same time allowing the organization to focus on its internal strengths. The partnering route does incur the additional overheads of contact and relationship management. However, this can be considered a small price to pay when considering the cost of the alternative—internally maintaining a leading-edge group in all aspects of the technology. Some of the issues surrounding outsourced development can be summarized as follows:

☞ Advantages of partnering

— Taps into existing expertise
— Gives access to a wider variety of external services
— Quickly gets up to speed
— Shares/builds expertise with vendor
— Facilitates internalization of learning
— Allows an organization to focus upon other issues, e.g., infrastructure

☞ Disadvantages of partnering

— Requires in-house skills to staff and manage the project (availability?)
— Requires business managers' commitment to achieve business and technology alignment
— Requires contract management costs to coordinate project

Bringing the Systems Back Inside the Organization—Insourcing

Some organizations have, since the inception of their Internet presence, moved through multiple development strategies. Some companies have outsourced only to subsequently insource once again. These early movers were often forced to outsource due to the classic problem of internal skill shortage that occurs in information technology deployment situations: The ability to acquire talent with the latest skill sets in a market where the talent is rare and expensive and often difficult to retain if internal training is given to existing employees. This problem is amplified when combined with a need for a rapid online presence. One travel-related company outsourced in order to be first in its industry to go online. This allowed the organization to build brand and gain valuable organizational learning while building its internal organization, infrastructure, and processes, all of these skills being learned when the competition on the Internet was less sophisticated and the development issues less complex. The company subsequently took its system development back inside the organization and built a successful, leading presence in its industry. Some of the issues surrounding the insourcing of development can be summarized as follows:

☞ Advantages of reinternalized development

— Internalize organizational learning while the vendor manages live system
— Gain time to understand the organization's processes and integration issues as they relate to the future online presence

    — Develop an understanding of the future internal IT infrastructure requirements

☞ Disadvantages of reinternalized development

    — Opportunity cost of mistakes
    — First-mover expense
    — Inexperienced vendors
    — Scarcity of IT skills resources may inhibit top-quality development
    — Vendor focus may be elsewhere

Summary: Development Issues

The strategy for development of an organization's Website is dependent upon several key factors:

☞ The maturity of the organization
☞ The access to skills among its internal technology group
☞ The necessity to create and develop proprietary technologies
☞ The flexibility of the content owners to drive, control, and harness change
☞ The time pressure to be online and compete in the organization's virtual marketspace or to lead its market in terms of service and brand

But consideration of these issues is secondary to determining the balanced strategy of the organization as a whole based on the *branding*, *technology*, *marketing*, and *service* leadership focus desired.

However, organizations are not fixed into one form of development relationship forever; furthermore, many organizations have moved from one development category to another over their online life span as:

☞ Organizations mature with respect to the medium.
☞ The markets in which the organization competes change.
☞ The nature of the Internet and its technologies change.

Thus these environmental drivers force all organizations to continually reassess their vision, strategy, and e-commerce execution paths. Table 8.1 summarizes the strengths and weaknesses of the three e-commerce development options covered in this chapter.

Table 8.1 E-commerece Development Options—Their Strengths and Weaknesses

	Major Strengths	*Major Weaknesses*
Internal Development	• Allows proprietary systems and technologies to be developed • Maximizes internal learning • Maximizes system integration	• Cost—can be very expensive to be first mover • Resource intensiveness—continuous need for new skills and technologies • Commitment—requires major commitment from all parties
External Development	• Taps into existing expertise • Offers a variety of external services • Gets up to speed quickly	• Cost—not a one-time cost; little payback in the form of internalization of learning • Cookie-cutter solutions—vendors using same ideas and formats over and over again • Difficulty monitoring and controlling • Service limitations—advantages gained through flexible partnering may be offset by the necessity to monitor and control those relationships
Partnering	• Offers variety • Gets up to speed quickly • Allows flexibility	• Lack of attention—partners may be overextended; too little time for each client • Lack of experience—experience of partners in new technologies possibly limited, raising risk concerns • Cost—integration costs, monitoring costs, and cost control issues

Hosting Options—Hosting Websites, Maintaining Control, and Managing Flexibility

The creation of a Website is the penultimate stage in the evolution of an organization's e-commerce strategy. The final aspect of deployment is the hosting of the site. Hosting can be defined as *the physical location where a company's Website and Internet system are stored, maintained, and monitored.* Several options are available, including:

☞ **Self hosting.** An organization takes responsibility for running, operating, and maintaining its own systems.

☞ **Colocation.** An organization maintains and monitors its own Website and systems but uses the facilities of a hosting company to physically locate its systems.

☞ **Dedicated hosting.** An organization outsources the management of its system and support activities to a third party, but the Website and systems are located on a server dedicated solely to that organization.

☞ **Shared hosting.** Similar to dedicated hosting, with the exception that the Website resides on a shared server.

An organization needs to consider several factors when making a hosting decision, including the following seven metrics relating to site performance as identified by IBM:[5]

☞ Performance

☞ Scalability

☞ Availability

☞ Reliability

☞ Simplicity

☞ Integration

☞ Security

The degree of impact and the extent to which these factors are supported (hosted) either internally or externally will depend upon the category of e-commerce the organization is participating in:

☞ **Enterprise level.** High volumes of commercial transactions servicing an extensive customer with a high degree of performance, availability, reliability, and security; e.g., eBay, Amazon, Charles Schwab, AOL.

☞ **Corporate Level.** The online provision of transactional systems, brand reinforcement, or informational systems. These vary in performance requirements, ranging from the high degree of reliability and availability needed from companies such as Royal Caribbean Cruises to the simpler requirements of a company wanting Web page availability in order to display a simple collection of pages.

---

5. www.as.ibm.com/asus/pmcpwaldnerfinal730.html

☞ **Entry Level.** Situations where scalability, integration, and security are among the key drivers for organizations developing their organizational e-commerce presence.

The ultimate goal for all Internet-based commerce is to deliver to the customer a high quality of service captured by the *end-to-end response time metric*. Figure 8.3 shows a model from IBM that identifies the factors contributing to a successful installation and delivery, as reflected through that metric. Three key drivers are present: application design, network topology, and server configuration.

Application Design

Depending upon whether the organization's e-commerce initiative is *enterprise*, *corporate*, or *entry* level, the application portfolio created by the organization will be assessed accordingly, as defined through its *Web traffic profile*. The highest demand will come from enterprise-level organizations, whose processes and Websites will be accessed upwards of 100 million times a day. As stated earlier in the book, the key drivers behind the demand for these pages will be *content*, *access*, and *format*. The higher the desirability of the content, the higher the potential demand.[6] However, the ease of accessing the information will be

Figure 8.3
Building an End-to-End Response Time (Reproduced with permission from IBM Website [www.as.ibm.com/asus/pmcpwaldnerfinal730.html] ©1999, International Business Machines Corporation, Internet Division, Somers, NY.)

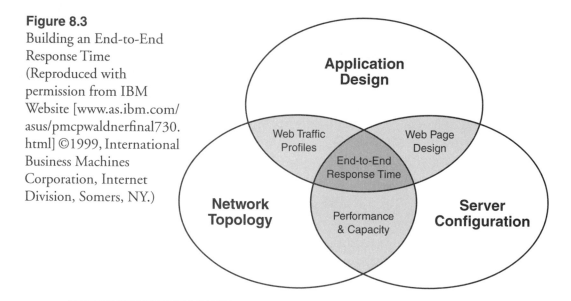

---

6. Reminiscent of the old saying, "Information about money is worth more than money."

dependent on the format of the application and the bandwidth the application demands upon request. Several application types are used in Website designs: HTML, CGI, and Java Script, to name a few. For enterprise- and corporate-level applications, these transactional sites will also have to interact with the back-end processing systems; this may slow down access. For instance it is necessary to transform the "buy stock" request placed through the Web browser into a suitable format for the organization's trading system. Thus the primary application design criteria in this situation will be to create applications that have optimal bandwidth overhead usage profiles for the network and architecture of the organization.

Network Topology

Again, depending upon the nature of the organization and its Internet strategy and on whether its initiative is enterprise, corporate, or entry level, the *Web traffic profile* driven by the external customer and internal user base will determine the *performance and capacity* needs of the organization's internal network topology. A network topology is the shape of the internal local area network (LAN) or communications system deployed by an organization in order to meet the information demands of its users. The performance and capacity of an organization's system have two key determinants. The first is the *bandwidth* of the interfacing connection to the external Internet, through an Internet service provider (ISP). The second determinant is the configuration of the internal network topology, which is usually based upon one of three basic configurations: a bus, a star, or a ring.

Figure 8.4 shows three companies (A, B, and C) each with a different network topology within its firewall. Company A is utilizing a bus topology, in which all devices, be they clients, servers, printers, or other device, are connected to a central network cable. The bandwidth of this cable can vary from a dedicated T1 line with a capacity of 1,500 thousand bits per second (Kbps) to ATM connections with 155,000-Kbps capacity depending upon the technology employed (10,000 Kbps for Ethernet, a T3 is 45,000 Kbps, and FDDI is 100,000).

The ring network has the advantage of being easy to install and relatively inexpensive for small- to medium-sized LANs. Company B has deployed a ring topology in which all devices are connected to one another through cabling on a closed oval or loop. The advantages of this topology stem from the fact that there is less signal attenuation than in a bus topology, but the downside is the

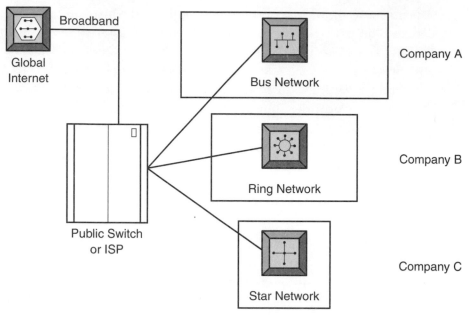

Figure 8.4
Network Topologies

necessity for every entity on the network to be functioning correctly as the signals are passed sequentially around the network. One outage could cripple the system.

Company C has chosen a star topology in which all devices are connected to a central hub. The hub is usually a file server and as such the topology facilitates centralized control of the network, with relatively low-cost equipment utilized at the nodes. The star topology has the advantage that it is relatively simple to install and manage. But the downside is that, due to the single point of contact for the incoming Internet pipe, the server may become a bottleneck at peak demand times since all data transfers pass through that point.

There are other network topologies utilized such as the mesh topology where all nodes in a network are connected to all others and the hierarchical network which layers the network. In practice organizations mix their topologies; for example, a bus may have a second bus as well as a ring hanging from it.

From this brief discussion of network topologies, we can see that an organization must determine its internal Internet needs and its external needs in order to develop a topology that will allow the performance and capacity needs of the organization to be met. If the network is to be an *intra*net alone, then the organization may wish to maximize general-purpose network traffic in which Web traffic is just a part. Should the organization have a high rate of external Web traffic, then a dedicated Internet-server hub would be required, which then connects outward to offload specific transaction requests and queries. The description of this analysis is highly technical and specific which, together with the dynamic nature of the technologies, precludes a more detailed discussion here.

Server Configuration

The nature of the server configuration is similarly focused upon delivery of optimum performance and the accommodation of user demand, central to which is capacity and the ability to accommodate peak demand. An illustration of this was the case with Charles Schwab & Company who needed to fly in extra capacity to accommodate the expected surge in demand following a Federal Reserve interest rate meeting (see case study following this section). The ability to satisfy capacity demand is a very complex process, based in part on factors such as

☞ **Disk Space.** The general rule is you can never have enough disk space in enterprise-level systems, but the actual amount required will be heavily dependent upon the interaction the user base is allowed, such as allowing the customer to store information at your site—e.g., personalized stock portfolio at a portal or grocery lists at an online supermarket. Similarly, the storage of digital sound and image files, even in compressed form, are memory intensive. The data type will also heavily impact the bandwidth requirement and the number of processors required in order to meet performance demands.

☞ **Memory capacity.** Following the secondary storage of data on disk, the degree and amount to which data can be held in cached memory is important. How many simultaneous connections can the system undertake without performance degradation? The aim is to understand this issue prior to a peak capacity experience when the server has a "meltdown" and crashes.

☞ **CPU requirements.** To provide ease of file retrieval (a Web page can be thought of as a file), the layout of the information on the server has to be considered. The way that the server is populated with information will have a significant effect on the accessibility and maintainability of the files, files that include many different data types and mixes: text, sound, images, graphics, movies, HTML, e-mail, compressed data, etc.

After our brief consideration of some of the issues in the three major areas impacting end-to-end response time, it is clear that this is a complex problem and that many factors need to be taken into account in order to achieve a satisfactory response time. One approach is to use *load balancing*. In networking, the term *load* usually refers to the amount of data traffic being carried by the network, while in systems programming *loading* refers to the process of copying data from the main memory into a cache memory. The two come together in load balancing—a technique that attempts to distribute processing and communications activity across a network, including both the transmission and processing components, so that no single element becomes a bottleneck or a localized focal point of processing. The load-balancing process also enables fault detection and recovery through fault tolerance procedures and facilitates system scalability without downtime. It also allows other areas of network control such as defining *single-host rules* which let you direct, for example, all client requests of a specific type to a single host, thus further refining load balancing among different applications.

The following case study of Charles Schwab demonstrates the intricacies of these drivers and the interaction of the different system processes. It was developed by IBM and details Schwab's infrastructure and technical systems development process, complementing our earlier discussion of Charles Schwab's strategy as presented in chapter 5.

Case Study: Charles Schwab—Expanding Internet-based Investing[7]

Charles Schwab & Co., Inc., one of the nation's largest financial services firms, provides discount securities brokerage and related financial services and offers trade execution services for NASDAQ securities to broker-dealers and institutional customers. Schwab serves 6.2 million active accounts, with $592 billion in customer assets through 310 branch offices, 4 regional customer telephone service

---

7. Reproduced with permission from IBM Website (www.2.software.ibm.com/casestudies/ swcsweb.nsf), ©1999 by International Business Machines Corporation, Internet Division, Somers, NY. This publication illustrates how one customer uses IBM products. Many factors have contributed to the results and benefits described. IBM does not guarantee comparable results. All information contained herein was provided by the featured customer. IBM does not attest to its accuracy. References in this publication to IBM products or services do not imply that IBM intends to make them available in all countries where IBM operates.

Table 8.2 Schwab's E-commerce Setup

Company	• $592 billion in customer assets • 310 branch offices
Website	• www.schwab.com • Data center in Phoenix, Arizona, services approximately one-third of all Internet trading
Application	• Deployment of IBM's WebSphere Application Server technology within Schwab's online trading site
Benefits	• Increased productivity for application development • Shorter development cycle • Lower development cost • Improved efficiency of hardware utilization • Lower long-term hardware costs
Technology	• IBM WebSphere Application Server • IBM CICS • IBM RS/6000 • IBM Global Services

centers, automated telephone support, and online channels. Table 8.2 gives a snapshot view of Schwab and its e-commerce setup.

Schwab has been an essential force behind the explosive rise of Internet-based investing and has gradually expanded its Web offerings. The expansion incorporates a full range of brokerage services online, including the distribution of advice and investment research. This case study addresses Schwab's use of IBM's WebSphere Application Server (WAS) technology to improve the productivity of its application developers and to maximize hardware resource utilization and efficiency.

Schwab recently added a new technology platform to its e-business solution using the WAS, a Java-based application environment for deploying Internet Web applications. Schwab's e-business solution leverages WAS's Java servlet infrastructure and Java Server Pages (JSP) support. As we will discuss in detail later in the case, Schwab opted to deploy IBM's WAS technology in order to achieve two strategic goals:

• Improved efficiency of Schwab's ongoing application development process
• Improved efficiency of hardware utilization within Schwab's trading site

Figure 8.5
Schwab's E-business Solution Profile

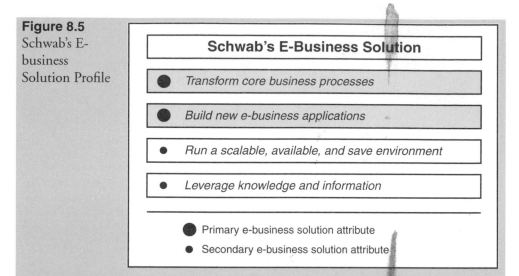

According to Purna Roy, director of Web Systems Availability for Schwab and the main driver of its adoption of server-side Java, it was important for Schwab to proceed cautiously in its deployment due to the sheer size and complexity of its online trading platform. "On a site as big as ours," he says, "we cannot make radical changes, especially to business-critical applications such as online trading. So to contain the impact of the first deployment and to use it as a learning experience, we decided to focus on a single, noncritical business application." Schwab chose the ability to open new accounts as its first application, which it deemed significant, yet not critical.

Schwab's history with IBM can be traced to December 1995, when Schwab established the formidable goal of implementing an Internet trading system within 90 days. Schwab selected IBM by virtue of its experience in building large-scale transactional sites, as well as the depth of its software and hardware solutions. Among the early solution components provided by IBM were RS/6000 SP AIX-based systems running CICS for AIX transaction server software, which was tightly integrated from the start with Schwab's existing mainframe OS/390 CICS-based applications. Other IBM technology elements added to the Schwab solution include Tivoli systems management software; IBM DB2 Universal Database, which stores store client personalization data and Web transactional information; and MQSeries, which was deployed to provide increased availability and scalability for Schwab's Web trading platform. In 1995, Schwab's original three RS/6000 systems grew to 24 in the first 9 months, and currently hundreds power the site, which, according to Roy, is considered the largest secure transactional site in the world.

Schwab's present infrastructure is a three-tiered system. The back-end systems run IBM CICS on mainframes; this serves as the platform for Schwab's business transaction applications and holds all of Schwab's business logic. Schwab's Web servers are located in two redundant data centers located in Phoenix, AZ, and form another tier. Between these tiers is an intermediate gateway tier, also comprised of IBM RS/6000 servers, which are collectively known as Schwab entry—or SEntry—servers, whose function is to link the UNIX and CICS domains within the Schwab IT infrastructure.

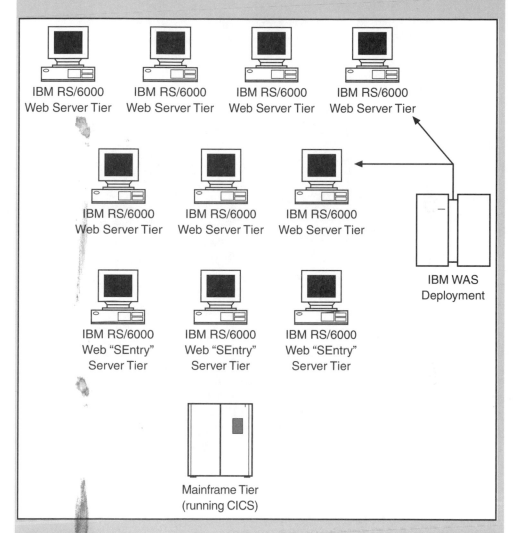

Figure 8.6
Basic System Architecture of the Schwab Platform and E-Business Solution (Source of information: Charles Schwab. Note that hardware configurations presented are for explanatory purposes; actual number of hardware units is not known. Reproduced with permission from IBM Website (www.as.ibm.com/asus/pmcpwaldnerfinal730.html) ©1999, International Business Machines Corporation, Internet Division, Somers, NY.

Schwab has rolled out IBM's WAS technology to all of its servers, including automatic alerts and backup procedures.

Late in 1997, Roy saw that servlet technology was developing quickly and that it might provide even better performance to Schwab than CGI. It then became Roy's next goal to establish the business case for deploying server-side Java technology and to identify where to deploy the technology (i.e., which applications). As Roy points out, the project's value proposition from the outset had been that the Java environment would lead to both higher developer productivity and increased hardware efficiency. "From very early, this was really considered an IT initiative because the benefits were mainly IT benefits," says Roy. This, in turn, was reflected in the people to whom Roy presented the concept.

Roy presented the concept more than a dozen times to groups that included Schwab senior management, senior- and middle-management committees from the technologies subgroup of the electronic brokerage division, the office of the CIO, and operations personnel. Roy also submitted the concept to Schwab's Technology Review Board, a group of senior IT managers charged with examining significant architectural change proposals. Developed to manage the accelerating change that had accompanied Schwab's rapid growth, the board seeks to ensure that technology decisions are always examined with an eye toward business value, supportability, and other operational issues. This approach, says Roy, is evidence of the importance of prudent technology adoption to Schwab. "We don't make changes that are going to cause a problem, and we only make changes that offer long-term business value to Schwab," he says. The final decision to go ahead with the WAS initiative was made by the senior vice president of electronic brokerage.

The decision of which application to deploy was driven by the cardinal rule that mission-critical trading applications must not be impacted, according to Roy. "The most critical applications for Schwab are those related to quotes and trade placement. Although the Account Open application is important to Schwab, if a problem or outage occurs, it will not impact Schwab customers to the same extent as more mission-critical applications." Indeed, trading downtime means lost revenue for Schwab, while would-be customers can always open accounts by downloading an application form over the Web or making a trip to the local Charles Schwab branch office.

As the Account Open Java initiative was proceeding, Schwab was also developing a separate Java desktop application for its active trader customer segment. Roy notes that the two projects created the opportunity to reap substantial benefits from the inherent synergy of the two Java-based solutions. "The server-side Java solution of IBM WebSphere Application Server presented itself as a perfect server-side complement for this experimental product. A major benefit of having Java on both sides was their ability to communicate using serialized Java objects instead of the large HTML documents filled with presentation directives. This made the product significantly leaner in the usage of Internet bandwidth." The new

Schwab product, known as Velocity, exhibits an almost threefold improvement in response time for a comparable transaction using a Web browser.

Prior to choosing IBM, Schwab also considered other vendors' application servers, including Sun/Javasoft, BEA/Weblogic, and JRUN. As part of its early research phase, Schwab contacted each of these vendors in order to obtain resources such as research hardware and consulting assistance. According to Roy, Schwab selected IBM's WAS solution due to IBM's early support for the JSP standard as well as the longer-term benefits that have accrued from Schwab's ongoing partnership with IBM, such as technical support. "Java server pages' capability was one of the key things that Schwab wanted, and IBM was one of the earliest vendors to provide full support for that," says Roy. "Strong support matters a lot to us."

Another key reason for choosing IBM was Schwab's desire to stay within its existing AIX environment, which, says Roy, "made it more beneficial to work with an IBM solution." Schwab also cited the sheer strength of the IBM WAS offering as a significant factor in the decision. "In terms of functionality, our critical need was Java server pages, and IBM's technology was well ahead of other vendors, including Sun Microsystems which developed the standard."

Goals and Business Drivers

Schwab's main goal for deploying the WAS technology on its site was twofold. First, Schwab wanted to use Java on the server side to improve efficiency of processing at the Web server level, thus reducing long-term hardware requirements. How do servlets benefit processing efficiency? "Servlets represent a more efficient way of processing request/response, which is a common scenario for a transaction platform such as Schwab's," answers Roy.

Schwab's second goal was to increase the productivity of its application development personnel by using WebSphere's JSP support to decouple the two components of the CGI development process: presentation (i.e., publishing) and logic (i.e., transactional). According to Roy, "By implementing JSP, the application development process becomes more efficient as tasks become more clearly separated in terms of skills and tools."

Schwab segments its Web development team into two skills-based groups: Web page designers and software developers. Prior to implementing WAS, much of the presentation logic was embedded inside the CGI programs along with the transaction logic. As a result, a task such as modifying a Web page often necessitated a complex coordination of tasks between the Web designers and software developers. Moreover, this crossfunctional interaction generally required each group to have a working knowledge of the other's functional area, further exacerbating the inefficiencies of the process. "By deploying server-side Java," says Roy, "Schwab can now make changes that used to require days within one-half hour to a day."

Underlying Schwab's JSP initiative is the acknowledged need to remain nimble in the fast growing, yet increasingly competitive online brokerage market. Roy comments: "Schwab needed a more efficient IT infrastructure to improve both time to market and hardware resources utilization. With the rapid growth of our online brokerage solution, we needed to start looking into more efficient ways to leverage our hardware and our development resources."

Implementation Timetable and Strategy

The initial phase of Schwab's server-side planning began in the first quarter of 1998 with the focus on funding and research. During this initial phase, Schwab assembled the internal team of Java and CORBA programmers required to assist in the deployment of WebSphere's JSP technology. Concurrently, Schwab also contacted IBM, Sun, and other vendors in order to line up hardware resources and consulting support. In the second quarter of 1998, Schwab began using both the Java Web Server (from Sun Microsystems) and Servlet Express, which was IBM's Java server product at the time, to create a demonstrable prototype of the application. Also in this time frame, the idea of deploying server-side Java technology was pitched to Schwab management to gain support and resources.

In the third quarter of 1998, the proposed system was still under review from management, which had lingering questions about such issues as supportability and the impact of using Java on Schwab's ongoing release process. Despite these concerns, the project grew worthy of further attention and additional resources from Schwab's development organization, which was used to make the reference implementation more realistic. At this point, Schwab also began more rigorous performance testing of the prototype application.

In the fourth quarter of 1998, Schwab's focus shifted toward resolving a broader range of issues related to the implementation of new technology architectures. These issues included questions on the likely impact of the new JSP technology on key areas within Schwab's IT organization, such as the quality assurance (QA) department, the development organization (especially issues related to developer training requirements), and data center operations management. By the end of the fourth quarter, these problems were resolved, largely with the assistance of IBM Global Services (IGS). For example, IGS assisted the development organization by teaching a training class for Schwab developers on the Internet brokerage side of the IT department. "IBM was also invaluable in reassuring the data center operations people in Phoenix," says Roy. One of the final tasks achieved during the fourth quarter of 1998 was the selection of actual projects for deployment.

The implementation phase of the project began in the first quarter of 1999, during which time the Account Open application was deployed across all of Schwab's transaction servers. Implementation of Account Open was completed in March 1999. While core programming was performed by internal Schwab personnel, IGS played the extremely important role of problem solver for such issues as run-time environment, JSP technology, and Java Virtual Machine. Although the IGS team on site at Schwab averaged 5 people, the virtual team swelled to 20 to 30 during the height of Schwab's JSP actual deployment process. "During a very important phase, IBM came through with a great amount of problem-solving support, working around the clock. Only a company with IBM's technical experience would be able to address such a broad range of problems in as timely a fashion," comments Roy.

In addition to general problem solving, IGS was an indispensable source of expertise and development advice throughout the process. "IBM was engaged all the way through," according to Roy. "For example, early on, IBM examined Schwab's code and gave some extremely useful comments. This set the tone of IBM's hands-on involvement in the project." Roy also sees IBM's Java expertise as a good foundation for its own planning, by allowing Schwab to capitalize on IBM's first-hand exposure to Java best practices seen in other IBM solution implementations.

Return on Investment

By deploying WAS within its Web site, Schwab expects to derive significant payback from two main areas: increased application development efficiency and higher levels of hardware utilization efficiency. Roy points out that the root of JSP's positive impact on developer productivity is its inherent separation between what will be built by the developer (mainly logic) and what will be built by an HTML author (mainly presentation content). "This means that Schwab can apply very specialized tools and personnel to different types of deliverables, while minimizing their interdependence. This makes it easier to administer from a personnel standpoint and will ultimate reduce development costs as Java skills increase."

Using WAS also benefits the application development process by shortening the cycle time significantly. Roy continues, "In fact, the Schwab developer who was working on the Account Opening application said that, had it not been for the WAS solution, meeting the deadline would have been next to impossible. This says something about the productivity benefit." According to Roy, the clear separation of logic and presentation content in a WAS application shortens the overall development cycle because it allows a programmer to quickly modify the presentation portion of the data as a response to a business requirement change, while obviating the need to change the logic portion. "You know exactly where to make the change to an application," he says. "The deliverable is more adaptive to changes in business requirement and maintenance."

Due to the relatively small scale of its present WAS implementation, Schwab has yet to fully realize the other expected benefit: increased run-time efficiency for WAS-based applications and the attendant cost savings due to more efficient hardware utilization. Nevertheless, Roy expects the increased performance to materialize before long. "The run-time efficiency, while so far unrealized, is expected to improve fairly rapidly over time and will ultimately surpass the C/CGI

Table 8.3 Benefits of Charles Schwab's E-business Solution[*][†]

Overall ROI Benefits	
Function	*Benefit*
Application development	Increased productivity of applications developers through increased specialization of tasks and tools
Cost savings	Lower development costs resulting from increased developer productivity
	Lower long-term hardware costs resulting from increased efficiency of hardware utilization
Time to market	Ability to bring new applications to market faster than through CGI-based application development process, thus increasing Schwab's competitiveness against a growing field of agile competition

[*] Source: Charles Schwab
[†] Reproduced with permission from IBM Website (www.as.ibm.com/asus/ pmcpwaldnerfinal730.html) ©1999, International Business Machines Corporation, Internet Division, Somers, NY.

environment." Roy explains that much of WebSphere's run-time benefits relate to lower start-up costs for programs because JSP Web pages—unlike HTML pages—remain in memory.

Roy is equally confident about Schwab's opportunity to save on hardware costs as WAS drives more efficient hardware utilization. "At our scale, if we can reduce our hardware utilization by, say, 2% per Web page, that represents a huge savings because of the number of times that Web page is executed. We expect the potential savings in hardware costs—as well as operations and systems administration costs—to be phenomenal."

Implementation Issues/Lessons Learned

As the Schwab and IGS team progressed in the planning and early implementation of the WAS solution, it became increasingly apparent to Roy that the success of the project depended upon allaying the concerns expressed by various IT constituencies. There was concern, for instance, within the development organization on how the proposed WAS deployment would impact future training practices as well as Schwab's release process. Similar questions were raised by the operations group on the issue of the supportability of JSP-based applications, while the data center operations group—the heart of Schwab's Web trading operations—needed reassurance that the initiative would not disrupt the normal flow. Roy's group worked assiduously with IBM to address these concerns, thus allowing sub-sequent development and implementation work to proceed.

Roy further notes that Schwab's WAS deployment experience taught important lessons on developing Java applications that will perform optimally. For instance, Roy points out that careless coding can easily lead to less-than-optimal application performance and maintainability, effectively neutralizing the inherent architectural benefits of WAS. Another key lesson learned was the need to recognize the relationship between servlet logic and performance optimization, especially as the size of the logic grows. "Nonoptimal coding of this logic may actually begin to offset the CPU savings, which are inherent architectural benefits of the server-side Java infrastructure," says Roy.

Future Plans

In the wake of its first WAS deployment, Schwab now plans to build on its success by deploying WAS across more applications, all the while incorporating its lessons learned. For example, Schwab is interested in utilizing the eXtensible Markup Language (XML) Document Services capabilities provided by WAS in other applications. Schwab has already begun an initial XML pilot where data from a Mutual Fund application is being converted from an Oracle database to XML to give Schwab more flexibility in accessing the data. Other projects using XML and the IBM XML4J parser, shipped with WAS, are also under consideration.

"We plan to work with IBM to review the effectiveness of our code. We will also identify our best practices and good application design patterns and incorporate those into new projects," Roy says. "Ultimately, the use of WebSphere Application Server will become an important part of many other Schwab applications. Once the benefits of the new approach to application development becomes clear, I expect that there will be a large rush to use it more widely within Schwab." By adopting IBM's Application Framework for e-business, Schwab has laid the groundwork for incorporating other next-generation capabilities in the near future.

Internet Strategy Effectiveness—A Scorecard Approach

As illustrated in previous chapters, creating a successful e-commerce strategy is a complex and intricate process. The strategy can vary from "let's start fresh—close all the bricks-and-mortar stores, and go online" to "we aren't going to sell online, but we want our site to reinforce our brand." The problem faced by executives whose organizations have yet to go online is "where on this spectrum should I position my organization's e-commerce strategy?" The executive whose enterprise is already online faces the question, "How do I evaluate the success of my organization's online strategy and our positioning of that strategy?"

This chapter tries providing some guidelines on how to approach these issues in a concrete and substantive manner. The approach advocated is based on three phases:

1. **Determination of the forces both internal and external to the organization that influence the organization's e-commerce strategy formulation.**

    In the first analysis stage, an organization must consider exactly which sectors of its business are most applicable to the e-commerce environment and whether these businesses will function as model B2C, B2B, or B2G. Furthermore, the options associated with the creation and execution of these business models need to be explored. This includes the possible development of partnering models or e-consortia models.

This macro-level analysis is based on the creation of models from the methodology presented in the earlier chapters of this book with the goal of finding a suitable overall strategy, one that balances out the four areas identified earlier as vital to a successful e-commerce strategy: *brand, technology, market,* and *service.*

Having completed this analysis, executives then have to formulate a set of e-commerce strategic goals based on the opportunities identified. These are the *value criteria* through which the effectiveness of the business plan, in the form of the operational system, is ultimately judged.

2. **Create a metrics program based on the use of value criteria in the form of an Internet effectiveness scorecard.**

   In order to determine the success of the system against the value criteria, the stakeholders must consider their e-commerce strategy from an activity-based ROI analysis. This is the objective of the second analysis stage, which encourages executives to develop and complete an *Internet strategy effectiveness scorecard* based on the value criteria.

   The scorecard provides jumping-off points for group discussion and reflection. A sample scorecard is presented in this chapter that organizations can use to develop their own scorecards, using fresh, innovative questions tailored for their own organizational situations. The scorecard provides the user with a framework from which a SWOT[1] analysis can be performed and the results used to improve the business.

3. **Determine the effectiveness of the value criteria at the ownership levels, the process levels, and the transactional levels.**

   The third level of analysis is based upon a second framework: the **e-value map**. This tool enables the e-commerce strategist to map out the issues surrounding each of the processes affected by the transition to Internet-based e-commerce or since the previous system iteration. Since each organization has a different set of procedures and associated process goals, the framework presented here is generic in nature, but can be effectively applied to most situations.

These three phases will now be considered in more detail.

---

1. The strategic e-commerce strengths, weaknesses, opportunities, and threats of the marketspace are compared and contrasted with those of the organization.

Forces Affecting Strategy Formulation—Understanding the Forces That Impact You Is Half the Battle to Overcoming Them

The creation of world-class e-commerce strategy is no accident; the executive leadership brings together varying mixes of

☞ Inspired thinking

☞ Clarity of vision

☞ Perfect judgment

☞ Superb timing

while the anchors that weigh down otherwise great companies include

☞ Complacency

☞ Inertia

☞ Regulation

In considering an e-commerce strategy we need all of the former and none of the latter. However, this is not always easy or possible—executives may feel threatened by e-commerce or they may not understand that this is more than the usual "management fad." Another problem executives often fall prey to in strategy formulation is the failure to balance the tactical with the positional. They get bogged down by internal politics and pressures that turn strategy formulation sessions from the *art of the possible* to the *art of the impossible,* with people giving more reasons against progress than breakthrough ideas that would move the organization forward. It is important at those times to remember and assert that the essence of strategy formulation is the ability to create corporate policy decisions that allow an organization to compete effectively in a changing market and that failure to meet those changes can be extremely detrimental. Two sets of factors therefore need to be considered—the ***internal*** and the ***external***—relative to a changing marketspace and the creation and execution of an organization's e-commerce strategy.

☞ The *external* factors or rivalry issues can be considered through the model detailed in this book, abstracting the technology, brand, market, and service parameters to model the industry rivalry as a whole and determining the strengths and weaknesses of the players in that marketspace. Figure 9.1 illustrates the direct influence that these *marketspace*

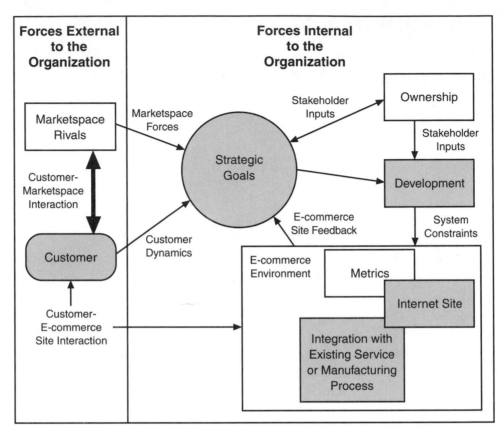

Figure 9.1
Forces in Strategy Formulation

rivals have upon corporate strategy formulation as well as their interaction with the *customer pool* as a whole, indirectly influencing the relationships customers have with the organization; for example, in the customer's comparison of one Website as a vehicle for e-commerce against that of a rival. Thus two external forces—the marketspace forces and the forces of the customer dynamics—influence our strategy agenda. These forces need to be constantly monitored and their impact upon organizational effectiveness calculated.

☞ The *internal forces* and their impact upon strategy formulation also have complex interactions, many of which we have discussed throughout the course of this text. A key internal facilitator to strong strategy formulation is to derive strength through the content and process owners, who understand the market dynamics. The creation of a small peer-to-peer executive council is often advantageous, the members of which work together to create the nimble and flexible e-organization discussed in detail in previous chapters.

The input of content owners is vital to the positioning of the strategy and the strategic goals of the e-commerce initiative; equally important is their interaction with the technologists in the development process. The content owners and systems engineers combine to play an important role in defining the art of the possible, constraining the conceptual ideas in such a way that their operational execution does not, over the short term, defeat the longer-term goals. For example, they would argue that maintaining and ensuring reliability and performance levels is more important than the incorporation of new "resource-greedy" applications that may cause system crashes or bottlenecks short term. This protects the brand as a whole and allows these greedy systems to be rolled out at the appropriate time.

Ultimately, executives, content owners, and the systems group will receive feedback from the metrics information associated with their site and their Internet strategy effectiveness scorecard measurement system. This valuable resource information can then be used to refine the system and business plan in an iterative manner.

The interaction of all these players and forces needs to be carefully considered in order to avoid unbalanced strategy and business plans. To assist in the formulation of a balanced and consistent strategy, a framework is now presented that will facilitate executives, managers, and organizational teams to determine the effectiveness of their organization's existing or proposed Internet strategy.

Internet Strategy Effectiveness—
The Creation of a Metrics Program

The key to a successful e-commerce organization is having a strong understanding of the ramifications of the business plan you are about to execute or currently execute. This is as true for new, born-on-the-Net organizations and move-to-the-Net organizations as it is for those that have been on the Net for a while. In this section we will discuss an approach, illustrated in Figure 9.2, to assist in the creation of a metrics program for monitoring the effectiveness of an organization's e-commerce venture.

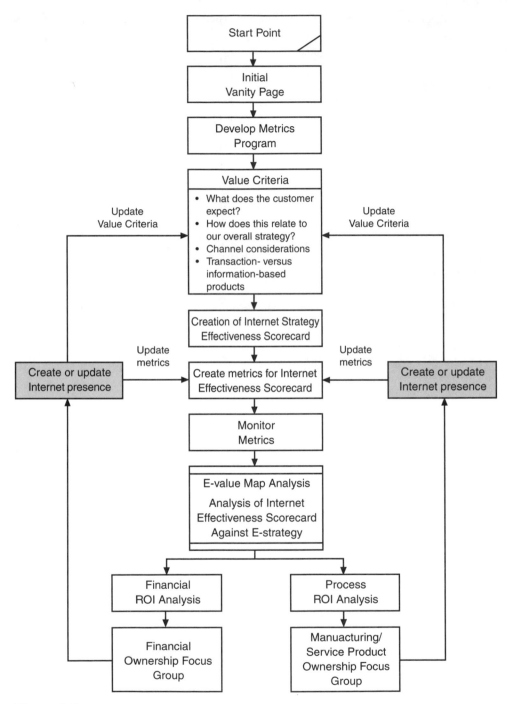

Figure 9.2
Creation of an E-commerce Metrics Program

In many instances organizations have undergone several metamorphoses since their original Internet (pre–e-commerce) business plans were developed. Many of the organizations researched for this book were in the first wave of online development—circa 1994–96. They often commenced by creating an initial *vanity page*, that said, "*look, world, we're here,*" and they learned as they went along, changing as the technology and market changed.

Today, however, when a corporation puts up a vanity or "splash" page, this usually indicates that much more structured activity is taking place behind the "under construction" sign or the cover page giving basic information about the company and photographs of the CEO. During this period, when the URL has been chosen and successfully secured, the focus is on the creation of the e-strategy and detailed business plan. Central to this activity will be, as we have detailed throughout the book, the need to identify the *value criteria* considered most appropriate for the marketspace in which the organization will function, this being a careful blend of the technology, brand, market, and service dimensions.

Having created and defined the value criteria, the next step is to create a mechanism to evaluate the operational effectiveness of the e-commerce system that represents the conceptual strategy. This is the role and function of the Internet strategy effectiveness scorecard.

The scorecard takes each dimension of the strategy and creates an effectiveness rating system for it. The purpose is for an enterprise, based upon its value criteria, to ask itself a series of rhetorical questions regarding its objectives and to define goals for those objectives.

For example, if a key to success for an organization is to reduce its costs through an online e-commerce presence, then in the **Financial Impact** section, the query:

> Did the strategy move call center volume to the online channel from the telephone channel?

could be posed. From this the appropriate metrics could be defined and measured against projected targets, e.g., call center volume, e-mail volume, and forecast volumes.

However, a determination of success cannot be made simply by using an individual metric. First, metrics need to be assessed against other metrics such as *industry-best-practice* data. Second, the impact of the value criteria query needs to be examined through all other associated metrics. For instance, a metric measuring the customer satisfaction index may reveal a negative customer reaction to the shift of emphasis from call center to online.

Thus, in order to establish the effectiveness of the organization's e-commerce activities toward achieving its goals, it is necessary to follow three steps.

1. Define a set of metrics that measures the progress to that goal as represented in the value criteria.

2. Have a clear, projected expectation for the metric concerned. This will force the metrics team to identify and hammer out assumptions upon which the metric forecast is based.

3. Create, wherever possible, an automated data delivery system for the actual results. This can then be compared to the internal company forecast as well as the industry-best-practice data.

From this, the effectiveness rating for each value criterion can be determined, based on a 10-point scale that ranges from *the strategy has a strongly negative impact upon reaching the goal* to *the strategy has a very positive impact upon reaching the goal.* The effectiveness rating for the section as a whole is the summation of the criteria ratings divided by the number of criteria. These can then be plotted on a *polar graph.*

By following these steps, an organization can make a strong determination as to the effectiveness of its strategy and can work to further improve its data and information metrics, together with its analytical abilities in an iterative manner.

Internet Effectiveness Scorecard

The scorecard is divided into the following seven sections.

- ☞ Financial Impact
- ☞ Competitive Leadership
- ☞ Brand
- ☞ Service
- ☞ Market
- ☞ Technology
- ☞ Internet Site Metrics

However, the organization can add more depending on circumstances.

Each section of the scorecard contains a series of starter questions the organization can use to develop its own specific questions. Suggestion: to be most effective, the organization should create a peer-to-peer policy team with cross-functional strengths to tackle these questions. In completing the scorecard, the organization needs to develop a metric to measure each issue, in conjunction with a forecast of the initial goal for that metric. Following metric selection, the organization needs to collect actual results and compare them to industry best practice where available. This comparison gives the team sufficient data to make an effectiveness rating. Effectiveness is ranked on a scale of 1 to 10 for each of the factors (see Table 9.1). If a particular factor was never aimed for, enter N/A (not applicable).

Table 9.1 Effectiveness Rating Scale

Scale	Effectiveness	Description
1	Ineffective	Had a strongly negative impact on reaching the goal(s) the organization was trying to achieve
2		
3	Negative	Had a negative impact on reaching the goal(s) the organization was trying to achieve
4		
5	Neutral	Had no impact on reaching the goal(s) the organization was trying to achieve
6		
7	Positive	Had a positive impact on reaching the goal(s) the organization was trying to achieve
8		
9		
10	Highly effective	Had a very positive impact on reaching the goal(s) the organization was trying to achieve

A model initial scorecard for each of the metrics is presented. The criteria in the scorecards reflect the type of questions an organization may ask itself after the first or second generation of e-commerce system has been developed and deployed.

1. Financial Impact	Metric	Forecast Initial Goal	Actual Results	Industry Best Practice	Effectiveness Rating
Was your strategy effective as a mechanism for reducing costs?					
Was your strategy effective as a mechanism for generating revenue?					
Was your strategy effective as a mechanism for transferring revenues to a low-cost channel?					
Was your strategy effective as a mechanism for increasing market share?					
Was your strategy effective as a mechanism for increasing transaction volume?					
					$\Sigma ER/5=$

2. Competitive Leadership	Metric	Forecast Initial Goal	Actual Results	Industry Best Practice	Effectiveness Rating
Was the effectiveness of your development increased by the involvement and support of the CEO, CIO, or other senior executive from the outset?					

2. Competitive Leadership	Metric	Forecast Initial Goal	Actual Results	Industry Best Practice	Effectiveness Rating
Did the technology effectively add value to your customers through provision of information services?					
Were the organizational and technology strategy plans effectively aligned?					
Was our approach to the sourcing of the development effective in achieving the goal of rapid system deployment?					
Did the Web technology effectively reduce the costs associated with updating our customers' information requirements?					
Did the technology effectively allow the organization to leverage its existing brand, products, and strategy?					
Is the technology effective in allowing the organization to get closer to the customer (and/or attain wider market coverage)?					
					$\sum ER/7=$

3. Brand	Metric	Forecast Initial Goal	Actual Results	Industry Best Practice	Effectiveness Rating
Was being an early mover in combination with high-presence visibility an effective strategy?					

3. Brand	Metric	Forecast Initial Goal	Actual Results	Industry Best Practice	Effectiveness Rating
By adding information surrounding the product to the site, did we effectively add value to the branding strategy?					
Has brand reinforcement been an effective intermediate strategy prior to offering online sales and services?					
Is brand reinforcement an effective strategy where we are prevented from selling online?					
Is continuous and innovative change of the information surrounding the products and the organization effective in adding value to the brand?					
Is mass customization as an approach to Internet branding an effective strategy for the organization?					
Is the Internet an effective mechanism for facilitating low-cost global branding?					
As an organization that has not created a brand position on the Internet, is it necessary to create an effective strategy as quickly and effectively as possible, and are we achieving this?					
					ΣER/8=

4. Service	Metric	Forecast Initial Goal	Actual Results	Industry Best Practice	Effectiveness Rating
Are established strategies of customer service still applicable and in effect?					
Is the effectiveness of Internet service strength derived from the added information provision to the customer on the customer's terms?					
Is the organization's Internet customer service effective in building a significant affinity relationship?					
Does the Internet service strategy provide an effective low-cost quality service channel opportunity with a global reach?					
Must an effective e-mail channel strategy be defined and planned for in advance, and did we achieve this?					
Must an effective virtual call center (at the Internet site) be defined well in advance of its potential implications, and did we achieve this?					
					$\Sigma ER/6=$

5. Market	Metric	Forecast Initial Goal	Actual Results	Industry Best Practice	Effectiveness Rating
Did we develop an effective Internet strategy prior to developing a Web presence?					
Did we develop an effective IT architecture to cope with and integrate the changes to the organization caused by the Web presence?					
In order to compete in the Internet space effectively, was it necessary to align the Internet strategy with the overall business strategy, and did we achieve this?					
Did our organization (regardless of product) need an effective Internet presence that offered value to the customer (visitor), and did we achieve this?					
Do changes in Internet marketing strategy need to be avoided to allow the customer to have an effective and consistent vision of the organization, and do we achieve this?					
Did we effectively achieve a coherent Internet marketing strategy that is necessary across all brands?					
To be effective do the product marketing and branding strategies need consistency in the eyes of the customer, and do we achieve this?					

5. Market	Metric	Forecast Initial Goal	Actual Results	Industry Best Practice	Effectiveness Rating
To be effective in getting closer to the customer, does the Internet strategy have to change over time to meet the changing demands of the customer and the market, and do we achieve this?					
To have flexibility and transactional capabilities, is it necessary to have an effective IT architecture, and do we have this?					
As a mass-customization-based company, was the effectiveness of the strategy based on the demonstration of market leadership through speed, innovation, agility, and technology?					
As a commodity-based organization, was the effectiveness of the Internet's added information value demonstrated?					
As a third-party provider, was the effectiveness of the Internet in its ability to enable the customer to be dealt with as they required?					
As a products-based company, was the strategy effective in allowing new information-based products to be offered through the low-cost channel?					
					$\Sigma ER/13=$

6. Technology	Metric	Forecast Initial Goal	Actual Results	Industry Best Practice	Effectiveness Rating
Did the technology infrastructure provide a flexible base to accommodate market change?					
Were the technology partners chosen responsive?					
Do the front office and back office systems interface effectively?					
What is the mean time between failures?					
What is the average bandwidth requirement?					
What is the mean time to upgrade a server installation?					
					$\Sigma ER/6 =$

7. Internet Site Metrics	Metric	Forecast Initial Goal	Actual Results	Industry Best Practice	Effectiveness Rating
The number of hits per month (as a measure of customers' interest and site potential value)?					
The number of purchases per registered customer per month?					
The average purchase size per transaction?					
The length of time a registered customer spends (as a measure of site information value)?					

7. Internet Site Metrics	Metric	Forecast Initial Goal	Actual Results	Industry Best Practice	Effectiveness Rating
The repeat visit rate by registered users (as a measure of site value)?					
The purchase/hit rate (as an indicator of interest converted to revenue)?					
Other (any other metrics you use for measuring the effectiveness of your site) Description:					
					ΣER/7=

Once the organization has developed a series of effectiveness ratings for each individual goal in a category, an overall effectiveness rating can be created. The results for these categories can be analyzed in several ways, one of which is through a polar graph (see Figure 9.3). The polar graph allows the organization to identify changes, period by period, regarding the effectiveness of its strategy. Figure 9.3 shows two time periods—the dashed line represents time period 1 and the thick line a subsequent time period. The separation indicates that there has been an improvement, based upon the value criteria, with regard to the effectiveness of the company's e-commerce strategy, as indicated by an increased effectiveness of the brand, service, and market criteria, with technology staying the same. However, the effectiveness of the site in terms of the organization's financial goals has decreased.[2] This may be a consequence of the changes the organization made to achieve the positive reactions in the other five dimensions. In order to examine this more closely, we will now look at another framework, the e-value map, which considers the impact of these value criteria at a more detailed process level.

---

2. This can also be validated through actual financial data reports; the aim of the framework is to provide a basis for strategy discussion that entails all processes and functions, not just numeric financial data.

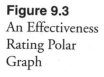

Figure 9.3
An Effectiveness
Rating Polar
Graph

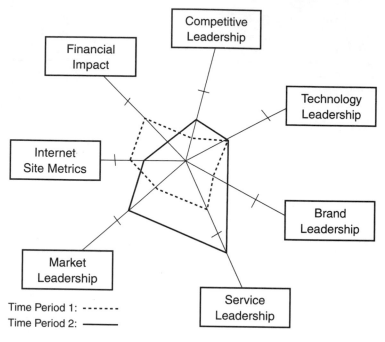

The E-value Map

Having completed an Internet effectiveness scorecard evaluation at the macro level, it is beneficial to follow this up at a finer level of detail. To accomplish this we can consider the value criteria through *e-value maps*. These maps allow each process in the value criteria to be examined, including the *process ownership*. The creation of this framework facilitates continued discussion surrounding evaluation criteria and forces the prioritization issues to be resolved. A suggested first step is to establish a value map at the ownership level.

Ownership Value Map

In this map the stakeholders at each level of the organization are asked to determine their three[3] most important success criteria. Clearly these will not

---

3. The use of three criteria focuses the discussion; more can be used. However a computational explosion in issues arises and distracts from the effective use of the technique. The mutually exclusive, collectively exhaustive (MECE) methodology of selecting criteria is suggested. For further reading see Ethan M. Rasiel, *The McKinsey Way*, N.Y., McGraw-Hill, 1999.

all be identical; however, they should all support the overriding goals of the senior management group. The CEO may for instance focus on *brand development* as the number one priority. The development of this objective may be formulated differently in the organization's individual divisions. In Europe, this may mean the brand is reinforced by providing a consistent pricing structure across different countries; in the North American division, this may mean perfecting customer service levels; and in Latin America the branding issue may be driven by market coverage and by building partnering relationships with e-commerce portals and providers. Each of these criteria is then passed through the organization to the next level of ownership—the country managers—and then down to their marketing-automation and technical groups.

Ownership Levels

At Level I, the executive level, the CEO may have branding as the most important value criterion; the corporate CIO security and the CFO revenues (multiple criteria for each member can be created).

This value-criteria set of metrics can then be passed down through the organization so that the regional managers and then the country managers can create their own metrics based on their directive as content owners.

The country managers then customize the processes to their own territory and develop a metrics program to drive their own content.

This process continues through all manager content-owner levels, addressing the same issue as identified as a value criterion at the executive level.

Process Value Map

The mapping technique is then continued and developed at the process level, the base of the analysis. This again involves metrics determination and effectiveness analysis. If we consider the situation where a grocery store in the United States is developing an e-commerce metrics base in the delivery of products such as perishables, it may initially develop the value map shown in Table 9.2.

In this small example the mapping process would be used to determine the effectiveness of the value criteria, through their associated metrics, for each of the processes against the previous cycle. The delivery of groceries has multiple

Level I: Senior Strategic Management Group

Owner	Value Criteria	Metric	Target	Results	Projected Change	Effectiveness Rating
CEO	Branding	Brand equity analysis	Top 100 brand ranking	First year of operation—Rank 164	7%	7
CIO	Security	MTBF	100% coverage	99.65%	-0.05%	9
CFO	Revenues	$ per registered customer	$15	$7	4%	6

Level II: Regional Planning Group

Owner	Report	Value Criteria	Metric	Target	Results	Projected Change	Effectiveness Rating
Director European Division	CEO	Brand	Price consistency with competitors	3% variance	5%	0.8%	8
Director North American Division	CEO	Brand	Customer service index	96%	94%	1.0%	7
Director Latin America	CEO	Brand	Market penetration	34%	36%	2%	7

Level III: Country Managers Planning Group

Owner	Report	Value Criteria	Baseline	Target	Results	Projected Change	Effectiveness Rating
Managing Director UK	Director Europe	Brand	Price consistency	3% variance	6%	1%	7
Managing Director Germany	Director Europe	Brand	Price consistency	3% variance	4%	0.4%	8
Managing Director Spain	Director Europe	Brand	Price consistency	3% variance	3%	0.7%	10

Level IV: Marketing-Automation Strategy Group

Owner	Report	Value Criteria	Baseline	Target	Results	Projected Change	Effectiveness Rating
Director of Marketing	MD UK	Brand	Price consistency	85% of customers acknowledge price consistency	78%	13%	7
CIO	MD UK	Brand	Price consistency	100% competitor sites scanned and the pricing updated at home site	97%	3%	8
VP Internet-Partner relations	MD UK	Brand	Price consistency	100% data and information exchange with partners	100%	0%	10

Level V: Technical Owners

Owner	Report	Value Criteria	Baseline	Target	Results	Projected Change	Effectiveness Rating
Hardware group	CIO UK	Brand	Price consistency	100% up time	99.9	0	10
Software group	CIO UK	Brand	Price consistency	0 errors	17 logged fatal errors	−0.2%	9
Telcom. provider	CIO UK	Brand	Price consistency	100% connectivity	100%	0	10

Table 9.2 E-value Map—Example

E-value Map: Strategic Perspective						
Product						
1. Perishable Products						
Process		**Value Criteria Metrics**				
		Baseline Targets		*Results*		*CSI**	
		Previous Cycle	Present Cycle	Previous Cycle	Present Cycle	Previous Cycle	Present Cycle
1.1. Logistics on-time delivery in-bound		97%	97.2%	96%	97%	89	91
1.2. Logistics on-time delivery to customer		67%	67%	64%	63%	65	67
1.3. Returns to manufacturer		4%	8%	7%	9%	NA	NA
1.4. Out-of-stock requested items		5%	7%	8%	12%	NA	NA

*CSI = customer satisfaction index.

product areas such as perishables, canned products, and wines, each with different process requirements. With the question "What is our ability to secure on-time delivery of the product to the customer within the time window specified?" having identified these issues, metrics can be created and evaluated against internal targets as well as against industry best practice. Again these issues will vary across processes and regions. From here the business case can be determined and the investment analysis considered. Further refinement in the effectiveness criteria may still need to be developed; this may be in terms of the effectiveness scorecard technique we discussed in this chapter or through another value map.

The creation of the value maps provides strong benefits for the organization, in that the varying perspectives allow the organization to have tight control over its operational e-commerce system. This may prevent damaging strategies from progress beyond critical boundaries, such as pursuing a low-cost strategy and alienating the organization's most valuable customer base. The top-down hierarchical nature of the maps also allows them to reflect a consistent policy from the top of the organization down through the organizational layers and content owners to the processes.

Summary

The Internet and e-commerce presents executives with a new variant on an old problem: determining "What am I getting out of this technology investment?" When faced with this question in the normal context of business activity, a concrete answer can be elusive. However, the ability to answer this question effectively clearly separates the successful e-commerce organization from the rest. Having faced this question with technologies such as data warehouses, ERPs, and knowledge management systems, successful CEO-CIO teams understand the value of an activity-based approach to IT ROI analysis, the basis of which has four stages:

1. The creation of an ROI value criteria
2. Creation of a metrics program to monitor the ROI value criteria
3. Data capture
4. Actual ROI analysis from the metrics data

The creation of a set of value criteria is vital. These criteria form the basis of the business case upon which the e-commerce process is developed. In this chapter we identified six areas in which metrics should be created: financial impact, competitive leadership, market, technology, service, and brand leadership. The value criteria are developed by senior executives together with cross-functional peer-to-peer teams and compiled into an Internet effectiveness scorecard. The scorecard allows metrics to be developed specifically for each of the criteria. The data capture for the metrics may be the recording of traditional organizational performance measures such as cycle time or cost per unit. Alternatively, the data may originate from an automatic software collection mechanism. The analysis of the activity or process against the projected organizational forecast or industry best practice allows the effectiveness rating of the e-commerce initiative to be considered.

The data can also be analyzed at the process level; this will result in a stronger vertical analysis. All parties should be involved in this, from the senior management strategy team and divisional planning groups to content owners. The goal is to develop metrics for each level of the organization that collectively drive the corporate objective forward. Results are assessed against the forecasts, and the strategy and systems are modified based on effectiveness and performance. The correlation between the business objectives and the metrics by which they are measured must be carefully assessed. For instance, the strategy to reinforce the brand could mean increasing customer service satisfaction levels in conjunction with an increased technology leadership position. However, it may lead to a negative metric in the traditional dealer sales channel.

The creation and maintenance of an assessment framework is vital for the creation and continued development of a successful and effective e-commerce strategy.

10

Waves of the Future— Issues That Will Shape the Formulation of Strategy

In this book we have examined the experiences of corporate Internet pioneers, drawing from their experiences to create the models detailed in the previous chapters. The 40+ organizations contributing to this study ranged from giants like Ford and Sony to organizations yet to go public. They provided a rich series of issues around which we created the models.

To create a model, it is necessary to learn from the past but to enable future issues to be debated within their context in a way that they do not become dated and redundant. Thus these models were constructed to enable future executives to formulate strategy through the methodology and philosophy of thought. However, executives and managers developing their corporate strategies from these models must tune them to meet the needs of their own corporate environments as well as to the technological environment of the hour.

In this chapter we will examine the waves of change that will impact future organizational e-commerce planning initiatives. By considering these changes when constructing and developing business plans, organizations can stay *nimble* and *agile*, modifying their directions, possibly influencing the waves of change rather than being overwhelmed by them.

The Agile E-commerce Organization

As e-commerce develops, over time organizations will have to become more and more agile. The critical factors for developing a strategic plan identified in the preceding chapters will be no less critical for maintaining a position in the organization's future marketspace. Figure 10.1 illustrates seven areas that are the key drivers of change, four of which are the leadership factors we have focused on throughout our study. These are impacted by many other factors, and two of the most important are

☞ Government and political change
☞ Changes in external relationships

These and other factors need to be recognized by the organization and its management, and adjustments must be made to the firm's strategy in order to accommodate them. While it is clearly impossible to predict all changes that will occur, several key issues in each of these areas can be seen as drivers of future change as well as challenges to management.

Technology Change—A Rising Tide Does Not Lift All Boats Equally

By far the most dynamic change agent is that of technology. This is an area where the only certainty is that there will be change, and that it will continue to increase in pace and scope.

Figure 10.1
The Seven Key
Drivers of
Change

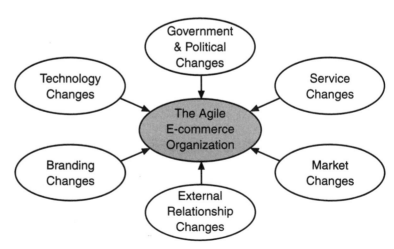

In terms of the future of technology, organizations can be broken down into two categories: *the creators of technology* and *the exploiters of technology.* The creation of technology is by far the most important lever for the global electronic economy and, as has become apparent in the past, those organizations that control those levers will be able to influence the waves of change and have the opportunity to exploit them. This factor is not just the province of "garage entrepreneurs" anymore. There has been a resurgence of effort by the past champions of pure and applied research. The reigning and undisputed heavyweight champion is IBM,[1,2] which was awarded a record number of U.S. patents during the 1990s, totaling over 15,000 more than triple the number of patents in the previous decade. IBM was awarded 2,756 patents by the U.S. Patent and Trademark Office in 1999 alone.

"While the sheer number of patents is impressive, what's even more important is that these technologies are firmly positioned to drive IBM's key strategic growth areas in the coming years—OEM technologies, software, and services," said Nicholas Donofrio, IBM's senior vice president and group executive of corporate technology and manufacturing. "We're making the right investments in the right technologies, and it's paying off with growing market share in the fastest-growing parts of the industry." Donofrio cited the role of IBM's patent portfolio in more than $30 billion worth of OEM agreements signed by IBM's technology group in 1999. In addition, patent and intellectual property licensing efforts generate more than $1 billion in revenue annually. According to Donofrio:

> Our commitment to research and develop the industry's most innovative technologies—and our ability to get these technologies to market quickly—is unparalleled. That explains why leading companies, ranging from Dell to Cisco to Nintendo, are lining up at the door to use IBM technology in their products and to get access to our intellectual property portfolio.[3]

It is this focus on making technology investments to drive growth in key areas that has become the modus operandi of those organizations with

---

1. Press Release: IBM, "IBM Leads in U.S. Patents for Seventh Consecutive Year, Top Patent Performer of the 1990s Again Sets Record," Armonk, NY, January 11, 2000.

2. IFI Claims Patent Services, Wilmington, DE.

3. www.ibm.com/press/prnews.nsf/Print/0E8FBD7E6AC8D12E85256863005A3D4C

enough capital to push and fuel pure research. In addition to hardware and components, IBM's 1999 patent portfolio includes more than 900 software-related patents that are fundamental to the company's e-business strategy.

Patents in Key E-commerce Technologies by IBM

US5926798: Method and apparatus for performing computer-based online commerce using an intelligent agent. Intelligent software agents perform e-commerce negotiations and transactions by committing services from multiple service providers and customers. This technology will play a major role in the future of e-business. The intelligent agents consider both the availability of the requested service, such as arranging for a vacation, and the business policies of the service provider, for example, the cancellation policy. The least severe cancellation policy is committed first while the most severe cancellation policy is committed last, giving the user the greatest possible protection in making arrangements.

US5870717: System for ordering items over computer network using an electronic catalog. This patent is a good example of IBM's leading technology for e-business. The e-business solution allows employees in a company to directly process orders for goods from another company by using catalogs and electronic purchasing methods. Users can bypass both the normal paper approvals and the manual verification of the order by the organization's purchasing department. This is achieved by means of an electronic catalog, accessible from the employee's own personal computer, and a computer network and associated services linking the company to multiple suppliers.

Source: www.ibm.com/press/prnews.nsf/Print/0E8FBD7E6AC8D12E8525-6863005A3D4C

IBM's leverage of its patents is also facilitated through the Internet, where potential licencees of a patent can identify and investigate the patent through the use of IBM's Intellectual Property Network Site[4] which offers free access to information on all U.S. patents granted to IBM since 1971. Full images of IBM's 2.1 million U.S. patents issued since 1974 are also available. In October 1998, the site added European patents and published international patent applications.

The development of patents and patentable technology brings the developer benefits in three areas:

---

4. www.ibm.com/patents

1. The development work itself facilitates intellectual thought and creativity ensuring that the organization's technology sight horizon is stretched to the maximum.

2. The organization can gain valuable revenue through its licences. IBM reported more than $1 billion in revenue from its patents.

3. The patents can be used as strategic weapons—locking the market out, for example—or to create strategic alliances through cross-technology licencing agreements which would otherwise be very expensive or prohibited by the other company.

This has been studied in the academic literature. An influential study by Zhen Deng and Baruch Lev of New York University and Francis Narin of CHI Research tested the ability of a set of patent-related measures to predict stock returns and market-to-book ratios:

> Our empirical results indicate that patent measures reflecting the volume of a company's research activity, the impact of companies' research on subsequent innovations, and the closeness of research and development to science are reliably associated with the future performance of R&D-intense companies in capital markets.[5]

Therefore the case can be made that to be sucessful in the technology arena it is advantagous to invest in and develop an R&D program in pure and applied research; without such a program, the time lag in adopting technology may be fatal as the speed of technology development increases.

Future Wave 1: Develop R&D programs that link pure and applied research with key elements of the organization's structure and strategy.

However, the cost of developing a research program may be prohibitive—after all, even governments sometimes have difficulty justifying pure research—in which case an alternative strategy is necessary.

If the organization is a born-on-the-Net, pure Internet company, then the very survival of the company may be dependent upon the technology deployed—its strategy must focus upon being *first*, *fast*, and *furious* in its product application.

---

5. Zhen Deng, Baruch Lev, and Francis Narin, "Science and Technology as Predictors of Stock Performance," *Financial Analysis Journal*, May/June 1999, pp. 20–32.

In essence this involves the purchase and rapid absorption of products from purveyors of technology, not always immediately deploying the technology, but with the intention to integrate the relevant components into the organization's business plan as far ahead of time as possible.

For move-to-the-Net organizations the absorption of the technology is potentially more difficult, involving the integration of technology and the alteration of existing processes. These organizations must be able to create value from their incremental deployment of technology. moving toward a collective goal or focal point. Again, as we said earlier in the book, the goal is to balance the four strategic areas—technology, brand, service, and market presence—not to develop one at the expense or detriment of the others. Therefore the vision will always be long range to tie together the compatibility of the technology over the long term rather than to "clean house" and switch entire operations from one technology to another overnight.

For the e-consortia the utilization of the technology development will be to identify technologies that will enable the often heterogeneous organizations to come together, form mutually beneficial alliances, and compete in the market, potentially against born-on-the-Net upstarts moving into their marketspace. This is ironic to a certain extent—the large service and industrial giants of the past were very much in an isolationist mode of thinking when the Internet opportunity presented itself; rather than form consortia to use the technology to raise the barriers to entry, building cohesive brands and market strength, they chose to "go it alone." Being less nimble and agile they failed to reposition quickly enough to maintain their previous strengths.

> **Future Wave 2:** Harness the power of others' technologies. Even if it is necessary to pay a license fee or purchase a package, immediate access to the technology outweighs the "build and play" model.

The technologies that are going to lead to significant developments in the near future will be driven in part by content needs, access needs, and format constraints. The Internet is fundamentally driven by content, and the interest apportioned to a site directly corresponds to the utility and value of that content. Thus the boundaries of content need to be examined, as these are the commercial and technical frontiers that the leaders of the future will be looking to explore and exploit. Organizations are limited in their ability to push out content in an audio and visual format by the access technologies and the formats they support.

The speed of Internet development requires that developers push their *technology horizon* as far as possible into the future. No organization can stand alone; no organization can develop the technology fast enough and across enough sectors that it can truly dominate the Internet in all its dimensions in the way that IBM dominated computing in the 1970s and Microsoft dominated operating systems at the end of the twentieth century. To facilitate organizational development it will be necessary to break down the defensive walls erected by organizations to protect their proprietary technology investments and increase their involvement in ***technology consortia***. The best known consortium is the World Wide Web (WWW or the Web), which was founded in 1994; the Web is led by Tim Berners-Lee, director (also acknowledged to be its creator), and chaired by Jean-François Abramatic. The WWW consortium aims to continue

> developing common protocols that promote its [the Web's] evolution and ensure its interoperability. The consortium is jointly hosted by the Massachusetts Institute of Technology Laboratory for Computer Science [MIT/LCS] in the United States; the Institut National de Recherche en Informatique et en Automatique [INRIA] in Europe; and the Keio University Shonan Fujisawa Campus in Japan. Services provided by the Consortium include: a repository of information about the World Wide Web for developers and users; reference code implementations to embody and promote standards; and various prototype and sample applications to demonstrate use of new technology. The consortium is funded by Member organizations, and is vendor neutral, working with the global community to produce specifications and reference software that is made freely available throughout the world.[6]

Membership, as they say, has its privileges, and membership in the consortium allows for participation in the workshops, symposia, and conferences organized for the membership, plus the ability to be involved in the processes that ultimately lead to the development of and adherence to the standards and technologies associated with the Web.

The World Wide Web consortium is an open forum for any organization to join, but there are many other forums that exist with the intent of creating

---

6. Copyright © 1994–2000 World Wide Web Consortium, (Massachusetts Institute of Technology, Institut National de Recherche en Informatique et en Automatique, Keio University). All Rights Reserved. http://www.w3.org/Consortium/Legal/

proprietary standards within the consortium companies such as the *digital transmission content protection* (DTCP) method.[7] DTCP is a specification developed by Hitachi, Intel, Matsushita Electric Industrial, Sony, and Toshiba that defines a cryptographic protocol to protect audio-video entertainment content from illegal copying, interception, and tampering as the content moves over high-speed digital buses. The companies leverage their collaboration through the creative use of licensing formats, having developed a dual licensing strategy: The *use license* is for system OEMs, and the *development intellectual-property license* for semiconductor companies.

> **Future Wave 3:** Power comes through consortium relationships and the collective knowledge that brings. To extend the technology vision of the corporation, two forms of consortium can be exploited: open-industry-based and closed-proprietary consortia; utilized intelligently this assists in the prevention of technology isolation.

The accessibility of the Internet will for the foreseeable future be the driver of change. The first technology wave for the leading Internet nations is already over and was based on static Websites that displayed text or basic graphical information. The second wave is the dynamic information provision in both an audio and visual format. To a large extent this wave is maturing successfully on traditional landline and networked devices such as workstations and personal computers, but the new frontier is wireless Internet device connectivity.

The utopian dream of a completely wireless world is still on the technology horizon, but the world will relentlessly and inevitably move toward it. The international marketing consulting company Frost & Sullivan predict that "the compound annual growth rate (CAGR) for wireless data from 1996 through 2003 is projected to be 35 percent. The market is expected to grow to ten times its current value and reach close to $2.5 billion by the year 2002."[8]

Along with the utilitarian use of the mobile phone for voice usage, and the acceptance by consumers that this electronic prosthesis needs updating every

---

7. Press Release: Sony, "Sony to Launch Single-Chip LSI Solutions for the Secure Transmission of Digital A/V Content," San Jose, CA, May 27, 1999.

8. Frost & Sullivan Research Report, "Mobile Data Services: How to Keep Your Customers and Profits Moving" and "North American Wireless Office Markets." www.frost.com/verity/press/telecom/pr289365.htm

few years, the potential market for mobile data communication beyond the "beeper" is immense. The battle for technological dominance in this space has been underway for some years and is still evolving, and both technology vendors and commerce organizations are preparing themselves for combat through this for this new channel.

The technological rollout of wireless service is eagerly anticipated by many organizations waiting for the day they can provide their information resources to a roving mobile user base, in both the vertical and horizontal user bases: The vertical user base will be focused within specific industries developing the marketspace of industry-specific handheld devices such as those used by truck drivers, such as a soft drink delivery person or a repair technician. The horizontal user base will focus on the so-called "road warrior" class of personal digital assistant devices (PDAs), pagers, and mobile data phones. Presently, however, several factors are contributing to the issues and problems of mobile data service to these potential markets. First, there is geographical coverage—as any business traveler knows, it is difficult (leaving aside Motorola's Iridium system) if not impossible to have a single cellular telephone connection at all locations in the United States today, hence the comparative difficulty in data transmission through this channel. Second, the proliferation of standards and devices is a deterrent to overcommittal to one technology; for example, at the service provider level ATT uses TDMA (time division multiple access), Sprint PCS uses CDMA (code division multiple access), Pacific Bell uses GSM (global system for multiple access), and Nextel uses iDEN (the integrated dispatch enhanced network). The debate and rivalry continues at the device level with the manufacturers lining up behind Microsoft's CE operating system and Palm's OS platform.

Future Wave 4: Develop a wireless dimension to your e-commerce online strategy. Imagine a customer anywhere on the planet looking for your product by wireless device and wishing to complete the purchase cycle. Could you fulfil the order?

The idea of a personal assistant is not new, but it has had limited applicability due to the incompatibility of standards that limit the interconnectivity among devices. It is also annoying for users that seemingly wireless devices need to be wired together to share data. Again the consortium concept is being embraced to solve this issue, the august International Telecommunications Union— founded in 1865 to standardize international telegraphy: equipment, procedures, tariffing, and accounting—is one of the bodies that is working toward a third-generation data transmission standard for wireless devices. Bluetooth, a consortium of leading technology companies, including Ericsson, IBM Corporation, Intel Corporation, Nokia, Toshiba Corporation, 3Com Corporation, Lucent Technologies, Microsoft Corporation, and Motorola Inc, is working to create a specification to facilitate interoperability between personal devices.

As the wireless dimension changes, so will the systems and software that run on these infrastructures and devices. And the more organizations attempt to push products to customers, the more defensive the customer will attempt to be. Just as we have caller ID at our homes to stop the annoying calls from stockbrokers desperate to make a sale before being displaced by the Internet, the future Internet user will hide behind his own personal firewall assistants, blocking unwelcome and time-consuming spam and enabling friendly agents to converse and negotiate on our behalf—perhaps negotiating for a hotel room rate with a sales agent in a Las Vegas clearinghouse, perhaps monitoring an auction house for that rare first edition. This will cause problems for the static organization reliant upon an advertising-based revenue model in the same way the TV remote control to a certain extent neutralized the power of TV advertising.

> **Future Wave 5:** Develop a strategy to interact with the intelligent agent of users in the future. Identifying sales leads, negotiating for the sale, and fulfilling the obligation with less human interaction on the part of the customer.

So how does this emerging situation impact the e-commerce organization of the future? It will force that organization to reevaluate its strategy from a global perspective. The Internet will become less and less "landlocked" to wired landlines; the rapidity with which previously closed markets will open up is going to increase; and only those who have this accessibility wired into their business plans will succeed. Already the user base in South America and Asia is growing exponentially; as the infrastructure in these regions continues to grow, by skipping technology generations, the user base and potential customer base will grow even faster. Thus executives will soon be facing questions about such things as: the positioning of their advertising on a cell phone display; their advertising-based revenue models for wireless devices; their collection and payment mechanisms for a global customer whose only contact point is an IP address; and how digital product layering will be rolled out.

Brand Changes—Brand Equity, the Currency of the Global Leaders

Amid the turbulent changes associated with technology, organizations will have to determine and develop a brand strategy. Earlier in the book we outlined four basic branding strategies that organizations utilize to position themselves effectively in their marketspace: brand creator, brand follower, brand reinforcement, and brand reposition. The branding strategy developed by the organization acts as a point of origin, a "true north" from which all future market movements by the organization are considered: Will this technology divert me from my brand position? Will the customer change her perception of our products if we change our customer relationship management strategy? What are the implications of the technology on the existing traditional brand drivers?

The parameters that drive branding and branding decisions are clearly going to become much more complex as the Internet continues to impact all organizations and their relationships globally. Key to managing brand in the future will be the determination of and management of *brand equity*, which can be defined as *a financially related value on the customer-based equity of brand images and associations.*[9]

In general terms the four major drivers of brand equity are

1. Brand name awareness. A brand has a degree of presence in the consciousness of the consumer.
2. Brand loyalty. The degree of customer preference for a brand association.
3. Perceived quality. A determination of customer service and satisfaction are the key metrics.
4. Brand differentiation. The separation between brands in a marketspace.

The ability to place a numerical value on brand equity has been the subject of much research, both in academia and industry, the premise of which is to determine the current valuation of future ownership of the brand.

---

9. Paul Dyson, Andy Farr, and Nigel Hollis, "Understanding, Measuring, and Using Brand Equity," *Journal of Advertising Research*, November 1996, pp. 9–21.

The global consulting firm Interbrand Gerstman+Meyers, has proposed one of the leading methodologies to measurement. Michael Birkin of Interbrand outlines the approach:

> The valuation of a brand, like that of any other similar economic asset, is the worth now of the benefits of future ownership. In order to calculate brand value one must identify clearly:
>
> - the actual benefits of future ownership—that is, the current and future earnings or cash flows of the brand; and
> - the multiple or discount rate which needs to be applied to these earnings to take account of inflation and risk.
>
> Interbrand's approach to brand valuation (one which is now widely accepted in many markets around the world) works on the premise that it is brand strength which determines the discount rate, or multiple, to apply to brand earnings. Thus a strong brand provides a high level of confidence that brand earnings will be maintained. High brand strength translates into a low discount rate or a high multiple. Conversely, with a weak brand, one's level of confidence in future earnings is reduced, so the discount rate to be applied to those earnings must be high, or the multiple low.[10]

Interbrand has identified seven key factors that together provide an indication of brand strength:[11]

☞ Leadership. The brand's ability to influence the direction of the market in which the brand competes.

☞ Stability. This metric reflects the stability of the consumer base and the loyalty the customers feel toward the brand.

☞ Market. This parameter is used to reflect the stability of the market as a whole in terms of future volatility and change; e.g., technology-based brands are more market sensitive than canned food brands.

☞ International scope. The more geographically established a brand is, the less vulnerable it is to the instability caused by relying on a single domestic market.

---

10. Michael Birkin, "Assessing Brand Value," in *Brand Power*, edited by Paul Stobart, New York University Press, New York, 1994, pp. 209–22.

11. Ibid.

☞ Trend. This is a measure of the ability of a brand to remain contemporary.

☞ Support. This metric aims at establishing a measure of the financial support an organization provides for a brand.

☞ Protection. This refers to the organization's ability to protect the brand through legal mechanisms.

> **Future Wave 6:** Develop a multicomponent strategy for the creation and protection of brand equity. Focus on brand leadership, brand stability, and global market positioning through proactive corporate policies.

Through this approach Interbrand produces valuations for organizations and annually compiles a league table of brands. The top five coming into the year 2000 were Coca-Cola, Microsoft, IBM, General Electric, and Ford.[12] The premier pure Internet company (prior to its merger with Time Warner) was America Online, ranked 35 with a brand valuation of $4,329 million, followed by Yahoo! at 53 with a valuation of $1,761 million and Amazon.com at 57 with a valuation of $1,361 million. It is interesting to consider these brands in more depth and to note that, for AOL, Yahoo!, and Amazon, their brands represent only 18%, 14%, and 7% of their capitalization respectively, compared to the percentage for more mature brands such as Coca-Cola (59%), Ford (58%), Disney (61%), and McDonald's (64%).[13] As youthful organizations, they have broken into the ranks of the world's major brands at incredible speed and are still undervalued as brands in terms of long-term profitability.

Let's consider Interbrand's seven factors in more detail with respect to e-commerce organizations.

Leadership

As we noted earlier in this book, it is advantageous to create a market and then lead that marketspace from the start. All three of the ranked e-commerce organizations (AOL, Yahoo!, and Amazon) were brand creators. Consideration of the top 50 branded organizations indicates that not only are they leaders in their traditional marketspaces but they are also active in adjusting their brand

---

12. Press Release: Interbrand, "Why Do Brands Matter? Because They Create Value," New York, NY, June 22, 1999. www.interbrand.com/valuebrands.html

13. Ibid.

position in light of the impact of the Internet; e.g., Microsoft, IBM, GE, Ford, and Disney, which rank 2, 3, 4, 5, and 6, respectively, are all successful in that space. It is interesting to note that, prior to its May 3, 2000, announcement of an interactive marketing initiative with AOL, Coca-Cola had been relatively low key in the B2C space, just reinforcing its brand through this channel while concentrating its efforts on its B2B channel.[14]

The strategy of building brand through first-mover advantage has paid off for the new ranked Internet organizations, but the marketspace is never still—the data from the Interbrand study indicates that maintaining a brand equity leadership position in the Internet marketspace requires significant investment in repositioning, and reinforcing brands for established organizations or in the creation of a new global megabrand for new entrants to markets, be they physical or electronic.

Ford and GM have both decided to leverage the use of the Internet toward maintaining their leadership positions. Ford has teamed with Internet company Yahoo! to develop personalized services for Yahoo!Autos specifically for Ford vehicles. The intent is to allow customers access to services including owner guides, recall notifications, Ford Motor Credit information, service reminders, vehicle maintenance logs, trip planning, and real-time traffic updates. Ford CEO Jacques Nasser comments:

> Our agreement with Yahoo! enables us to reach customers where they spend their time online, to better develop an ongoing relationship with vehicle owners throughout the lifetime of their ownership. The world is moving online and we want to ensure that we meet the customers there, meeting their needs in the virtual world as well as the physical world, this is another element of our totally integrated e-business strategy. We are connecting with consumers through multiple touch points on their turf, at their time and on their terms.[15]

Similarly GM, the world's largest industrial corporation, and America Online, the world's leading interactive services company, have announced a major strategic alliance designed to bring consumers an easier and more convenient per-

14. Press Release: Coca-Cola Company, "Coca-Cola and America Online Announce Global Marketing Alliance," May 3, 2000. media.web.aol/media

15. Press Release: Ford Motor Company, "Ford and Yahoo! Team to Serve Customers Online," Dearborn, MI, and Santa Clara, CA, January 9, 2000. www.ford.com/default.asp?pageid=106&storyid=622

sonalized car shopping and lifetime ownership experience. Bob Pittman, AOL's president and chief operating officer, commented:

> For the first time, AOL members can learn about new GM cars and special offers, immediately find the car they want from available inventory at a dealer near them and then buy it, enabling AOL and GM to deliver the most trusted, personalized automotive experience.[16]

Clearly both organizations are taking notice of the new channel. Figures from Forrester research indicate that, the use of the Internet as a mechanism to shop for an automobile will increase from 2 million online households in 1998 to 8 million households by 2003.[17]

Stability

For an established brand such as Kodak the insurgence of new substitute digital products may erode market share and decrease profits. Consequently the organization's brand equity will decrease. A repositioning and reinforcement of the brand to limit the drift of customer focus to new or previously marginal brands must be enforced; e.g., Kodak.com and digital equipment/services.

Market

The factor most impacted by the Internet is that of *market*, in which the volatility of a brand's market position is measured. The Internet has made the marketspace much more volatile for traditional organizations. This can be seen in the way the giant automobile manufacturers are fighting to dominate this channel, a channel extensively utilized by what is probably their most profitable demographic customer base. Alternatively, for some traditional organizations like Kodak, the determinant of future market success is dependent upon how Kodak captures the market for new-technology-based products as this market displaces the old film-based technologies.

---

16. Press Release: General Motors, "General Motors & AOL Announce Major Strategic Alliance," Detroit, MI, and Dulles, VA, January 9, 2000. www.media.web.aol.com/media/press_view.cfm?release_num=15100391&title=General%20Motors%20%26%20AOL%20Announce%20Major%20Strategic%20Alliance

17. James L. McQuivey, The Forrester Report: "New-Car Buying Races On-line," January 1999. www.forrester.com

The market is also potentially volatile for born-on-the-Net organizations—overdependence on a single product or technology may leave them vulnerable to any radical subsequent changes or trends of technology in the space. This has in part led to the significant volume of mergers and acquisitions within the domain of pure Internet companies, which individually were struggling for brand recognition, scale, and market share, but as merged organizations with greater market scope the problem may be more manageable. An example of this can be seen in the online equity trading market where there is a fierce battle for market share as illustrated in Table 10.1. In such a market the ability to run with the technology is key to maintaining position. The strong market leader Charles Schwab, as we have seen during the course of the book, is an example of an organization that is able to assimilate technology and bring it to market rapidly and in a form that the consumer wants. Technomarket moves from Schwab include:

☞ Teaming with TD Waterhouse Group, Inc., and Ameritrade Holding Corporation, together with leading venture capital firms (Kleiner Perkins Caufield & Byers, Trident Capital, and Benchmark Capital) to form an e-consortium in the form of a new online investment bank.[18]

Table 10.1 Market Share in the Online Equity Trading Marketspace

Brokerage: Online Equity Trading 4Q 1999	Assets Under Management (Billions)	Average Daily Trades	Total Active Accounts
Charles Schwab	725	234,000	6,600,000
Fidelity	269	55,417	3,500,000
TD Waterhouse	150	190,000	2,372,000
E*TRADE	44	133,000	1,551,000
Ameritrade	31.6	81,000	686,000
DLJ Direct	21.7	30,500	795,000
Datek Online	10.6	81,004	339,798
Brown & Company	—	34,000	—

18. Press Release: Charles Schwab & Company, "Schwab, TD Waterhouse and Ameritrade Join Forces with Three Venture Capital Firms to Build New On-Line Investment Bank," San Francisco, CA, November 15, 1999.

☞ Allowing its best retail customers who participate in IPO purchases access to Internet viewing of road shows by organizations wishing to be brought public.[19]

☞ Creating new Web-based tools designed to provide Schwab customers with more robust mutual fund research capabilities. A *MutualFund Screener* allows customers to screen all funds rated by Morningstar, Inc., using specific selection criteria, and a *Fund Details* feature captures a rich range of information on funds, including tax efficiency and performance data.[20]

All of these continue to add value to the customer relationship and improve the acquisition, revenue generation, and retention of its customer base.

International Scope

The most universally known commercial product in the world is Coca-Cola, established in 1886 and now sold in over 200 countries worldwide; the power of the brand is undeniable.

The international dimension of the Internet is rapidly causing the new born-on-the-Net organizations to grow in both brand scope and brand strength.

For traditional organizations, international scope and growth has always been an interesting challenge; investing in an area and developing the brand have always been important but also very expensive. Through the Internet it is now possible to reach previously inaccessible markets—this might be in the form of information, product supply, or a supplement to existing retail channels. BMW, for example, has Websites in eight languages serving its established and developing markets. The British Broadcasting Corporation has global reach providing news and audio in 43 languages and developing the brand BBC World to compete for international recognition against other global media giants such as CNN and News Corporation.

For new born-on-the-Net organizations such as Yahoo! the challenge is the same. Yahoo! has developed content in Europe (Denmark, France, Germany,

---

19. Press Release: Charles Schwab & Company, "Schwab Announces Access to Internet Road Shows for Retail Investors," San Francisco, CA, November 15, 1999.

20. Press Release: Charles Schwab & Company, "Schwab Introduces New Online Mutual Fund Selection and Screener Tools," San Francisco, CA, December 22, 1999.

Italy, Norway, Spain, Sweden, UK, and Ireland) , the Pacific Rim (Asia, Australia, New Zealand, China, Hong Kong, Japan, Korea, Singapore, and Taiwan), and the Americas (Brazil, Canada, and Mexico). Focusing on its global brand as a key to future earning and future brand equity, Yahoo! has transformed itself into a global organization, taking its "brand creator" model and applying it to the global marketspace. Already its listing on the Japanese stock market has become the first stock to trade above the ¥100 million ($948,000) mark, trading up approximately 4,700% in the period 1998–99 on increased pretax profits of ¥584 million for the fourth quarter of 1999, up 430% over the same quarter of the previous year. The brand is very powerful. Thomas Rodes, an analyst at Nikko Salomon Smith Barney states that "approximately 87% of Japanese Internet users go to Yahoo!Japan at least once a month. No other media get that kind of reach."[21] Yahoo! has clearly demonstrated the utility of a first-mover strategy tied into an omnipresent information source and content base.

Trend

The ability of an organization to maintain the relevance of its product and brand in light of changes in society, technology, and culture is more than ever a measure of its agility in the marketspace. For established organizations this first requires a careful consideration of the brand itself and its repositioning in the marketspace over time. Second, it requires the use of the Internet to best leverage that position. In the traditional marketspace, organizations such as Bang & Olufsen (B&O), the high-end technology company, change their products to reflect the market demands, but they never dilute their brand by following a trend. Rather they *create* solid trends. The CEO of B&O has commented on the impact of market forces and B&Os branding initiatives going forward:

> B&O a/s is in the middle of a cultural change that has turned out to cause problems in the long term with regard to achieving the profit objectives we have set.…This cultural change implies that we change from being a typical Danish production company that manufactures different products for audio/video distributors to being an internally oriented brand. In order to create an international brand we must have an unambiguous and international message. Not only in our products but also in the shops, in our marketing, and actu-

---

21. Source: Alexandra Nusbaum, "Yahoo!Japan: Demand Hits Record High," *Financial Times*, January 20, 2000. www.FT.com

ally in everything that we do. This means that we not only invest large resources in products which set new standards in terms of design and operation, and which are being copied in cheap versions by other manufacturers. We are now investing in becoming just as innovative and trend-setting with our shops and with our communications in general.[22]

This *exclusivity of brand* is reflected in B&O's Website, which is creative and informational, maintaining the products' exclusive appeal by not selling online, keeping them above "the crowd" of impersonators. The power of the brand is the *mysticism* that surrounds B&O's retail outlets. Detract from the experience and you detract from the brand.

As we have already discussed in the book, the ability of organizations to maintain their products' brand strengths in light of market conditions is thus vital to their success. For example, Sony manages to move its brand ahead both in the marketplace and in the marketspace of the Internet. For the pure online organizations such as Yahoo!, Priceline.com, or TheStreet.com, the ability to stay focused on their market demands that they stay one step ahead—this is the key to their branding efforts.

Support

The primary vehicle for brand support is promotion and advertising via traditional media channels such as TV, direct mail, and radio. The advent of the so-called "new media" as a mechanism for promotion has increased the pressure on the marketing and advertising agencies to find new and creative ways to position themselves and get noticed in the ever more crowded Internet space. The phenomenon that initiated the media blitz can be pinpointed to the 1998 Super Bowl, the most sacred and most watched sporting event in the United States, which succumbed to the Internet. Victoria's Secret, the lingerie company, took the initiative with a 15-second slot to promote a live supermodel fashion show on the Internet,[23] an event probably more memorable than the

---

22. Press Release: Bang & Olufsen, "Anders Knutsen (UK) Speech," Struer, January 26, 2000. www.bang-olufsen.com/default.asp?id=1198

23. Further Reading: C. Allbritton, "Victoria's Secret Net Show a Bust," The Associated Press, February 4, 1999. www.cnn.com/TECH/computing/9908/18/vicwebcast.idg/index.html

game itself. By Super Bowl XXXIV only two years later in January 2000, with an estimated 130 million viewers, the excitement and conversation was as centered around the dot-com advertisements airing during the game as it was around the game itself, each company paying out a record $2.2 million each for a 30-second slot.[24]

For the traditional organizations the impact of the Internet has been immense in terms of its consequences for their products and their customer relationships. The ability to nimbly move the business into this new economy has been the key to competitiveness. IBM for example has been working to recreate itself, focusing its strategy on the e-business mantra, while Ford has labeled its vehicles as *communication tools* and developed relationships with new media companies such as Yahoo! as a part of its "e-troit" strategy, a strategy to make its vehicles more attractive to the emerging e-generation of consumers. Some organizations have been more hesitant to embrace an Internet strategy and have been forced to play catch up in a variety of ways: The banking giant Chase Manhattan acquired Hambrecht & Quist[25] to develop its technology investment skills and evolve to meet new market demands. Toys R Us created an independent division in 1998.[26] GM created a partnering relationship with AOL. The internal development and support of these ventures have been immense; supporting the brands in this way ensures that they remain in the game.

While the traditional organizations have been restructuring and developing their online strategies through internal growth, acquisitions, mergers, and partnering relationships, the born-on-the-Net community has been rushing to spend hundreds of millions of dollars in advertising, both traditional and online, in order to develop and reinforce their brands. The Internet has become the electronic version of a land rush, with all parties intending to stake out a visible and memorable claim. With an estimated $3 billion[27] spent on online and offline advertising, the long-term sustainability and effectiveness of these campaigns has to be questioned. The leaders in online branding

---

24. For the record, the final score was St. Louis 23, Tennessee 16.

25. Press Release: Chase Manhattan, "Chase Completes Acquisition of Hambrecht & Quist," New York, NY, December 9, 1999.

26. www.toysrus.com/

27. "Interactive Year in Review: Dot dot dot," *Advertising Age.* www.adage.com/interactive/articles/19991220/article1.html

have two strengths: they were usually first movers with a strong product, and they have enormous advertising budgets. The e-organization leaders in ad spending in 1999 were Schwab and E*TRADE—each with $300 million, Ameritrade—$200 million, HomeGrocer.com—$120 million, and Altavista, TD Waterhouse, Value America, and WebVan Group, each with $100 million.[28] While the ability to spend hundreds of millions of dollars on advertising is beyond most traditional organizations, ironically it is not always beyond all start-up IPOs and pre-IPO Internet ventures. Ad revenues have also had an effect in being a significant catalyst for the growth of the Net itself, with advertising banner ads and pop-up windows funding many other online ventures. However, this catalyst for Web growth may be about to change as the sophistication of measuring Internet advertising effectiveness increases. The Internet Advertising Bureau, an industry association that reports on ad revenues, identified that, in 1999, 72% of advertising revenues went to the top 10 online sites and networks (up from 70% a year earlier), with the top 25 sites attracting 84% of revenues.[29] This focusing of financial resources could limit the growth of organizations planning business strategy based upon Web ad revenues in the future.

There has been a further consequence for the Internet e-commerce organizations that, through their need to define themselves quickly in the space, spent wildly on advertising with insufficient strategic planning with regard to the consequences. The advertising caused demand to wildly exceed estimates, leaving the organization fighting to satisfy online customers' requests for service. The inability to match projected volume with actual volume is nothing new, but what *is* new is the impact that a missed calculation can have on an organization and a brand. In traditional channels, it is possible to develop models over many years to predict consumer demand cycles; the Internet has not been so benevolent. Some organizations spent heavily on advertising prior to Christmas 1999 to "grab the space" only to find they could not supply the volume, leaving disappointed customers. Wal-Mart, on the other hand, delayed the relaunch of its e-commerce site until after Christmas rather than risk disappointing customers: *"We have a brand that is trusted and we want to extend that to our web store,"* a spokeswoman said. *"Part of that is recognizing that a bad first*

---

28. "Ad Age Estimates and Company Reports (Annualized Spending); Competitive Media Reporting (Measured Spending)," *mad.ave.dotcom.* www.adage.com/dataplace/archives/dp398.html

29. Internet Advertising Bureau, *IAB Internet Advertising Report 1999.* www.IAB.com

visit might be the last."[30] Thus support requires the full attention of the organization; the coordination of all aspects of the value chain, internally understanding the company's ability to meet demand and match customer expectations, is a key to stable, controlled growth in this sector.

> **Future Wave 7:** Successful nimble and agile organizations will rely on speed to market and continuous innovation rather than protection under the law.

Protection

The ability of an organization to protect its brand is key to its survival. Any infringement may reduce the *perceived quality and brand differentiation* positioning efforts by the organization in terms of the product's *brand name awareness.* As a consequence, the brand loyalty and the brand equity may suffer.

The legal frameworks surrounding the Internet have been attempting to catch up to this rapidly developing space and to adapt and amend existing statutes as well as to develop new case law. Brand protection comes from two primary areas of law: trademarks and copyrights.

Trademarks

The development of standards in trademarks can be traced back to the first U.S. patent granted in 1790 to Samuel Hopkins of Philadelphia for "making pot and pearl ashes," a cleaning formula used in soap making.[31] The U.S. Patent Office defines a trademark as "either a word, phrase, symbol or design, or combination of words, phrases, symbols or designs, which identifies and distinguishes the source of the goods or services of one party from those of others. A service mark is the same as a trademark except that it identifies and distinguishes the source of a service rather than a product"[32] which is different from a copyright or a patent. A copyright "protects an original artistic or literary work; a patent protects an invention."[33]

---

30. Richard Karpinski, "E-Retailers Balancing IT, Marketing," *Internet Week,* January 10, 2000.

31. www.uspto.gov/web/menu/tm.html

32. www.uspto.gov/web/offices/tac/doc/basic/basic_facts.html

33. Ibid.

The U.S. Patent Office states that trademark rights are established either from actual use of the mark, or from the filing of a proper application to register a mark with the Patent and Trademark Office (PTO) stating that the applicant has a bona fide intention to use the mark in commerce regulated by the U.S. Congress. Federal registration is not required to establish rights in a mark, nor is it required to begin use of a mark. However, federal registration can secure benefits beyond the rights acquired by merely using a mark. For example, the owner of a federal registration is presumed to be the owner of the mark for the goods and services specified in the registration and is presumed to be entitled to use the mark nationwide.

There are two related but distinct types of rights in a mark: the right to register and the right to use. Generally, the first party who either uses a mark in commerce or files an application with the PTO has the ultimate right to register that mark. The PTO's authority is limited to determining the right to register. The right to use a mark can be more complicated to determine. This is particularly true when two parties have begun use of the same or similar marks without knowledge of one another and neither has a federal registration. Only a court can render a decision about the right to use that mark, such as issuing an injunction or awarding damages for infringement. It should be noted that a federal registration could provide a significant advantage to a party involved in a court proceeding.

Unlike copyrights or patents, trademark rights can last indefinitely if the owner organization continues to use the mark to identify its goods or services. The term of a federal trademark registration is 10 years, with 10-year renewal terms. However, between the 5th and 6th year after the date of initial registration, the registrant must file an affidavit setting forth certain information to keep the registration alive. If no affidavit is filed, the registration is canceled.[34]

The patent office has been developing a series of guidelines surrounding the issuance and use of an Internet-based trademark such as those used by online organizations like Amazon.com and Priceline.com or by government institutions such as Whitehouse.gov (see appendix A). However, issues are developing to influence the market.

---

34. Ibid.

Jurisdiction

The jurisdictional dimension to trademarks disputes will become more apparent as we are able to scour more and more remote corners of the world due to advances in Internet technology. There will be increases in conflicts such as Miss King's Kitchens, a Texas restaurant chain—it bakes cakes under the name "The original Texas Yahoo! Cake Company"[35] and took the California Internet portal Yahoo! to court over trademark infringement. These jurisdictional issues will also become international in nature. Bodies such as the World Intellectual Property Organization (WIPO) Standing Committee on the Law of Trademarks, Industrial Designs and Geographical Indications will no doubt take a leading role in future trademark policy and the creation of international law. One area in which international practices have been standardized and used effectively is that of *cyber-squatting*—individuals became *cyber name squatters*, taking the name of a famous brand hostage by purchasing the URL first, only to release it for a large sum of money or "ransom." Both the U.S. courts and administrators of domain name services such as ICANN, the Internet Corporation for Assigned Names and Numbers, have recently effectively addressed this problem, preventing the practice and prosecuting offenders.

Association

The continuous protection of a brand is a vital dimension to all organizations. The Internet has brought another dimension to the struggle to ensure that the product, its image, and the purity of the official corporate message are not impinged upon. In the physical marketplace, Harley-Davidson has successfully been defending its brand from the accessory and T-shirt makers who might lessen the value of its "official products." Just as damaging for organizations are "unofficial" Websites that have a look and feel of an "official" site, through the misuse of trademarks and misrepresentation of interests. This is especially a factor in developing markets where a site may give the impression that it is an "affiliated" site through the high usage of hyperlinkages to branded sites or associated brand images. For example, a Website advertising "brake components" may attempt to convey that the components are produced by an automobile manufacturer by plastering the site with images of the automobile in the style reminiscent of the manufacturer's site. This misrepre-

---

35. Computer & Online Industry Litig. Rep. (Andrews Publications) 23, 107, 23153 (October 15, 1996). No. 396-CV0963-D (N.W. Texas, Dallas Division motion for preliminary injunction filed August 28, 1996).

sentation of the product is extremely damaging to the brand not only of the automobile manufacturer but of all the official original equipment manufacturers licensed to produce that part.

Copyright

The second major area of concern for all users of the Internet and for commercial ventures on the Internet is the copyright. The way in which copyright protection is secured is frequently misunderstood in that no publication or registration or other action is required in the Official U.S. Copyright Office to secure a copyright. There are, however, certain definite advantages to formal registration.

> Copyright is secured automatically when the work is created, and a work is "created" when it is fixed in a copy or as the Copyright office still quaintly terms it fixed on a "phonorecord" for the first time. "Copies" are material objects from which a work can be read or visually perceived either directly or with the aid of a machine or device, such as books, manuscripts, sheet music, film, videotape, or microfilm. "Phonorecords" are material objects embodying fixations of sounds (excluding, by statutory definition, motion picture soundtracks), such as cassette tapes, CDs, or LPs. Thus, for example, a song (a "work") can be fixed in sheet music ("copies") or in phonograph disks ("phonorecords"), or both. If a work is prepared over a period of time, the part of the work that is fixed on a particular date constitutes the created work as of that date.[36]

However, not everything can be protected by federal copyright in the United States, including:[37]

- Works that have not been fixed in a tangible form of expression (for example, choreographic works that have not been notated or recorded, or improvisational speeches or performances that have not been written or recorded)
- Titles, names, short phrases, and slogans; familiar symbols or designs; mere variations of typographic ornamentation, lettering, or coloring; mere listings of ingredients or contents

---

36. www.lcweb.loc.gov/copyright/circs/circ1.html#wci
37. Ibid.

U.S. Copyright Office
Library of Congress
101 Independence Ave., S.E.
Washington DC 20559-6000

WHAT IS COPYRIGHT?

Copyright is a form of protection provided by the laws of the United States (title 17, U.S. Code) to the authors of "original works of authorship," including literary, dramatic, musical, artistic, and certain other intellectual works. This protection is available to both published and unpublished works. Section 106 of the 1976 Copyright Act generally gives the owner of copyright the exclusive right to do and to authorize others to do the following:

> To reproduce the work in copies or phonorecords;
> To prepare derivative works based upon the work;
> To distribute copies or phonorecords of the work to the public by sale or other transfer of ownership, or by rental, lease, or lending;
> To perform the work publicly, in the case of literary, musical, dramatic, and choreographic works, pantomimes, and motion pictures and other audiovisual works;
> To display the copyrighted work publicly, in the case of literary, musical, dramatic, and choreographic works, pantomimes, and pictorial, graphic, or sculptural works, including the individual images of a motion picture or other audiovisual work; and
> In the case of sound recordings, to perform the work publicly by means of a digital audio transmission.

In addition, certain authors of works of visual art have the rights of attribution and integrity as described in section 106A of the 1976 Copyright Act. For further information, request Circular 40, "Copyright Registration for Works of the Visual Arts."

It is illegal for anyone to violate any of the rights provided by the copyright law to the owner of copyright. These rights, however, are not unlimited in scope. Sections 107 through 121 of the 1976 Copyright Act establish limitations on these rights. In some cases, these limitations are specified exemptions from copyright liability. One major limitation is the doctrine of "fair use," which is given a statutory basis in section 107 of the 1976 Copyright Act. In other instances, the limitation takes the form of a "compulsory license" under which certain limited uses of copyrighted works are permitted upon payment of specified royalties and compliance with statutory conditions. For further information about the limitations of any of these rights, consult the copyright law or write to the Copyright Office

Source: lcweb.loc.gov/copyright/circs/circ1.html#wci

- Ideas, procedures, methods, systems, processes, concepts, principles, discoveries, or devices, as distinguished from a description, explanation, or illustration
- Works consisting entirely of information that is common property and containing no original authorship (for example: standard calendars, height and weight charts, tape measures and rulers, and lists or tables taken from public documents or other common sources)

And as with trademarks, the ability to enforce international copyright is of vital importance to the owner of the copyright. The European Commission, for example, has attempted to address the harmonization of copyright laws in accordance with the guidelines of the WIPO through its "Proposal for Directive on Copyright and Related Rights in the Information Society" initiative. The initiative identified that a breakdown of copyright law could occur due to the new digital infrastructure which has become a conveyer of copyrighted materials and that this would discourage the creation of an electronic commerce marketspace.[38] The directive was amended in 1999, the aim being that it "would establish a level playing field for copyright protection in the new environment, and in particular cover the reproduction right, the communication to the public right, the distribution right, and legal protection of anti-copying and rights management systems."[39]

As we have discussed throughout the book, possessing high brand equity is a significant step toward a successful e-commerce presence. However, the ability to position a brand is becoming increasingly more difficult for pure e-commerce *brand followers* with products that offer little in the way of differentiation. In the Internet space, first-mover advantage remains the key to success; even being a strong brand in the traditional markets does not guarantee success or strength of brand through the new media. However, the ability to maintain a strong and definitive trademark is a fundamental necessity in the Internet space; executives and organizations will need to monitor their brands constantly and adjust their strategy accordingly. Brand in part equals success, and defending that brand is of paramount importance.

---

38. European Commission, Internal Market Directorate General: "Copyright and Related Rights in the Information Society—Proposal for Directive/Background" (10 December 1997). www.europa.eu.int/comm/dg15/en/intprop/intprop/1100.htm#faq

39. European Commission, "Amended Proposal for Directive on Copyright and Related Rights in the Information Society," www.europa.eu.int/comm/dg15/en/intprop/intprop/copy2.htm

Service Changes—Evolving to Meet the Changing Expectations of the Customer

The role of customer service and relationship management is going to increase in parallel with the importance of the e-commerce channel for organizations in the future. The drivers behind these changes are based both on the changing customer-organization relationship and on the technology upon which that relationship is managed and conducted. It is important to determine what the future holds for this aspect of e-commerce because, as was noted at Wal-Mart, a poor customer service experience may be the last customer experience shared by the customer and the company. To consider this we will return to the customer service value chain we described earlier in the book (see Figure 10.2). This value chain models the development of an organization's relationship with a customer over time.

Customer Acquisition

The *prepurchase support period* in the e-commerce space is going to be driven more and more by the brand of the product, which translates to mean that the technology has to support the customers as they locate that product and its vendor on the Internet. As the scale of the Internet and the number of Websites it contains globally continues to grow, consumers will grow ever more sophisticated in their usage, and consequently their expectations and demands will grow. To match these expectations, organizations will need to utilize technology in continually more creative, sophisticated, and adaptive ways.

Figure 10.2
Internet Service
Value Chain

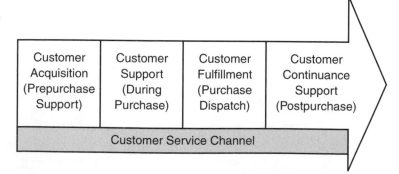

Location, Location, Location...

The mantra of the real estate business has always been location, location, location. The location of large, established public and private organizations on the Internet is relatively straightforward—most adopt their established brand as their URL ".com." For the small business and born-on-the-Net organization, creativity and adaptability are the key. The small business will have to make the decision as to which brand name is more important—its potential as an Internet brand or its established moniker. Many small businesses in the future will be clicks-and-mortar companies—this will compound the difficulty of the decision-making process, and much will depend upon the hinterland from which the business draws. An example of creativity is Soft-Aid, a medical billing company that grew from being a provider of traditional client-server-based billing systems to providing billing systems through the Internet. In order to expand and build its brand-name recognition, Soft-Aid changed its name to Manage.MD and registered its URL domain name in Moldova—a creative solution to a branding issue brought about by the new medium.

Future Wave 8: Change is the only constant (adapted from Heraclitus 540 B.C.) but, to keep the customer-organization constant, the organization and its use of technology must change constantly.

Having identified and established a quality brand-name URL, the next goal is to gain preference on the search engines. To a certain extent the battle for location on the first-generation search engine is almost over; without significant amounts of investment or brand equity, it will continue to be difficult to find premier space on the search engines. The strategies they employ to search for a topic are becoming less and less helpful as the volume of Websites increases. The new form of customer relationship focus will develop from a powerful tripod of concerns and relations: the customer, the intelligent portal, and the organization. The move on the *consumer side* has to be toward secondary specialist information sources or to use intelligent agents that do the searching on behalf of their owner. On the *portal side*, specialist portals are destined to evolve—whether they are from traditional portal sites such as Yahoo! or from fresh new entities remains to be seen. This is especially relevant for emerging markets such as South America and Africa—where a U.S.-based customer may wish to purchase an object but have no idea of where to begin a search. For example, a wine connoisseur in California may wish to buy a bottle of rare wine from Chile but may have little meta-knowledge about how to solve this problem, as well as not knowing Spanish. In order to continue to facilitate search queries and transactions, the portals will need to establish a language-independent search engine and assisted search strategy. The beginnings of such a portal strategy can be found in sites such as AskJeeves.com which perform rudimentary parsing of natural language texts. It is feasible to conceive that a portal initiate a natural language discussion with the customer to preprocess the search and search space. The third leg of the tripod upon which the relationships are made is the vendor or *organizational side*. This is where an organization can make a valued customer connection, and it depends on an organization's ability to perform business intelligence data mining. The ability to locate the space in which their customers are most frequent visitors and are most active is vital to the future success of all organizations, which will need to focus their advertising more intelligently as the Internet space continues to evolve. Organizations need to advertise on the Internet in a specific location in a specific time slot to capture individual customers based on preference and demographic profiling with the minimum of intrusion.

Customer Support—During Purchase

Once a customer has located a potential vendor, the customer holds the power of continued connection or the ability to terminate the relationship. In the traditional model—for example, in the purchase of a car—the slick, white-shirted salesman would attempt to make a customer stay in the showroom, almost against his will, with lines like "what can I do to make this sale happen today?" In the Internet model, this is no longer the case—one click and the customer is gone, free to purchase elsewhere.

In their early use of the Internet many organizations based their customer support strategies on the misconception that an online channel was a low-cost channel and that customers would understand this. Their online customer service was like that of a low-cost grocery store—"The reason our costs are low is that you have to bag your own groceries"—fine for some customers but a definite turnoff for others. Many organizations have realized this and have changed their strategy to be more open and welcoming or they offer different fee structures for different levels of human involvement in the transaction in the manner of the online trading companies. However, generally in retail this is not feasible due to competitive pricing issues, so vendors will continue to develop second-generation technologies aimed at integrating human customer service representatives with a variety of channels and technologies. The goal is to relate to customers on their terms and through the technology that they find most useful, ranging from zero physical, person-to-person interaction to full-service capability through a physical bricks-and-mortar channel. Technologies such as live chat, where customers can talk through their computers via the Internet to sales representatives using either voice communication or text (the equivalent of instant messaging), will become pervasive. Two-way interaction is inevitable, including the customer service representative taking control of the customer's Web page and cursor, manipulating the site remotely, even sending to customers new images that are available only from the service representative. The company of the future will be prepared for this and will adapt to it.

From an organizational perspective the objective has always been to provide first-class service at minimal cost. Software being developed that enables automatic routing and analysis of e-mails together with Web-based queries will facilitate this, giving the customer access to expertise and maximum resource utilization. The question of how much an organization will spend on all this, however, is still strongly related to volume—if your site generates a million hits a day and if 5% make requests, that can still represent a significant cost to manage on a continuing basis. Hence the human cost element is one area in which bricks-and-mortar stores have an advantage, leveraging their existing resources to field local customer requests for information, acting as conduits for specialized customer queries through systems that can reroute the queries invisibly to the organizations expert in that particular subject area. In this way a financial advisor could field a query in a local office of a major firm and immediately build the customer relationship through the delivery of first-class advice instantaneously.

The challenge, therefore, for the organization of the future is to integrate the customer service system of the company to include as rich a talent pool as possible, facilitated by systems to reduce the costs. One way costs can be reduced is to create a knowledge management system that customer service representatives can access during user interactions alongside their Web-based systems and traditional customer database systems with easily locatable best practice and Q&A issues. The ability to service the customer is key to a successful and developing relationship. Technology cannot be the sole answer but, in conjunction with a human specialist, technology can be a powerful lever.

Customer Fulfillment—Purchase Dispatch

The ability to make a sale is only a part of the customer relationship value chain. The timely delivery of the good or service is an important part of matching customer expectations. A challenge for established organizations and for start-ups alike is to identify and satisfy the logistical needs of their customers. The continued development of tracking systems will enable customers to continue to monitor and control the shipment of their purchase in new ways, and it will be those companies agile enough to respond to the customer logistic needs in changing markets that will gain an edge.

UPS is a wonderful example of an organization that has changed from being a *package delivery company* to an *information-based delivery company* providing added value services to its customers based on flexibility of product offerings derived through its information systems. For example, should a customer request a change in her shipping option midjourney, upgrading from 5-day to next-day delivery, UPS can offload the item at the next scanning point and transfer it to the new mode of transportation and fulfill the customer request. Further, UPS has identified the impact of e-commerce on its customers and has moved preemptively, spending $10 billion over the last decade to satisfy developing needs.[40] This has been achieved through informational assistance for new e-commerce vendors as well as new product offerings that are physical and software oriented in nature.

One e-commerce growth area identified by UPS[41] and other logistics solutions providers is that of the online grocery store, a problematic domain that we have discussed throughout this book. The online grocery business involves bulk, perishable, age-restricted, and regulated items, along with a customer base that most likely cannot be delivered to during the regular workday. Webvan, HomeGrocer, PeaPod, and others have spent hundreds of millions of dollars addressing the problem. The agile, nimble mind that solves this logistics problem holds the key to victory. The solution path will require e-consortia and partnering on a new scale, utilizing the talents of the grocer, the logistics specialist, storage specialists (refrigeration, etc.), and security consultants. It

---

40. Lea Soupata, "Managing the Speed of Knowledge," address to the Business Women's Network at the 1999 Global Business Summit, Washington, D.C., October 18, 1999. For UPS press release, see www.ups.com/news/speech/speed.html

41. Press Release: UPS, "On-Line Grocers Choose UPS's Roadnet Technologies for Complete Delivery Solution," Baltimore, MD, January 4, 2000.

may be that the future model is not home delivery at all, but the creation of a new business concept such as a *home services station*. Just as we would go to a gas station for all services related to our car or to a general medical practitioner for all services related to our general health, we might go to a home services station to facilitate our daily lives and chores, including all the duties once performed by a valet and maid. It could take care of our dry cleaning, mail, and pharmacy needs, as well as being our Internet workstation, gas station, ATM, and banking station. And it could provide storage for our shopping items delivered by the logistics company from an intermediary such as Webvan. Perhaps it may even be Mail Boxes Etc. or the oil companies that will win in the home grocery wars of the future.

> **Future Wave 9:** An e-consortium will develop to supply the customer-centric environment with all its needs, focusing multiple organizations and their products through one information hub.

Customer Continuance and Support

The final stage in the customer service value chain is that of postpurchase support. The agile company will be able to identify potential uses of technology to fill customer needs on an ongoing basis, such as using the Internet to check the mechanical status of an appliance like a refrigerator or even using a wireless telephone or communication device to check the family car. Should the system identify a problem and if it is feasible, a fix could be downloaded in advance of the item breaking down, or alternatively the customer could be informed in advance of a critical problem. This would reduce the organization's costs by scheduling service on its schedule rather than the customer's and would build the customer relationship by preventing problems from growing into more expensive ones in the future. By integrating itself into the fabric of a consumer's life, the organization can obtain a richer understanding of its customer's behavior and can create products and services around that knowledge base.

Market Changes—The Rapid Evolution of Global, Segmented Systems-based Markets

The market of the future will continue to be impacted by three major factors (see Figure 10.3):

Figure 10.3
Three Factors
Impacting Market
Change

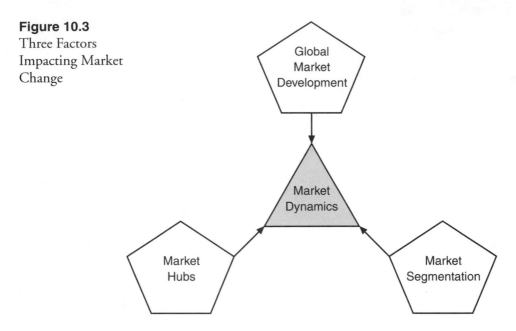

☞ Market segmentation
☞ Development of global markets
☞ Emerging market hubs

Market Segmentation

As markets continue to divide and segment, the twenty-first century will see the dawn of a new industrial species—the *agile* organization. Agile organizations, as we have discussed, compete through competitive flexibility in all aspects of their internal value chain and through an extended value system with their suppliers and customers. This agile competitive position is obtained through maximizing the use of information systems to enable flexibility, both internally through a virtual value chain[42] and externally through extended interorganizational relationships within an electronic community of commerce.[43] The movement of organizations from traditional mass production entities of the industrial society to agile organizations of the virtualized

---

42. J. F. Rayport and J. J. Sviokla, "Exploiting the Virtual Value Chain," *Harvard Business Review*, November–December 1995.

43. Further reading: T. W. Malone, J. Yates, and R. I. Benjamin, "Electronic Markets and Electronic Hierarchies," *Communications of ACM* 30, 1987, pp. 484–97.

information economy of the Internet is gaining pace as the decreasing cost of technology allows the creation of an infrastructure in which these organizations can establish themselves.

The status of agile enterprise is not necessarily on the evolutionary road for all of today's organizations. The ability to move down this road will be determined by several factors, the most important of which are flexibility, innovativeness, and the ability to overcome existing inertia—inertia that results in the perpetual repetition of negative and detrimental industrial practices that prevent organizational renewal. The agile enterprise will adopt information technology to facilitate its flexibility through a smaller, more adaptive organizational structure, one that links together all of the organization's employees (knowledge workers) in a common goal—the creation of an innovative solution to any problem.

The organization of the future may bear only a slight resemblance to its industrial society image, having shed the entrenched functions that detract from the adaptive and agile philosophies of the organization in its information economy form.

The move to the agile form has been long predicted, Ronald H. Coase who was presented with the 1991 Nobel prize in Economics for his "discovery and clarification of the significance of transaction costs and property rights for the institutional structure and functioning of the economy"[44] stated as far back as 1937 that the organization may not be required to be composed of all aspects of the value chain[45] and that the "entrepreneur" may outsource all functions if they wish: "In the Lancashire cotton industry, a weaver can rent a power and shop room and can obtain looms and yarn on credit."[46]

> **Future Wave 10:** The status of agile enterprise is not necessarily on the evolutionary road for all of today's organizations.

It is the ability of entrepreneurs and owners of traditional organization to coordinate activities through the use of information technology via the Internet that has allowed the agile entity to become a reality. This is further enhanced

---

44. www.nobel.se/
45. M. E. Porter, *Competitive Advantage*, Free Press, New York, 1985.
46. R. H. Coase, *The Firm, the Market, and the Law*, University of Chicago Press, 1990.

by the Internet's ability to facilitate the development of and connectivity to communities of economic interdependence. The ability to exchange information and market intelligence among the community is of vital interest to all organizations, but especially to the agile organization developing on the Internet in the e-commerce space. Kenneth Arrow, the 1972 Nobel Laureate in Economics, identified the relationship between uncertainty and the value of information where "information is merely the negative measure of uncertainty"[47] and observed that organizational behavior is based upon the observation of signals upon economic variables. Extrapolating from Arrow's propositions it becomes apparent that in order to survive, the agile organization of the future will need to be increasingly information intense, facilitating the flexibility of the organization to cope with uncertainty. It is interesting to consider that as agility increases, the ability of the projected negative costs of dealing with uncertainty is lessened. Commenting upon the value of information Arrow states: "1) That information or signals have economic value and therefore are worth acquiring and transmitting even at some cost; 2) that different individuals have different information."[48] This emphasizes the need for an agile organization to belong to a community of commerce, preferably electronic, where an exchange of information can be facilitated at lowest cost.

Thus we can see that, in order to cope with the turbulent market dynamic of the future, organizations are going to become increasingly information rich and connected to other organizations, either in temporary partnerships or through e-consortia, that can continuously complement each other with more information and product. This agile web of organizations will become an agile collective that will thrive in changing markets. Survival outside this collective, even for today's megaorganizations, is uncertain.

Global Markets

The continuous progression and deployment of the Internet is not just a phenomenon of the United States, Europe, and Japan. The global rollout of the Internet continues wherever there is a telephone dial tone. Trade knows no boundaries (other than those imposed by political constraints) and will continue to flourish through the new media. Two regions where the potential

---

47. Kenneth Joseph Arrow, *The Economics of Information (Collected Papers of Kenneth J. Arrow)* 4, Belknap Press of Harvard University, Cambridge, MA, 1994.

48. Ibid.

for investment, growth, and technology innovation is high are Latin America and India.

Latin America

The Latin American market continues to grow at a rapid pace; International Data Corporation, a research firm in Framingham, MA, projects that the market will grow from \$167 million in 1998 to more than \$8 billion by 2003.[49] The roots of this growth can be seen emerging from the intense interest large Latin American organizations have in developing their e-commerce markets. A primary vehicle for this growth is through partnering relationships with U.S. portals and domain experts with experience in developing markets.

One example of this is the relationship between Commerce One, a leading provider of global B2B e-commerce solutions,[50] and Banacci, Mexico's leading financial group. Banacci's vision of the future is to attract Mexico's growing Internet users to its site by providing banking and other services.[51] The partnering relationship has allowed Banacci to get up to speed faster than its own internal systems development would have permitted and gives Banacci immediate access to Commerce One's expertise.

Its close proximity to the United States makes the Latin American countries ripe for growth in the Internet space. André Vanyi-Robin, president and CEO of Visualcom, the largest Latin American solution provider, describes the challenges and rewards offered by the Latin American market:

> There are five fundamental differences between e-commerce in the United States and in Latin America on the Internet usage:
>
> The first one is that in Latin America in 1995 you had 300,000 Internet users which were predominantly University professors, students, or government officials, whereas in the United States you had 10 million Internet users which we now call "critical mass" in the U.S., which is when Amazon, Netscape, etc., took to the scene. After that you had the creation of portals such as Yahoo! They were

---

49. Andrea Peterson, "Opening a Portal, Ecommerce Targets Latin America but It's a Tough Sell," *The Wall Street Journal,* January 25, 2000, p. 1.

50. www.commerceone.com/news/US/banamex.htm

51. Press Release: Banacci and Commerce One, "Banacci and Commerce One Announce Joint Venture for Business-to-Business E-Commerce Network," Mexico City, Mexico, and Walnut Creek, CA, December 14, 1999. www.commerceone.com/news/US/banamex.htm

formerly known as search engines that were there to create order out of chaos. In Latin America this was not the case; there was no Internet market per se, and in 1996 with the advent of StarMedia you had a massive advertisement campaign that took $200+ million to start educating the Latin America population that there is such a thing as the Internet, that there is such a thing as living and buying online, and that you had to join it. So in reality the culture was created from scratch as opposed to having been organically born, as was the case in the United States—that is really one major issue.

The second major issue is that in Latin America contrary to the United States you do not have consumer protection laws or the necessary legal framework to be able to facilitate the purchasing of products online, such as in the United States where you have "lemon laws" that protect buyers from defective products or you have credit card protection laws to protect consumers from fraudulent use, etc., etc. So, as this was not the case in Latin America, this had to be built from scratch.

The third point is that the tradition of buying from catalogs, which in the United States dates back to the late 1800s (Sears, for example), did not exist in Latin America. The idea of buying without touching, of buying remotely, without having to see the goods or have a relationship with the vendor, did not exist in Latin America and so this also had to be created from scratch.

The fourth point is the payment method, which, contrary to the United States where one credit card will serve you throughout the 50 states, in Latin America credit card usage was limited by three different factors: 1) high interest rates—which do not incite the use of credit cards or the holding of debt and thus limited penetration; 2) credit cards could not be exported to other countries; and 3) access to credit cards for the vast majority of people was limited. And so Latin America had to identify and create methods of payment to be able to provide the ability to do e-commerce.

The fifth point, and perhaps it is a very important point, is that there were a dearth of options online to be able to meet the needs of Latin Americans, and this is strictly a fact because there was no Internet culture at the time. So, since there was no Internet culture, the only sources of information or product were American sites in English and Latin Americans could go to those sites. A perfect example is that the largest bookstore online in Argentina is Amazon.

This is the competitive landscape with which we are faced, however. In Latin America they have the ability and tendency to "leap frog" technologies, and they can adopt a best breed or practices approach from the experiences of their U.S. counterparts who have already absorbed the expense of passing through the learning and experience curves.

In Latin America it was necessary to build the Internet market from nothing, led by companies such as StarMedia. This commenced with heavy advertising in traditional media. It has to be remembered that you are creating the Internet culture in Latin America, you are creating the infrastructure for payment, you are creating the infrastructure for consumer protection, you are finding the payment systems. And where do you look [if you are a business in Latin America]? You look north to find the best in products, people, and resources and take that expertise and "know how" to Latin America.

Vanyi-Robin also comments upon the nature of the legal systems, deregulation of markets, and partnering relationships as stable platforms through which to perform business:

The governments of Latin America are obviously very excited by what is going on and are doing their best effort not to interfere, and if they are, they are going to do so in the positive sense where they are going to legislate to facilitate e-commerce online. For example, at the Organization of American States meeting on e-commerce in Washington, D.C. [January 2000], the governments present were there to talk about how the laws will be impacted by e-commerce and what to do so that they do not interfere with e-commerce but encourage it, and governments are very conscious that they have to work with private industry to help build the necessary infrastructure, in terms of legal environment, for online business. The biggest boon is that you are taking 480 million people, and because they adopt the technologies by "leapfrogging," which implied best of breed and best of methodologies, you are going to be analyzing Latin Americans within 18 months in terms of profiles as opposed to rich and poor.

The first tier of countries leading e-commerce in Latin America, according to Vanyi-Robin, are

> Brazil, Mexico, and Argentina—Brazil having 4.5 million users, Mexico 1.5, and Argentina 400,000. The second tier is Venezuela, Colombia, and Peru, Chile being between first and second tier only due the fact of its size; however it is one of the most advanced countries with regard to technology, infrastructure and legislation.[52]

India

With an annual compounded growth rate of 42.35%[53] over the last 10 years, the Indian software industry is a key export industry for India that is estimated in a McKinsey report to grow from about $3 billion in revenues to $85 billion by 2008.[54] Recognizing the importance of this industry, the Indian Government Department of Electronics created a *software technology park* scheme. Located in Hyderabad, dubbed "High Tech City," it is intended to become the Silicon Valley of India. With a depth of talented systems engineers from outstanding universities such as the Indian Institute of Technology, the country is already experiencing a growth of Internet-related start-ups, and the movement of U.S. technology companies into the space has commenced. An example of the Internet thrust can be found in S. Kumars Group, formerly a textile company that has diversified into many sectors including power, retail, and financial services generating $250 million in revenues. S. Kumars' goal is to establish its own nationwide telecommunications network based on VSAT satellite technology in order to facilitate e-commerce through its 30,000 retail outlets.[55] Its mission is to "eventually enable the remotest and smallest of villages in India to have access to urban centers and the world. The project thus overcomes the constraints of inadequate cable infrastructure, shortage of personal computers and validation of transactions which are critical for e-commerce to flourish."[56] With the world's largest national population as a potential audience, the opportunities look strong indeed.

---

52. Source: Personal Interview, Miami, Florida (1 February 2000).

53. www.stph.net/scheme/stps.html

54. S. Fidler, "Indian Software Capital Praised for Its Growth," *Financial Times*, January 20, 2000.

55. K. Guha, "Satellite-based Internet Trading Plan for India," *Financial Times*, November 23, 1999.

56. www.skumars.com/

There Are No Commercial Barriers to Entry Anymore, Only Political Ones

As the emerging Internet nations are creating their infrastructures and looking for internal growth, so the visionary organizations of the leading Internet nations are planning strategies to move into these markets at the appropriate time. The Internet-based financial services firms E*TRADE and DLJ Direct are adding customers by moving into the relatively sophisticated European markets. This move will be a fertile learning ground for the companies' predicted future move into emerging markets such as Latin America and Asia. Christos M. Cotsakos, chairman of the board and CEO of E*TRADE Group, Inc., states, "Leveraging our technology to a consumer base that is significantly greater than the home market is what globalization is all about." Clearly, the CEO of the future has to have global vision of the marketspace, technology in order to plan for growth, and development opportunities no matter where they occur on the planet.

Market Hubs

The stagnant state of Internet search engines is a major roadblock to the development of a more dynamic Internet market. The current search engines (frequently renamed *portals*) rely primarily upon two strategies: creating directories and power searching. Some search engines, when you type in a query, just search their database of links and match the query to the best degree possible and present you with the results. Others have already searched the database and created tree directories with the known links contained within them. Clearly there are limitations to both these strategies. With the first you never know how close you are going to get to a desired set of acceptable solutions; with the second, the directory structure may limit the search categories you can achieve.

The search mechanisms are primarily based on pattern matching of key words, headers in the HTML code describing a Web page, a technique that has been available since artificial intelligence (AI) pioneer Joseph Weizenbaum wrote the ELIZA program in 1965 at MIT.[57] ELIZA was a system that allowed patients to discuss their problems with a psychologist, in which the

---

57. Joseph Weizenbaum, "ELIZA—A Computer Program for the Studying of Natural Language Communication between Man and Machine," *Communications of ACM* 9, 1966, pp. 36–45.

psychologist was actually the program. The program worked by matching key words in a limited domain and improvising conversation by remembering words from the conversation and introducing them where necessary to continue the conversation. Since then there has been a significant amount of research in the area of knowledge-based systems and artificial intelligence, but the basic problem of *cognition* within a program still remains an elusive goal. Some researchers such as Boris Katz and his associates in the Infolab within the MIT AI Laboratory are pushing forward with the problem of natural language interfaces to the World Wide Web. They have created a natural language system START[58] to answer English questions related to information from the MIT AI Laboratory and from the World Wide Web. However, the first generation of search engines have primarily been driven by "brute force," relying more on syntactic analysis than semantic cognition.

> **Future Wave 11:** Information hubs of a specialist nature will cut down on the search requirements and effort needed to locate data as the Web continues to expand.

The frustration of search and the cost benefit of assisting in that search space will drive future developments. This may very well be in the form of information hubs that are monitored by experts or organizations that are dedicated parties. For example, the American Medical Association or the U.S. Department of Health and Human Services may wish to create a Web hub that is an authoritative medical authority for advice for U.S. citizens, free to all as a primary care service. The UK government has a help phone line that acts in a limited capacity in this way. Specialized hubs may be created in domains and fostered and created in e-communities.

The e-community concept can be traced back to the development of electronic data interchange and interorganizational systems. The concept of these systems was originally captured by Kauffman in 1966[59]—he urged organizations to "think beyond [their] organizational boundaries—extra corporate systems" and which prior to the Internet took the form of a closed system of proprietary linkages. This has been superceded by the concept of an electronic

---

58. www.ai.mit.edu/projects/infolab/

59. J. Kaufman, "Data Systems that Cross Corporate Boundaries," *Harvard Business Review*, January–February 1966.

community, which can be defined as *a collective group of entities, individuals, or organizations that come together either temporarily or permanently through an electronic medium to interact in a common problem or interest space.*

Within the e-community concept, an organization is either a *participant,* using the network of the community to exchange information for either a commercial or noncommercial objective, or a *facilitator.* A facilitator may be either a formal or informal organization that coordinates the development, operation, or use of a network or part of a network for exchange among participants. Examples of large commercial facilitators are AOL and Prodigy; other facilitators may be much smaller, running their information hub through the larger service provider—for example, a cancer support group (www.cancer.org/). A participant in the simplest form could be defined as any individual who, for instance, associates with others in a mutual interest through a chat room or bulletin board.

There are three sectors in the world of e-communities, each with its own subdivisions:

1. Commercial sector
   — private regulated communities
   — open regulated communities

2. Noncommercial (nonprofit) sector
   — closed and regulated communities
   — open but regulated communities

3. Public sector
   — commercial
   — noncommercial

The first category, the *commercial, private regulated community,* is a space in which private communities and subcommunities exist. The communities are private in the sense that the members share in a common value system for the production of goods or the creation of services, and membership to the community is by invitation or contract only. The community exists on a regulated network that can itself be private, value added, or through an Internet provider who regulates access. Subscription news providers are examples of this type of community.

The *commercial, open regulated community* is open to any individual or group that obeys the rules of the regulator of that community. The regulating bodies are the providers of the networks, who can thus control its partitions, prevent data/information encroachment and the unauthorized access of data by external parties. Examples of these regulatory agents are Internet service providers such as AOL and Prodigy. The ISP that regulates the for-profit sector of the community usually charges the participants a fee or takes a commission from other commercial partners in the community. The "free" ISPs, for example, gain revenue through the commissions generated from the telephone networks on which the service runs. The facilitator in the form of ISPs not only creates the systems that allow the hub to function but also enforces all the security and hardware defenses and regulates the system. The open regulated environments also offer a place for those organizations not yet able to form a private community of their own to come together under the technical auspices of the regulated provider.

The *noncommercial, nonprofit closed and regulated communities* frequently focus on providing research and development information. These communities include bodies such as the Advanced Research Projects Agency (ARPA), and consortia projects that are collaborative ventures between, for example, universities and federal organizations. These communities are closed and regulated, accessible only to those who sponsor them, or are supported by that sponsor, and the data, information, and resources are closely regulated for access and usage by the parent body. However, some access may be available to public users for technology transfer. An example of this is the ARPA net—primarily government-funded research that became the Internet.

The *noncommercial, open but regulated community* includes, for example, government agencies and research institutions whose data must be made available to the public under the U.S. Freedom of Information Act or other form of disclosure mechanism. However, the data area may be *read only* because the regulating body may not want changes to be made to the data; e.g., Securities and Exchange Commission's electronic data gathering analysis and retrieval (EDGAR).

Finally there are the *public commercial and noncommercial community*, comprising the vast majority of cyberspace. It is at best an unstructured and continually evolving community. The community is primarily composed of individual users who have created home pages on the World Wide Web through the spectrum of Internet service providers. In these unregulated communities, hubs often start out as not-for-profit groups with common interests, such as online focus groups, e.g., environmental communities. If successful, they increase in size and decide to move to a more regulated environment such as that found in the commercial sector, where facilities such as group media-tors are accessible and available.

Thus the growth of hubs through these e-communities and the specialization of hubs is likely to continue. The portals are likely to continue to act as focal points for the online communities, facilitating their creation, drawing them together and channeling audiences toward them, perhaps acquiring them as they grow, thus forming a new information value chain.

> **Future Wave 12:** Intergovernmental issues on privacy, access to information, and free trade will become more important as e-commerce becomes increasingly global and lucrative.

Future Directions: Agile and E-organization Confluence

The virtual economy will reshape the very nature of organizations, forcing them to transform themselves from rigid structures to agile structures. They will move from competitive strategies based on scale of economy to competition based on low-volume, mass-customized production and from vertical and horizontal structures to polymorphic structures composed of communities of collaborative electronic commerce.

The tactical changes that organizations underwent during the 1990s, combined with the growing ability to connect through information systems, is the precursor to the next strategic opportunity—that of being involved in an electronic marketspace integrated together in an e-consortium or through one or more e-communities. However, to be a successful predator in this environment, organizations must plan ahead and consider their evolutionary path so that they utilize information and technology in the most appropriate ways, leveraging that agility in ever expanding connectivity

Change in External Relationships—It Is the Company We Keep That Determines Who We Are

The Internet and its impact on commerce have been pervasive, and its effects will continue to be felt. An area in which this is destined to continue to have a significant impact is that of interorganizational relationships. The industrial era created an order to the society that had the giant multinationals at the top, then the tier-one suppliers, followed by tier two, and so on down the "food chain." The dependence of each supplier on its customers was total, and the profit margins were substantially fixed in these layers. The Internet has changed and challenged this (and will continue to) as organizations in the supply chain become more flexible and agile, increasing their market's scope and size.

Former heavy-industry suppliers, such as those in the automobile industry, have over the past few years become more agile and flexible as they have adopted the flexible work practices of the mass-customization management style.[60] Similarly service industries such as insurance and banking have begun providing services in sectors previously off limits (such as those provided by CitiGroup). Both these and other sectors have realized that the Internet is a new frontier with enormous opportunities. However, the former pecking order is being challenged and the rules changed through the access and connectivity of the Internet.

The Battle for Information Supremacy: The Information Hub

It has long been known that the interconnectivity of computer networks can lock in customers and act as barriers to entry in markets. MBA students have for the last 25 years studied the classic business cases of American Hospital Supply Corporation, American Airlines, and others were using their computer networks to do just this in the 1980s. However, this time the "genie is out of the bottle," and CEOs and CIOs are formulating strategies to ensure that their organizations take maximum advantage of the Internet opportunity within the boundaries of intercorporate relationships. A classic battle is unfolding in the automotive industry; both Ford and GM have created *information hubs* or exchanges aimed at facilitating the supply chain. Ford, in a joint venture with Oracle, created AutoXchange[61] while General Motors Corporation, in conjunction with Commerce One, announced its intentions to create its own hub, TradeXchange. Both of these information exchanges focus on B2B supply chain services. Ford wants to cut its $80 billion purchasing

---

60. R. Plant, D. Feeny, and H. Mughal, "Land Rover Vehicles, the CB40, a Project in Nimbleness and Flexibility," European Clearing House of Cases: Case 600-001-1.

61. Press Release: Ford, "Ford and Oracle Create Multi-Billion Dollar Business-to-Business Internet Venture," New York, NY, November 2, 1999.

transaction costs associated with its 30,000 suppliers and $300 billion extended supply chain. Ford's goal is to "dramatically reduce Ford's purchasing costs and increase its operating efficiencies through an integrated Internet supply chain system. Further, it will extend Ford"[62] core business into a virtual e-business enterprise allowing direct market connections of the supply chain to the consumer to reduce Ford's "time to market." GM, which spends approximately $87 billion annually with its 30,000 suppliers worldwide, wants to "be able to quickly create stronger, leaner and more efficient supply chains. The goal with GM TradeXchange is not to move the costs around the supply chain, but to reduce the costs of all of our suppliers," according to Harold R. Kutner, GM's group vice president of worldwide purchasing.[63]

Future Wave 13: The battle for ownership and control over the virtual intercorporate value chain will become a new venue for competitiveness.

By the spring of 2000, though, Ford and GM had realized that suppliers might not wish to join proprietary "Xchanges" through which a manufacturer minimizes its supply chain costs at the expense of suppliers' margins, pushing the pressure up the supply chain while maintaining the sales prices of its vehicles and increasing its profits. The relationships inherent in the Xchanges require careful consideration by suppliers: Join one or both? What will that do to our overhead? Which other automobile manufacturers will join these hubs?

Taking these concerns of their suppliers into consideration led to a rapid consolidation in this B2B space, with Ford, GM, and DaimlerChrysler joining together to form a B2B integrated supplier exchange. As G. Richard Wagoner, Jr., president and COO of GM commented: "As we continued to build our separate exchange sites, we quickly realized traditional, individual stand-alone models weren't the winning strategy for us, our industry, our suppliers and, ultimately, our customers....By joining together we can further increase the pace of implementation, thereby accelerating the benefits to everyone involved. We are excited about the opportunity to build on what each of us started separately and create the best trading exchange in the world."

---

62. Ibid.

63. Press Release: General Motors Corporation and Commerce One, "General Motors and Commerce One Add i2's Business-to-Business Supply Chain Services to GM Trade-Xchange," Detroit, MI, January 19, 2000.

Even in light of this massive B2B effort on the part of the manufacturers, some component manufacturers such as the $12.8 billion Dana Corporation are determined to press ahead with their own systems. Partnering with Ariba, Inc., and Aspect Development, Dana is developing a global e-procurement system that will allow Dana to manage its $8 billion annual worldwide purchases more efficiently. Joe Magliochetti, Dana's president and CEO, commented:

> Using this technology as a base, Dana will also explore the possibility of partnering with other automotive, heavy-truck, off-highway or after market suppliers to create an independent "services" exchange for B2B transactions…the creation of an electronic business exchange could provide significant value to our common customers and suppliers through reduced transaction costs, aggregated purchasing and value added services, such as supplier design collaboration, logistics, and vendor managed inventories. This will better position us to easily integrate with other industry specific exchanges, many of which have been announced recently.[64]

Regardless of who wins the battleground for the B2B information hub, the anticipated benefits are immense and include increased value with preferred suppliers or customers; significantly reduced transaction expenses; and consolidated information on customer contacts, supplier performance, and reduced inventory requirements.

The information economy will make all organizations reassess their positions with respect to their customers-supplier relationship. The e-strategy that an organization adopts is clearly the defining factor, a factor acknowledged by Minoru Makihara, chairman of Mitsubishi Corporation, a company still in the early stages of developing an e-strategy. He states: "I think if things are left as they are, we could miss the [Internet] boat. E-business is bound to come and unless we are able to cope with the changes in this world, our competitiveness will decline."[65] This is a clear testament to the power of the new information-based economy and a warning to all companies that inertia must be overcome and change embraced.

---

64. Press Release: Dana Corporation, "Dana Announces Global E-Procurement Initiative," Toledo, OH, January 13, 2000.

65. Michiyo Nakamoto, "Mitsubishi Corp Keen to Board Internet Boat," *Financial Times*, November 23, 1999, p. 18.

23 11 1999 COMPANIES & FINANCE: ASIA-PACIFIC:
Mitsubishi Corp keen to board Internet boat
By MICHIYO NAKAMOTO
TOKYO

Mitsubishi Corporation, Japan's pre-eminent trading company, is struggling to define a strategy to adapt to the new Internet era, Minoru Makihara, chairman, admitted yesterday.

"I think if things are left as they are, we could miss the (Internet) boat," Mr Makihara said.

"E-business is bound to come and unless we are able to cope with the changes in this world, our competitiveness will decline," he said.

His comments highlight a common problem among Japan's established companies, which have failed to respond swiftly enough to the rapid spread of the Internet and its impact both on business and consumer behaviour. Mitsubishi officials concede that they had not been able to identify a sufficiently clear strategy for taking advantage of the Internet's rapid spread by spotting new business possibilities or lucrative investment opportunities.

Although Japanese trading companies have been active investors in advanced technology sectors, particularly in cable and satellite TV, they have fallen far behind more nimble start-up companies, such as Softbank, in the Internet world.

Softbank's market capitalisation was standing at Y7,550bn (Dollars 71bn) yesterday, compared with Mitsubishi's Y1,398bn.

Mr Makihara conceded that Masayoshi Son, president and founder of Softbank, had a "respectful" strategy of investing in promising Internet start-ups and using that as a basis for new businesses in Japan.

In particular, his decision to link up with Tokyo Electric Power to provide Internet services was very clever, Mr Makihara said.

Mitsubishi itself has invested in a number of small Internet companies and has set up online businesses as well.

However, Mr Makihara indicated that in order to benefit from the Internet phenomenon, the company needs to take greater advantage of its position as a member of one of the most closely-knit keiretsu, or corporate groupings, in Japan.

"I think Internet commerce is one area where each company (in the keiretsu) doing separate things doesn't make sense," he said.

Another way in which Mitsubishi could enter the Internet market was to use its brand value, said Mr Makihara. In Japan, where the credit card system is not as widespread as in the US and trust is important, "the name of Mitsubishi, or our standing behind a business-to-business or business-to consumer business is a valuable asset", he said.

Source: *Finanicial Times*, London Edition, p. 31, November 23, 1999, copyright © Financial Times Ltd., 1982–1997. Reproduced with permission.

Government and Political Change—The Visible and Invisible Hands That Influence Commerce

Governments and politics have a great effect on the waves of change in the e-commerce space. Clearly the Internet would not have been created without these two factors. It was the U.S. government that funded the ARPA-net project from which the Internet arose, and it was the European Organization for Nuclear Research, a laboratory founded in 1954 and now jointly funded by 20 member states, where in 1989 Tim Berners-Lee and Robert Cailliau created the World Wide Web. However, as the power of information on and access to the Internet grows, so will the recognition by political interest groups that they can gain political power by controlling and influencing the medium.

The United States of America

The United States is the driving force in e-commerce and Internet development. The White House in July 1997 wrote a defining document, "A Framework for Global Electronic Commerce," which states its position and philosophy through five principles:[66]

1. The private sector should lead.

Though government played a role in financing the initial development of the Internet, its expansion has been driven primarily by the private sector. For electronic commerce to flourish, the private sector must continue to lead. Innovation, expanded services, broader participation, and lower prices will arise in a market-driven arena, not in an environment that operates as a regulated industry.

Accordingly, governments should encourage industry self-regulation wherever appropriate and support the efforts of private sector organizations to develop mechanisms to facilitate the successful operation of the Internet. Even where collective agreements or standards are necessary, private entities should, where possible, take the lead in organizing them. Where government action or intergovernmental agreements are necessary, on taxation for example, private sector participation should be a formal part of the policy making process.

---

66. www.ecommerce.gov/framewrk.htm#2. Governments should avoid undue restrictions on electronic commerce.

2. Governments should avoid undue restrictions on electronic commerce.

Parties should be able to enter into legitimate agreements to buy and sell products and services across the Internet with minimal government involvement or intervention. Unnecessary regulation of commercial activities will distort development of the electronic marketplace by decreasing the supply and raising the cost of products and services for consumers the world over. Business models must evolve rapidly to keep pace with the break-neck speed of change in the technology; government attempts to regulate are likely to be outmoded by the time they are finally enacted, especially to the extent such regulations are technology-specific.

Accordingly, governments should refrain from imposing new and unnecessary regulations, bureaucratic procedures, or taxes and tariffs on commercial activities that take place via the Internet.

3. Where governmental involvement is needed, its aim should be to support and enforce a predictable, minimalist, consistent, and simple legal environment for commerce.

In some areas, government agreements may prove necessary to facilitate electronic commerce and protect consumers. In these cases, governments should establish a predictable and simple legal environment based on a decentralized, contractual model of law rather than one based on top-down regulation. This may involve states as well as national governments. Where government intervention is necessary to facilitate electronic commerce, its goal should be to ensure competition, protect intellectual property and privacy, prevent fraud, foster transparency, support commercial transactions, and facilitate dispute resolution.

4. Governments should recognize the unique qualities of the Internet.

The genius and explosive success of the Internet can be attributed in part to its decentralized nature and to its tradition of bottom-up governance. These same characteristics pose significant logistical and technological challenges to existing regulatory models, and governments should tailor their policies accordingly.

Electronic commerce faces significant challenges where it intersects with existing regulatory schemes. We should not assume, for example, that the regulatory frameworks established over the past sixty years for telecommunications, radio and television fit the Internet. Regulation should be imposed only as a necessary means to achieve an important goal on which there is a broad consensus. Existing laws and regulations that may hinder electronic commerce should be reviewed and revised or eliminated to reflect the needs of the new electronic age.

5. Electronic Commerce over the Internet should be facilitated on a global basis.

The Internet is emerging as a global marketplace. The legal framework supporting commercial transactions on the Internet should be governed by consistent principles across state, national, and international borders that lead to predictable results regardless of the jurisdiction in which a particular buyer or seller resides.

The White House also discussed nine areas or "issues" where

international agreements are needed to preserve the Internet as a non-regulatory medium, one in which competition and consumer choice will shape the marketplace. Although there are significant areas of overlap, these items can be divided into three main subgroups: financial issues, legal issues, and market access issues.

- **Financial Issues**
  - customs and taxation
  - electronic payments
- **Legal Issues**
  - "Uniform Commercial Code" for electronic commerce
  - intellectual property protection
  - privacy
  - security
- **Market Access Issues**
  - telecommunications infrastructure and information technology
  - content
  - technical standards[67]

---

67. Ibid.

The incubation of the Internet and e-commerce by the U.S. government has clearly paid enormous dividends and has been taken very seriously as a function of government through the U.S. Department of Commerce.[68]

One of the most important areas and stimulators of e-commerce and trade has been the government's approach to taxation of commerce performed on the Internet. The White House position discusses customs and taxation stating:

> ...the Internet lacks the clear and fixed geographic lines of transit that historically have characterized the physical trade of goods. Thus, while it remains possible to administer tariffs for products ordered over the Internet but ultimately delivered via surface or air transport, the structure of the Internet makes it difficult to do so when the product or service is delivered electronically.
>
> Nevertheless, many nations are looking for new sources of revenue, and may seek to levy tariffs on global electronic commerce.
>
> Therefore, the United States will advocate in the World Trade Organization (WTO) and other appropriate international fora that the Internet be declared a tariff-free environment whenever it is used to deliver products or services. This principle should be established quickly before nations impose tariffs and before vested interests form to protect those tariffs.
>
> In addition, the United States believes that no new taxes should be imposed on Internet commerce. The taxation of commerce conducted over the Internet should be consistent with the established principles of international taxation, should avoid inconsistent national tax jurisdictions and double taxation, and should be simple to administer and easy to understand.[69]

This clarifying document and the government's subsequent stance to uphold this has been a key stimulator of the Internet's growth. However, not all agencies and states have adopted this philosophy. One area in which taxation on the Internet is hotly debated is that of the wine, liquor, and beer industries. In this industry a three-tier distribution system is enforced (grower/producer to distributor to retail) that has its roots in the repeal of the 18th Amendment to the U.S. Constitution—prohibition. The 21st amendment which reinstated

---

68. www.ecommerce.gov/

69. See note 66 above.

the legal sale of alcohol, however, gave the states the authority to regulate the production, importation, distribution, retail sale, and consumption of alcohol within its borders under the auspices of the Federal Alcohol Administration Act and regulated Bureau of Alcohol, Tobacco and Firearms. However, this legislation has become a focal point of debate, with some states supporting the growers' and Internet direct shippers' contention that this law limits free trade and needs to be amended and others dismissing the argument. Clearly, the tax and tariff issue will be a key issue.

However, the U.S. government is not resting on its laurels; under the auspices of the U.S. Department of Commerce, Technology Administration (a Federal agency), and the National Institute of Standards and Technology (NIST), it is investing heavily in research and development to reap the rewards at some time in the future. The Advanced Technology Program, a partnership between government and private industry, aims to "accelerate the development of high-risk technologies that promise significant commercial payoffs and widespread benefits for the economy."[70]

Two such projects are: A National Knowledge Infrastructure and Pen-Based User Interface for the Emerging Chinese Computer Market. Through the knowledge infrastructure project, AI researcher Doug Lenat and his group at Cycorp, Inc., of Austin, TX, hope to

> develop tools and technology to support a large knowledge base of widely-shared "common sense" information, to facilitate a large array of software applications and services, including online information searchers that carry on clarification dialogues to better understand a query posed to them, and then gather and integrate information from numerous sources; spreadsheets that highlight improbable values; and email systems better able to filter, prioritize, summarize, and annotate incoming messages.[71]

If successful, this ultimately will impact many dimensions of e-commerce. Meanwhile Communication Intelligence Corporation of Redwood Shores, CA, is working to

> develop data, algorithms, and software necessary for a pen-based character-recognition interface for the Chinese language with a goal

---

70. www.atp.nist.gov/atp/overview.htm

71. www.atp.nist.gov/itao/

of enhancing the exports of U.S. computer hardware and software to Chinese-speaking countries.[72]

This is clearly a visionary project that ultimately will be profitable not only for the company but for the U.S. e-commerce market as the project provides the means of interfacing with potentially the largest Internet market in the world.

Future Wave 14: International treaties and trade groups will become less potent as the customer takes control of markets through the Internet.

The key to a continued prosperity for e-commerce in the United States is for the government and leaders to have vision and be bold enough to act upon that vision. However, the role of Government is also to protect the people and businesses from adverse conditions. To this end the U.S. government has acted to consider issues of trade, ranging from the consideration of First Amendment issues (freedom of speech) to the prevention of illicit financial transactions over the Internet. An example of this is the FBI's Washington, D.C., field office's Infrastructure Protection and Computer Intrusion Squad who are

> responsible for investigating unauthorized intrusions into major computer networks belonging to telecommunications providers, private corporations, United States Government agencies, and public and private educational facilities. The squad also investigates the illegal interception of signals (cable and satellite signal theft) and infringement of copyright laws related to software. As part of its ongoing mission to prevent cyber-based crime and improve the security stature of private and public networks, IPCIS works with industry to assess the potential damage a network intrusion may inflict upon the Washington D.C. area telecommunications infrastructure.[73]

This office, in conjunction with the FBI's National Infrastructure Protection Center and the Department of Justice's Computer Crime and Intellectual Property section, works both as a center for information on potential threats to networks and as a law enforcement agency to protect free trade. Similarly, other agencies—such as Financial Crimes Enforcement Network of the Department of Justice, which looks into treasury issues including the Internet; and the FBI,

---

72. Ibid.

73. www.fbi.gov/programs/ipcis/ipcis.htm

which focuses on cybercrime, transnational crime, and intellectual property—work to maintain a positive environment for the Internet and e-commerce.

Global Issues

The global omnipresent nature of the Internet ensures that, if some of the world's governments ignore it and the regulatory framework it needs to grow to fruition, they will do so at their peril. To this end, various trade organizations and the United Nations have attempted to influence and guide policies in the area of electronic commerce:

☞ The United Nations—through the Commission on International Trade Law Working Group on Electronic Commerce—has created a draft legislative guide on privately financed infrastructure projects and uniform rules on electronic signatures for its members.

☞ The World Intellectual Property Organization is an intergovernmental organization with headquarters in Geneva, Switzerland. It is a specialized agency of the United Nations responsible for the promotion and protection of intellectual property throughout the world. It works toward this through cooperation among the member states. Its objective is to develop, create, and implement multilateral treaties that deal with the legal and administrative aspects of intellectual property. An example of this organization's work is the Arbitration and Mediation Center which resolves disputes over domain names applicable to the generic top-level domains (.com, .net, and .org) under the Uniform Dispute Resolution Policy adopted by Internet Corporation for Assigned Names and Numbers.[74]

The Eighth Principle

A leading issue among governments is the free traffic of information and data between nations and organizations. This issue breaks down into two major components:

☞ Security of the data during transmission

☞ The rights of the individual, whose information is "owned" or stored by an organization

---

74. www.wipo.org/

The protection and security of information is clearly a major concern for organizations passing sensitive and proprietary information between their divisions, suppliers, partners, and customers. It is the role of governments in this data transmission that is becoming a sensitive issue between organizations and governments as well as between individuals and governments. In the European Union (EU), the prevailing view is that tight data protection is necessary. European law mandates that the nations of the EU have data protection. The Data Protection Act of 1998 is primarily based on eight data protection principles that govern the use of data within the EU.[75] However, it is the proposed Eighth Principle that will cause the greatest problems for corporate executives and nations in the future. The Eighth Principle of the Act states:

> Personal data shall not be transferred to a country or territory outside the European Economic Area unless that country or territory ensures an adequate level of protection for the rights and freedoms of data subjects in relation to the processing of personal data.[76]

In the preliminary view of the Data Protection Registrar, "The Eighth Principle prohibits the transfer of personal data to any country or territory outside the EEA ('third country') **unless** the third country in question ensures 'an adequate level of protection for the rights and freedoms of data subjects' ('adequate level of protection') for those personal data in the particular circumstances of the data transfer operation or set of data transfer operations ('transfer') in question."

For countries like the United States, this could potentially be a considerable issue. What if you are an international organization that wishes to transfer information from your EU data center back to the United States? Options are available—*data striping* centers are in operation that desensitize the data in order to pass EU law requirements; these work for the individuals whose data is protected, but would clearly be detrimental to the interests of organizations wishing to use their global corporate reach to advantage. The United States has no official data protection act, and U.S. policy tends toward self-

---

75. The Data Protection Act of 1998, Part 1, Schedule 1, Principle 8. www.dataprotection.gov.uk

76. Data Protection Act of 1998, the Eighth Data Protection Principle and Transborder Dataflows. www.dataprotection.gov.uk/transbord.htm#_Toc458329491

governance by commerce or public interest watchdog groups such as the American Civil Liberties Union.[77]

A second area of concern is that of data transmission and data security. Again, this is a difficult area for governments in the creation of policy. The issue of allowing organizations to use varying levels of encryption strength has been a pressing issue in the United States for many years, with the arguments ranging from the government's need for access to the public's rights to use encryption, as outlined in a White House statement:[78]

> The strategy announced today continues to maintain the balance among privacy, commercial interests, public safety and national security. This approach is comprised of three elements: information security and privacy, a new framework for export controls, and updated tools for law enforcement.
>
> First, the strategy recognizes that sensitive electronic information—government, commercial, and privacy information—requires strong protection from unauthorized and unlawful access if the great promise of the electronic age is to be realized.
>
> Second, it protects vital national security interests through an updated framework for encryption export controls that also recognizes growing demands in the global marketplace for strong encryption products.
>
> Finally, it is designed to assure that, as strong encryption proliferates, law enforcement remains able to protect America and Americans in the physical world and in cyberspace.

The U.S. government has also recognized the need to relax export control of encryption technologies. The statement continues:

> Any encryption commodity or software of any key length may be exported under license exception (i.e., without a license), after a technical review, to individuals, commercial firms, and other non-government end users in any country except for the seven state supporters of terrorism.

---

77. www.aclu.org/privacy/

78. Press Release: The White House, Office of the Press Secretary, "Administration Announces New Approach to Encryption," September 16, 1999.

> Any retail encryption commodities and software of any key length may be exported under license exception, after a technical review, to any end user in any country, except for the seven state supporters of terrorism.
>
> Streamlined post-export reporting will provide government with an understanding of where strong encryption is being exported, while also reflecting industry business models and distribution channels.

This allows U.S. software vendors access to new markets and greater security for American individuals and firms in their data transactions.

While the United States is decreasing the complexity of enacting security measures, other nations are increasing them. China's policy is the antithesis of that of the United States. In January 2000 China announced that, without approval from the State Encryption Management Commission, no work unit, company, or individual may produce or sell encryption products. Furthermore, the sale of foreign encryption products is banned, with the exception of sales to foreign diplomatic and consular offices. This movement to tighter control was enacted on October 7, 1999, when Premier Zhu Rongji signed a decree to implement the Regulations for Managing Commercial Encryption, which were published in the *People's Daily* (in Chinese) on October 15, 1999. The decree was followed by a commentary three days later that set a January 31, 2000, deadline for registering at a new office of the State Encryption Management Commission. However, very few organizations were prepared for such an event or for the impact it would have on their business plans.

The Chinese legislation on Internet policy has been subject to large shifts in position with little or no warning and has resulted in an unstable atmosphere for foreign investors. This was especially evident following the announcement that the encryption standards would be enforced and the *positive investment sentiment* following the U.S.-China trade agreement reached in November of 1999,[79] when it was felt that the opening of China's telecommunications sector, including the Internet market, to foreign investment (with an initial maximum of 49% foreign ownership) would be beneficial for the investment community.

---

79. Press Release: Department of Commerce, "Statement by U.S. Commerce Secretary William M. Daley on Historic U.S.-China Trade Agreement," Washington, DC, November 15, 1999. www.204.193.246.62/public.nsf/docs/6B8214F81B2BAA0D8525682B0052273A

The situation in China with respect to the stability and long-term viability of law and trade practices implies that the zone, while carrying the potential for high rewards, also has serious risk implications. The Chinese government has indicated[80] that it may force companies that sell encryption systems in China to divulge proprietary information with regard to these systems with the consequential risk of the product being *reverse engineered*. This is contrary to the World Trade Organization's agreement from the Uruguay Round of the Multilateral Trade Negotiations, held in Marrakesh in 1994. In this document the issue of intellectual property rights were addressed, the signatories agreeing that:

> The protection and enforcement of intellectual property rights should contribute to the promotion of technological innovation and to the transfer and dissemination of technology, to the mutual advantage of producers and users of technological knowledge and in a manner conducive to social and economic welfare, and to a balance of rights and obligations.[81]

This issue is a major concern for WTO member countries and it needs to be addressed prior to allowing those countries with unstable technology policies to become members.

Trade is not the only global driver impacted by governmental and political factors. The ability to have access to human capital is also heavily influenced by governmental policies. In the United States the demand for Internet workers has been so strong that Congress has been lobbied extensively to increase the number of work permits available to overseas applicants. In the UK the government has been lobbied to reconsider pending tax legislation that may impact IT consultants and which could lead to an IT brain drain of up to 40,000 people from the high technology workforce.[82]

Governments and business have also encouraged the move to build and retain intellectual capital, in the form of science parks which have flourished all over the world in an attempt to mirror Silicon Valley through start-up incubator projects and tax incentives.

---

80. James Kynge, "Encryption Rules Will Hit Chinese," *Financial Times*, January 28, 2000.

81. World Trade Organization's agreement from the Uruguay Round of the Multilateral Trade Negotiations, Marrakesh, April 15, 1994.

82. "'IT Exodus' Threat over Tax Rules," *Financial Times*, January 21, 2000.

As the world becomes more connected, the ability of a government to block mergers and takeovers will become meaningless because organizations will be able to eliminate paper trails and change tax zones instantaneously to take advantage of the global economic environment. Enlightened governments will encourage or are encouraging the creation of international joint ventures such as joint stock exchanges and trading systems. Data will not be kept locally; therefore, governments will not be able to identify ownership; thus any attempt to control the data will ultimately be counterproductive and isolationist. Such a stance when measured in Internet years could lead to significant economic and long-term developmental damage to a country as well as instability in its long-term political and governmental position.

Commentary on the Road Ahead

This chapter has attempted to view the future in regard to six factors, each considered central to e-commerce and strategy formulation: technology, branding, service, market, government, and external relationship changes. The future is never known, of course, but it is a vision of the future to which the brave and the curious will be drawn and who will create the new and the dynamic organizational forms in the next stage of the online revolution.

As we have discussed in this book, no organization is immune to the contact and presence of the Internet and the technology that surrounds it. Those organizations that are successful going forward will be those who manage to balance their strategy in all of its areas; those organizations that are very successful will be those that manage not only to live within the waves of change but to influence them.

11

Views from the Edge—Conversations with Executives

In this book we developed a methodology to assist executives and managers in the creation of e-commerce strategy. The methodology is based on interviews and discussions with hundreds of individuals and companies, together with a synthesis of the data and information that permeates the business literature. The methodology attempts to define

☞ The conceptualization of strategy: building a overview of the complex interactions that need to be considered in the marketspace before a strategic plan is created

☞ The forces that drive strategic thinking within the framework of electronic commerce: both the positional forces of market, service, technology, and brand as well as the bonding factors of leadership, infrastructure, and organizational learning.

☞ Organizational issues such as the need for adaptive organizational structures

☞ Technology considerations

It also stresses the need to keep current and abreast of the potential waves of change that may impact the e-commerce organization of the future.

We have also attempted to bring these issues to three primary types of organizational strategy formulation:

- ☞ Organizations being *born on the Net*
- ☞ Organizations *moving to the Net*
- ☞ *E-consortia,* a new form of organizational structure that leverages the individual strengths of consortium members to deliver added value to the customer in a manner that none of the individual member organizations could on their own

However, the field of electronic commerce continues to progress and move forward every day, and thus it is vital to return to the individuals and companies that have contributed so strongly to the formulation of this book and its philosophies one more time in order to determine what they foresee as the road ahead.

The responses and commentary are diverse and thoughtful and reflected the continuing change found in this marketspace space. Among them are the perspectives of senior executives at start-ups with substantial lines of credit such as:

- ☞ Far & Wide Travel, founded in March 1999, backed by Wellspring Capital Management LLC, a New York–based $275 million private equity partnership
- ☞ LightPort.com, founded in 1997, an organization that has built and now manages Websites for more than 200 firms that together manage over $100 billion for nearly 250,000 clients
- ☞ SoftAid, a computer medical billing system founded in 1992, has over 250 clients in a rapidly growing marketspace

and more traditional organizations such as:

- ☞ Florida Power & Light, a power group founded in 1925 which, 75 years later, has more than $6 billion in revenues, more than 3 million customers, and a market capitalization of $7 billion
- ☞ Motorola, Inc., a global brand established in 1920, which manufactured and sold over $30 billion of electronic equipment and components in 1999, including communications systems, semiconductors, electronic engine controls, and computer systems

Executive Interview #1: Travel Related Services

FAR&WIDE Travel Corporation

www.farandwide.com
Executive Vice President: *Mr. Barry Kaplan*
Vice President, E-Commerce Marketing: *Ms. Annette Hogan*

Summary

FAR&WIDE Travel Corporation is a company privately held by Travel Industry Partners Corp. Founded in 1998 and headquartered in Miami, FL, the new company is led by veteran travel industry and business executives Phil Bakes, chairman and CEO, and Andrew McKey, executive vice president. FAR&WIDE plans to be a leading provider of midrange and upscale leisure travel products, offering a full array of travel experiences including customized and independent foreign travel, as well as escorted, cultural, educational, adventure, ski, and fitness vacations. The firm plans to grow both internally and through additional acquisitions.

Its lead investor and majority owner is Wellspring Capital Management LLC, a New York–based $275 million private equity partnership. Travel Industry Partners Corp. also has established a substantial credit line with a group of banks led by BankBoston, one of the country's largest banks. More than $115 million in capital is earmarked for the acquisition and growth program.

Plant: Perhaps you could give me a little of the background, evolution, and philosophy of the company and how e-commerce plays a part in the endeavor.

Kaplan: In 1997 two co-founders, Phil Bakes and Andrew McKey, surveyed the landscape of the travel industry at large, seeking an opportunity to take advantage of the sea of change that had started in a number of sectors including hotel and airlines as well as commercial travel agencies. They focused upon leisure travel since the demographics suggested "opportunity," and there had not yet been any consolidation or integration as had been seen in other sectors. By mid-1998 it was clear that the value-added tour operators' sector was the most fertile ground open, offering the greatest opportunity to create value for shareholders by integrating a very fragmented marketplace. Would-be sellers, by and large, built profitable entities that were often founded by entrepreneurs who are expatriates who brought to the U.S. their expertise and skills on product and destination knowledge. They all had created a nice business focused primarily upon sales and product development and less on marketing and technology and the kind of operations that would allow those businesses to scale to a large level. Demographics suggest that this is a significant growth sector. Particularly among aging baby boomers who wanted experiential or value-added travel. A number of tour operators who were running profitable businesses had developed them based upon their destination and product knowledge, focusing upon sales relationships with local vendors and product development, but had either neglected or underinvested in technology and systems as well as direct marketing databases and, of course, the operational infrastructure necessary to scale the business to grow. So we have a collection of entrepreneurs, most of whom were not born in the United States, all of whom are very sales- and product-development driven, some of whom do have some sophistication in other areas, but are looking to Far&Wide to develop the platform consisting of sophisticated marketing, technology, and systems within an operational infrastructure to scale the best practices that have been developed among the various business units that are now part of Far&Wide. Most were eager to turn in their entrepreneurial hats and become business unit leaders within a new and evolving organization. That being said, all of them—and I left one of your questions until last—all of them recognize that a major threat to their viability as a small participant in a fragmented industry that has seen quite a bit of consolidation was e-commerce. E-commerce is looked at as a threat to their business but also an opportunity that they wanted to but didn't have the resources to leverage. So, not only did Far&Wide present an excellent strategy for purposes of monetizing some of the wealth accumulation, not only did Far&Wide present a career opportunity for them to continue to build wealth but it also created an opportunity for them to avoid what they regarded as the unknown threat and the unrealizable opportunity to take advantage of e-commerce. Part of Far&Wide's business plan is to address all of those needs: systems and technology, marketing, operational infrastructure, and organizational effectiveness and of course e-commerce. And we recognize that while we may not need to be a pioneer, we certainly need to be an early leader in the development of our e-commerce strategy and the implementation of a significant presence in e-commerce.

Plant: I'd be interested from your position and perspective of what you see as some of the challenges that lie ahead perhaps to the successful use of e-commerce as a complementary channel or as a global proposition in the longer term. Perhaps you could comment on regulatory issues and how you perceive their influence on e-commerce going forward. Perhaps you could also comment on your B2B strategy and the wholesaler channel you are developing.

Kaplan: Yes, in terms of our constituent audiences: certainly business-to-business we'll address travel agents and we will address directly the consumer. We will address our employees, certainly at least in an Internet fashion. We will certainly address our suppliers to use it for connectivity purposes in a more efficient manner than other links, so it becomes an extranet in that regard. We will also use it for preferred customers and suppliers so it becomes an opportunity for us to build loyalty programs with consumers and to arrange for some preferential treatment with suppliers for travel and nontravel. So in that regard we're using the Internet both as a tool and an engine. We also recognize that it can be a driver, it can also be a facilitator with respect to making sales. We also recognize the vast opportunity for it to create an experience at Far&Wide. In some cases it will be an exclusive experience that folks have with us before they are travelling. In other cases it will be a supplemental one, but in all respects, we want to focus both on the transaction and the relationship experience that the Internet creates with the customer (or supplier for that matter) and it becomes a source of information about the company, its products and services and in all respects it will be a promotional device to support the relationship and also cross-sell other brands and other nontravel products that might accessorize the travel experience. And finally we recognize that it's an appendage to everything that we say and do, whether it be in the form of communication or in the form of the way that we deliver the travel experience. So content is important but so is forum so it is consistent with our target branding strategy from the way we write to the way we speak to the way we deliver the experience. Our main approach to the Internet is "it's new, but in some respects it's not new" —we've been communicating forever. We can look at it as a new model or we can also look at it as an extension and we're doing both.

Plant: Perhaps we could talk about some of the challenges going forward from an e-commerce perspective.

Hogan: I will be very frank, I think that the biggest issue today is cost of entry; any kind of e-commerce strategy today involves big technology and marketing dollars. Actually Gartner has a statistic out there which indicates that if you spend between five hundred thousand and a million dollars that puts you on par with average organizations. If you want to get above the general pack you have to spend up to three-plus million dollars, and if you really wish to differentiate yourself, your spending will look more like five million dollars and above, but bottom-line meaningful initial Web presence is expensive these days.

Plant: Yes, that is definitely the case.

Hogan: So, cost of entry being one of the biggest challenges, you need to see where you seek your funding, as well as how well can you use your money. These efforts need to be aligned with how to position that spending from a Board of Directors point of view, so that your web initiative is not just a "leap of faith." Metrics need to be put in place—some "stakes in the ground"— to measure the success of when the Website goes live and actually lives. So what that tells me is that we need pre-Web build research. As you know, I'm a big proponent of research. We started our research early in the business process, finalizing our Statement of Work (SOW), which is a document that outlines what we are doing in the year 2000 and in the year 2001. We are really studying what to do in marketing, technology, content, and initiatives we feel will help differentiate ourselves, like Amazon.com's claim to the "one click" purchase.

Plant: Yes. How can you "prioritize" your processes, or what are the processes that you need to protect legally?

Hogan: You first need to put a Website out there that has been supported by research that tells you what your audiences want from your brand, as well as how people will shop for and purchase your products. You then perform and analyze iterative research once the site has launched. Once you think you have a "special recipe" you keep improving.

Plant: I'm very interested in your views on technology rollout and how it impacts the CIO, especially the issue of how the alignment between the technology vision and the corporate vision occurs. It is clearly one of the most difficult things to continually achieve. Maybe in your case, where you are starting from a good strong position, if you're coming from a traditional organization or somebody with a lot of inertia you may have significant challenges ahead.

Hogan: I think that for me this has been one of the most appealing things about joining an organization like Far&Wide from the ground floor because when you have a long-standing existing structure it is often more difficult to create the nimbleness it takes to move quickly. More than ever and especially moving forward in time corporate visions are and will be enabled because of technology. That is why you see a lot of companies (with all the pros and cons) creating their dot com entity, whether it is Wal-Mart or whoever, as a separate unit. Spinning off a brand to form a dot com is good because you gain a lot of speed to market. But there is a lot of danger in doing things that way, because just from a process and integration point of view you're creating a business unit that may not reflect the parent company. Nonetheless, I support that it is a better alternative for an e-commerce group of an organization to help re-engineer an existing structure to incorporate the right infrastructure to support e-commerce. An organization that does do that will be significantly ahead of their competition because commerce is commerce, and the "e" in e-commerce will eventually go away because commerce is commerce. I'm fortunate at Far&Wide to work with a management team that sees and supports that.

Plant: Yes, it is just as interesting to create a dot com inside an existing organization as it is to bring a new dot com to market.

Hogan: Yes, but there are new challenges. The stock prices of some of the successful dot coms have been dropping. Investors are more sophisticated and they are saying "all right, we know these are new models, we know that we measure success in different ways, it's not the classical return of investment, but what is it?…and I don't know if I'm going to keep investing this much money without understanding what the return is." I'm oversimplifying, but today and I believe more so moving forward, investors are challenging Internet-based ROIs; therefore the economic realities are looming over the dot com efforts.

Plant: I think that argument is very interesting; it is a major problem for Wall Street to create valuations on companies and to identify the return on investments.

Hogan: That's correct: economic realities are setting in.

Plant: As a manager, someone who straddles the two sides between technology and strategy, what are some of the issues that you are finding most challenging? Is it the proliferation of technology? Is it HR element? Is it bringing things to fruition quickly enough to be effective? What do you think are the challenges that you face in that area?

Hogan: Well, I think all of the above. Web initiatives shoot across all the disciplines within a company: marketing, sales, customer service, operations, etc. Therefore, actually bringing something to implementation is quite an accomplishment. There are lots of solutions out there that you really have to evaluate on an in-depth basis. For example, you have a lot of companies out there from the technology side that are good at tapping into one repository of information such as a central reservations system. The challenge is to find technologists that have the expertise of going into multiple environments. We will need a Web solution that will interface to a reservations system to digitize assets, a data warehouse for customer information, and bring all that toward enabling a Website. So the requirements of technology and using it for knowledge as sites become more dynamic and can handle much more complex requests, like the next generations of personalization, and aspects of that nature are to satisfy the increasingly demanding needs of consumers. Today you need to find e-commerce technology shops that can handle that complexity. The role of marketing folks is to become knowledgeable in a whole new way of enabling initiatives, and technology is the enabler.

Plant: You think that the move in the immediate future will be to partner, go outside for the reasons that you just described.

Hogan: Yes, I believe that.

Plant: Because the technology is changing, because the talent pool is focusing and gravitating in on those, because they want to have options themselves, they want to get involved in a start-up, contribute and get returns on that and if they went to an individual company as a technologist they would not be compensated in that way.

Hogan: Exactly.

Plant: The market is driving skill set towards these "centers of excellence" if you want to call them that.

Hogan: Yes.

Plant: But I think that is also the case that the leading vendors themselves are turning down business because even they cannot fulfill their HR needs.

Hogan: Yes, and you most definitely have to search and perform due diligence to find some very precious companies out there that not only offer the right expertise, but also who are able to give you the right level of attention. Far&Wide has the breadth of experiential travel product and such an opportunity for the Web that the "rubber meets the road" in actually executing it. Thirteen companies responded to our Request for Proposal. After extensive due diligence our short list highlights companies that have experience in complex e-commerce technologies, as well as from a marketing perspective have information architecture expertise, which is the science of placing the right information, at the right time, to the right audience. Just apply the need for information architecture to your own life: you get voice mails, e-mails, billboard displays, television, newspapers, etc.—all throwing massive bits of information at you. At some point in time, the filter—your brain—will only accept a certain amount, or only certain pieces of that information will be used, or impress you. So the science of understanding how a specific audience will digest the information (about a specific product, for example) will lead them closer to a comfortable shopping experience and hopefully then a purchase. When you really "boil it down," it's using quantitative and qualitative research of your intended audiences as to how they will digest information to reach "your goal." My goal is sales conversion.

Plant: Because the old models may not correlate to the new media?

Hogan: No, Far&Wide is not about a commodity, "shopping cart" approach. We are about planning for an experience such as a beautiful African safari.

Plant: And you will have a global customer base I would imagine.

Hogan: We are primarily, right now, "outbound travel," meaning North Americans traveling outbound. But as we acquire companies more and more we are touching outside North America for potential customer sourcing. Again, information architecture plays a key role here. We're focused on North American traveling public. If and when we grow into sourcing outside North America those audiences will need to be researched.

Plant: Yes, you are charting some uncharted waters here in terms of marketing, and the marketing research approach and what people could have gotten away with in the first generation, first wave of e-commerce, IT development. You can't try doing that level of predevelopment research today and hope to get away with it. Especially now as you have said if you are spending millions of dollars upon a venture, you have to start up with a strong analytical framework.

Hogan: Absolutely, and it is really a living piece of work. It is really "how do you start structuring yourself?" You need good information architecture, it's the blueprint (like a good house), and then you execute beautiful creativity against that blueprint, and use good technology to enable and support it. Once you have your Website up and running you have the best focus group in the world, a living Website. Good metrics tools and analysis to assess the business intelligence you are garnering are key for deciding on iterative development, new features, and marketing initiatives. That business intelligence can help you cross sell and identify trends, etc. Analysis of that business intelligence gives you the rationale as to why you're doing it and helps you establish how to measure the success.

Plant: Thank you for sharing your insights.

Executive Interview #2: Financial Services

LightPort.com

www.lightport.com
Founder, President, & CEO: *Mr. Jonathan Bentley*

Summary

LightPort.com, a private company founded in 1997, is the leading Web services vendor in the United States to independent financial advisors and money managers. LightPort has built and now manages Websites for more than 400 firms managing over $125 billion for nearly 165,000 clients. These firms have uploaded to LightPort over 2 million secure client portfolios. The company's online directory of independent financial advisors is the largest on the Web, with searchable listings for more than 14,000 advisors managing over $17 trillion for over 1 million clients.

Plant: Perhaps you could give us an insight into the philosophies behind LightPort.com and your background.

Bentley: The appproximate cause for the company forming was two things coming together in late 1995, early 1996—first, the Netscape IPO, which got everyone's attention in the middle of 1995. August 1995 was one of those watersheds for the investment industry—that was where everybody said, "what is this?" and probably for the first time started seriously thinking about the Internet as a broad, big deal, not just something that academics used to send e-mail.

Also about that time, having been in the securities industry for a long time—I began as a broker in 1979—I was really losing bearings on how to value securities—equities in particular—using all of the standard Ben Graham, Warren Buffet, value kinds of things that we learned as a part of our training. They are very sensible principles whenever you have normal markets but not when you have the exuberant kinds of things that are going on now, where people seem unusually inclined to extend a lot of faith in the future, wholly unlike typical human fear.

Things started to break loose about that point. I honestly started to have concerns about how to deliver value in what my primary occupation was, which was securities recommendation, advisory work. At the same time I have always been a bit on the "geeky" side; I have always spent more money than all my friends on the newest and fastest computer and I went through them, one a year it seems like, for a decade.

So that, in addition to having a liberal arts background—I was a literature major, and also for a while I taught architectural design—there was this "artsy geeky" part of my personality that was magnified by the Web, and right at that time—it was the beginning of 1996—those things converged. I was not sure that I could deliver value in what I had been doing for a decade and a half, and this new thing looked awfully interesting. The first step was the Website I developed for my investment advisory firm; they saw the result and said "gee, this is pretty good." Comparing it against what is out there now, where everything is far beyond my individual design capability, it was nothing outstanding. But at that time, when really everything was so thin and poorly developed, it stood up quite well.

At any rate, that was where LightPort began. And typical of an entrepreneurial personality, even though we were easily a year early, I had this sense of "we have to hurry, it's too late, we have to hurry up and create this thing." In retrospect it's hard to quantify whether or not it was truly too early because it also allowed us to begin talking to some important strategic relationships that developed that now set us as an old-time player that has been around for a while. Maybe you can't have that if you come to the game later. Starting that early meant "spilling a lot more blood," burning more capital. But having to endure without any customers also toughens you up and makes you listen to the market more carefully. That's the history of how we started.

Plant: Perhaps you could share with us some of your insights as to the core strategic strengths developed and utilized by your company as it has evolved.

Bentley: In terms of what I would consider core or key strategic insights, one is how incredibly important it has been for us to have a narrow vertical focus. From an academic level, I'm sure you have studied this time and time again, but having a constrained vertical space to operate in accelerates two critical efficiencies—the efficiencies of product development and cost economies. When you have a constrained group of potential customers, you can narrow down the range of expectations the market requires and capitalize your product development cost over more iterations. You accelerate learning and development efficiencies. These efficiencies translate into better margins and more pricing flexibility. But that's not Internet business, that's just business, and it applies to the Internet as it does anywhere else.

The other key efficiency of a tight vertical focus is your branding and reputation. If you have limited dollars, you need the reference point feedback you gain in a vertical space that you can't get in broad spaces. Industry word of mouth is a very important thing. Beside all that was the fact that it was common sense to develop something for a professional that I understood, for an industry that I came out of.

A vertically constrained space is the only practical option—if you have constraints on capital, you can't throw a ton of money at it—and then by extension the second key point, focal point, for me has been that, to really make this work, you can't go out and build a reputation on your own. You really need to organically integrate your process to existing players in the space. For that reason, early on we targeted the number one and number two providers of brokerage services to money managers and the number one and number two providers of software solutions. We began knocking on their doors and trying to develop contractual relations, and we ended up securing the number one and number two in broker-dealer services, Schwab and Fidelity, and the number one and number two in the software area, Advent and Performance Technologies, which was a subsidiary of Schwab.

So that has done immense things. The Advent relations, probably more than any of the others, allows us to begin with credibility when we talk to a prospect. They appreciate that they are talking to somebody that is allied with a company that they have relied upon for years to run their core information, their portfolio management component. This is mission-critical stuff, and it allows us to start a mile and a half ahead of any unbranded, unaligned competitor that shows up at their door.

Plant: Perhaps you could share with us some of your insights as to the challenges faced by e-commerce strategists going forward.

Bentley: I think the fundamental intellectual problem facing my industry is: how do you automate the process, automate services without losing the human touch? I would bet that it would be as true for many industries, and the more intangible the product offering the more significant this problem is, with financial services being almost purely intangible. This is a core problem; in a sense the Web is the first serious shot in automating human intimacy in some ways, and the whole intimacy-touch thing, which is foundational to the trust that facilitates the delivery of intangible services, is a completely different intellectual challenge from automating a production line for bolts and widgets and automobiles. Or even for Amazon's books.

All the pathways that people rely on for developing trust in a physical consultation—especially in something as delicate as financial advising, which is so dependent upon comprehension, context, and confidence, something such as giving advice to a client to stay in an equity position—the industry is very far away from figuring that out. It is one thing to throw a lot of charts and financial graphs and historical things onto a Website, but you're probably creating information overload, creating confusion in a lot of cases, or at least false senses of security that will quickly evaporate in more difficult market conditions.

So the primary challenge that we have is: how can we take this ancient process of delivering advice that still today, the beginning of the twenty-first century, is like it has been for over 50 years: full human interface, talking, meeting face to face or by telephone with periodic paper statements and other physical backup. So the question is how can you take the qualitative elements of what it takes to trust an advisor and deconstruct it and determine what can be effectively automated into this broadband communication channel, and what cannot efficiently be put there. Figuring that out, finding out where those boundaries are and what are the new rules and means for advice is the key element of future success.

Plant: How do you see going forward, the government and political regulatory issues impacting? Is that something that you feel will have a bearing or do you think the laissez-faire, hands-off approach that we have in the U.S. will continue to stimulate the e-commerce environment?

Bentley: My sense is that laissez-faire wins, but it will not be a "layup" and there will be a lot of struggles where we get close to the brink, be that taxation or regulation, but ultimately "bits" and the network are so "quicksilver" fluid that they will flow wherever they have the freest ability to flow. I don't think that ultimately politicians will have the ability to constrain it, so they will back away from tight controls and encourage it through an open market strategy.

Plant: You are clearly a leader within your space in the early partnering mode, partnering with leading companies very early on and successfully. How do you see the partnering relationship changing in the future? Do you think organizations will change partners through looser relationships or do you think it will be a consortium approach? How do you see the landscape there?

Bentley: My belief is that you will have a folding back into traditional or larger businesses—maybe AOL–Time Warner is an example—but once larger, more established companies that have market depth and market share build internal competencies, I think the opportunity for the kind of thing that we have done then "recedes back into the surf." What David Pottruck at Schwab terms "clicks and mortar." Merrill Lynch was late to the game but Merrill has enough depth and enough mass and intelligence that they will figure out how to come to the electronic marketspace.

I think that there will continue to be plenty of opportunities for companies that are established, like we are, but ultimately I think you have these business opportunity gaps open up, and the Internet may be the most massive one of these in recorded business history, where the technology runs so far ahead of the ability of large businesses to "inculturate" that change. You have an amazing window for new companies to exploit. It stems from the gap between what the technology can do and the slowness of large bureaucratic enterprises to adapt to it. The wider that gap is, the more room there is for the ferment that creates companies like ours. But it is only at these inflection points that these things open up so massively. Once the nature of the new paradigm is known better and the technology gathers more of a stride, I think that the larger companies have an opportunity to exploit what they have, which is the branding and financial depth to come back in and regain share.

Plant: Do you think that the door is slowly closing upon smaller companies coming to the Internet in markets where the giants are awakening? Unless they have a true differentiation?

Bentley: I do think that it is closing, but slowly. The Internet is a watershed change in communications more than technology. Communications has such an overreaching effect on all industries and business processes that human comprehension, business methodologies, and service and structural responses will take years to catch up. And in terms of defining which doors are closing, I think the ability to brand a new business-to-consumer model is already closing; we will not have another Amazon. But in terms of the business-to-business reengineering opportunities that will enable the established brands, I think those opportunities are gaining momentum and the kind of business it represents probably favors smaller, intelligent, fast-moving companies.

Plant: Thank you for sharing your insights.

Executive Interview #3: Power Utility

Florida Power & Light

www.FPL.com

CIO: *Mr. Dennis Klinger*

Summary

FPL Group, Inc., provides electricity-related service. Florida Power & Light (FPL), one of the company's main subsidiaries, is engaged in the generation, transmission, distribution, and sale of electrical energy throughout most of the east and lower west coasts of Florida. More than half of the company's business is derived from residential customers, and the balance is generated from commercial and industrial clients.

Plant: What I was hoping was that you could give me some of your thoughts on what are the main challenges that lie ahead for e-commerce strategists, perhaps in your industry but more in general across the board—what people are really facing, as they mount an e-commerce strategy going forward in the next 18 months to 2 years. What are the issues? Is it too late to come into the electronic marketplace?

Klinger: I don't think it is too late to come into the e-marketplace, but digital markets are certainly starting to explode now. The challenges are large and complex. I think of these challenges in two major groupings. First, how can we use e-commerce to give our company an advantage either by improving internal operations and cost structure or by increasing revenue through e-commerce-related products and services? In either case, it is likely many different partners and partnership structures should be considered, which adds to the complexity. Second, what could a competitor, including competitors from totally new areas including pure dot-com, do to us to change the competitive balance or totally change the game? Issues I think about often are how to help our company think, decide, and act at Web speed and how to source, reward, and retain the kind of people required to compete and succeed in this new environment. Partners clearly play a part in the sourcing decision.

Plant: That's interesting, and it's interesting in that people now think more about retaliatory moves than they used to; it used to be just go ahead and do what you can, but now it's about thinking much more directionally.

Klinger: I don't know if "retaliatory" captures the whole thought. With the capabilities of e-commerce and the speed with which things can happen, you need to think about more than just responding to a competitor's move. You need to think about structural changes to your whole marketplace including who and what your competitors are.

Plant: Oh absolutely. I think your industry is very interesting because of the government regulatory framework that was put in place, and it really stimulated the environments—your environment—which traditionally we would think of as being quite staid. As one of the leading areas, really, how do you see government and regulatory policy moving forward in the sense of its impact?

Klinger: At this point, regulation is a consideration in e-commerce as it impacts the currently regulated component of our business. The issue is not so much that regulation impacts e-commerce directly, but rather it limits who can sell what to whom, including e-commerce. We will move at the pace regulation will permit and take advantage of opportunities that present themselves. There is no doubt in my mind that electricity could be sold profitably on the Web. This is already happening where allowed, although I don't think any money is being made yet. Moreover, it could be sold by nontraditional players such as retail stores with exciting portals, specialized digital marketplaces, or very customer-friendly dot-com businesses with no bricks and mortar at all. You will probably see what I would call a virtual utility with no physical assets. I would guess that we and a host of others are now getting all the right capabilities in place so that, when regulation allows, we hit the ground running.

Plant: In terms of the unfolding e-commerce marketplace, perhaps you could describe the issuers and relationships as you see them in the residential and business consumer channels.

Klinger: We are certainly looking at both B2C and B2B. In the B2B space I see two thrusts. The first is where we are the buyer. In this case, we are looking at buying consortiums that include partnerships with other buyers to leverage volume, partnerships with sellers to gain special deals, and partnerships with technology providers so we can move fast in this area without worrying about reinventing the wheel. The second is where we are the seller. In this case, we are trying to use e-commerce techniques and capabilities to make it easy and rewarding for our customers to do business with us. We can and will exploit the buy side immediately. The sell side of B2B and B2C can be practiced in some situations and in unregulated states now, and we will move as appropriate within our overall business strategy in this case. We will be ready when Florida opens up.

Plant: As far as the industrial consumer is concerned—the Wal-Marts, the Goodyears—they presumably will be interacting with you more and more, growing a business-to-business relationship.

Klinger: That is true. We have an e-commerce offering we call EDMpro.com that focuses on providing value-added products and services to large commercial customers now. When we are allowed to sell the commodity through this medium, we will be ready.

Plant: So in reality then, having the vision to understand how those changes are going to impact your organization is key; for example, deregulation...

Klinger: The deregulation initiatives in our industry and the changes that e-commerce could bring are separate and unrelated in their original intent. However, I think with the proper vision, the relationship or, maybe better said, the opportunities and threats are large. As an example, today companies cannot sell retail electricity against us in our territory because of regulation. However, as soon as there is deregulation, e-commerce will make it possible for anyone, not just an electric utility, to sell against us, and they will have totally different cost structures.

Plant: As a CIO, a manager of technical issues and a large organization internally, what have been the challenges that you have faced there and how are they moving forward? Is it a human resources issue? Is it a keeping-up-with-the-technology issue?

Klinger: As a CIO I have always been the focal point of technology for the companies I have worked for. However, as the chief technologist, I have always said people and not technology are the number one critical success factor. Applying people and technology to making the business successful has always been key. I think e-business causes things to move at tremendous speed, but the same things are still key. In summary, I think that the companies with the best people and intellectual capital will win.

Plant: Yes—attempting to employ the best people, with a shortage of talent available...

Klinger: Good people have always been in short supply. Now, with the speed of e-business and the need to be out of the box all the time, that is even more true. We will need to source, reward, and develop in more aggressive and more creative ways. We will also have to partner to fill appropriate gaps.

Plant: Do you find that partnerships are really the only solution to understanding and growing through all of the technologies that are out there?

Klinger: Partnerships are not the only answer, but they are certainly a part of the answer. I think this is true for at least two reasons. One is that it is almost impossible to have all the skill and talent you need as quickly as these things change and as quickly as we must move. Also, business structures will morph continuously. I see partnerships as a way to easily build, disassemble, and rebuild businesses quickly, which I believe will be mandatory. The concept of virtual companies is going to become even more clear as we move forward. E-business allows the business structure behind the scenes to change without impacting the customer.

Plant: Thank you for sharing your insights.

Executive Interview #4: Telecommunications

Motorola

www.motorola.com
Director, Internet Business Group: *Bob Clinton*

Summary

The company provides embedded electronic solutions, software-enhanced devices, and communications solutions, including wireless telephone, two-way radio, messaging and satellite communications products and systems, and networking and Internet-access products. The company has annual revenues in excess of $30 billion.

Plant: What do you think are the main challenges that lie ahead for e-commerce strategists?

Clinton: There are quite a few. Understanding the evolving needs of your key constituencies—whether they are customers, suppliers, analysts, whoever—is always important. Also, strategists must stay current on emerging technologies. In other words, strategists must be both "right brain," and "left brain." It is the rare e-business strategist who can clearly identify a core constituent or market need and then match it to the optimal enabling technologies.

The third and most important element is evaluating how the strategy not only ties into the business, but drives it. It is an ongoing challenge to tie the strategy, and its subsequent execution, to some quantifiable measurable manner, so that it impacts the bottom line—efficiency, quality, or consistency of message. You have to be able to make, and proselytize, those connections.

As you and I have been talking [in the research for the book] the supply chain space has changed tremendously. Many B2B segments and enabling infrastructure market plays (i.e., ERP/CRM) are fragmenting their focus into "vertical portals" and "trading hubs." You're seeing aggressive "go vertical movement" now in specific industries like fluids, oil, and gas, which traditionally were not leading-edge enablers of technology. Coincident with this movement is the integration of those industries' dynamic pricing structures. I expect you'll see this carry over into the more staid businesses.

From an evolving technology viewpoint, the logical extension of the Internet into the wireless space is just beginning. If you think that the Internet revolution is big, the wireless Internet surge will take it to the next level of adoption. Wireless implies a number of things: mobility, ubiquity, and untethered productivity. Think of the Internet as making organizations irrelevant. Adding a wireless component, whether a cell phone, pager, PDA, Palm Pilot, or whatever device, adds that element of mobility. It's the ultimate virtual company. The whole concept of organizations gets even more amorphous.

Plant: And you see that growing, especially in emerging markets such as Latin America?

Clinton: Yes, especially so. In areas where geography or terrain is an obstacle, like Latin America, Indonesia, and China, technology infrastructure deployment presents a challenge. You're also combining a relatively young populace with technologies that are liberating, both technologically and politically. It's going to be very interesting.

Plant: And how do you see the wireless world progressing? Handheld devices becoming the norm? Will the devices be in the phone?

Clinton: Handheld devices will be the norm and will be everywhere. Most studies today indicate that the phone is the preferred platform moving forward, probably due in part to its ubiquity and the total number of cell phones sold. Then again, the distinction among these devices and their capabilities are starting to rapidly blur.

Let's say that there are potentially three devices: phone, pager, and handheld computer/PDA. Each of these has advantages and disadvantages. The cell phone is readily acceptable, widely available, and offers immediacy of information. However, data entry and screen size in its current format is a challenge.

Two-way paging is a growth area and pagers are inexpensive, but there are response-time (latency) and service-coverage issues.

Then there are the multifunction Personal Digital Assistants (PDAs), which include devices like the Palm, Handspring Visor, or Microsoft Pocket PC. They have a nice user interface and can perform many functions.

As for cell phones, and more specifically, the first generation of Wireless Applications Protocol (WAP) phones, most of those are pretty limited in terms of their screen size. In the next three years, you are going to see the operator's cellular infrastructure evolve so the available bandwidth will increase from 64K or 144K up to a full two MB. Japan is moving aggressively in this direction, and Europe is not far behind due to its Global System for Mobile Communication (GSM) network standard. The U.S. is a little bit behind the curve, but is moving aggressively to catch up. In terms of cell phone devices, Nokia, Motorola, Ericsson, and others are cutting alliances with the architecture folks that should accelerate the drive toward a common global standard.

Plant: Do you think the challenge in this area for strategists is to be constantly aware of the changes in technology and changes in Government regulatory frameworks and be responsive to these changes?

Clinton: Yes. For example, planning a strategy for a wireless device (phone/pager/PDA) may have different implications than for a wired device (computer). You must also consider the service and the access portal.

Wireless devices use wireless frequencies or spectrum that is controlled and allocated by the government. Wireless devices like WAP-enabled phones are dependent upon that allocation of spectrum, as well as its rate of deployment and ubiquity. In Japan, there is available spectrum controlled by the government, so deployment will be faster. In the U.S., it may be more of an issue of reallocation of existing spectrum (i.e., the lower end of the FM band currently reserved for not-for-profit organizations). For wired devices, the debate has been going on for quite a while about phone and cable company access to the home. Also, don't discount satellite Internet access to the home.

The access portal presents, or personalizes, the information that is relevant to you. These are the "my.xxx.com" sites. The issue here is about your preferences and patterns and who has access to your "profile."

Consider China. China recently enacted an Internet policy. Users and businesses are required to register with the government. The Internet user's rights and privacy issues are coming more to the forefront. DoubleClick, a very successful ad company in New York, drew a lot of flack because they were very successful at data mining user information and enabling companies to cross-link it to their traditional non-Internet marketing databases. This allowed companies to cross-correlate online and offline profiles. This unsettled many people who liked the perceived anonymity of the Internet.

Conversely, other companies are moving forward to simplify the online experience. One company is piloting "drag and drop" credit card icons based on previously stored-on-the-site credit card information. Very simple: enter your info once, and no need to rekey at every site you visit. Very powerful as well. Folks hate to fill out forms. On business-consumer e-commerce sites, that's where the high dropout rate is.

Plant: Transitioning between what has been happening in e-commerce over the last year or so and looking into the future as a manager, how have you found the issues? Are they centered on keeping up with technology? Or trying to acquire the best talent—an HR issue? What is going to be the challenge going forward? Is it the continually evolving landscape and in bringing in different team members to meet those needs?

Clinton: Yes. The HR issue about lack of skilled resources has been written about pretty extensively. The challenge is in retraining workers in co-operation with the government, re-evaluating work visa requirements, and encouraging our students to enter these fields.

New technologies and approaches are emerging every day, every minute. The challenge is to stay focused on your business end goal, and the technology approach will become self-evident. The businesses that can anticipate the needs of their customers and use applications and technologies to improve processes in an optimal manner are the ones that will succeed. Technology deployments will be in increasingly faster, iterative cycles. The opportunities will be in finding discontinuities in the marketspace and "webizing" them.

As we move into progressive waves of Internet change, the role of the strategist will become more of the role of the visionary. The early waves were easy. Find unserved needs and fulfill them via the Internet. Or transition Old Economy companies with New Economy processes. Subsequent waves will require envisioning new approaches. This involves new arenas like anticipatory approaches, collaborative behaviors, and approaches that tie together multiple intelligent systems. Overlay on top of this security challenges, financial transactions, biometrics, and telematics and we've got a lot of opportunities to keep us busy for quite awhile.

How we tie it all together and harness the wireless Internet is going to be fun.

Plant: Comment upon the technology a little if you can.

Clinton: Forget Gameboys, Palms, DVD players, cell phones, and all of those devices of today. Three to five years from now you will have a supercharged version of all of those devices, rolled into one, in your hand. These third-generation, or 3G devices, will be incredibly intelligent and will communicate wirelessly at incredibly fast speeds. Video will be real-time, high quality, in full color. Prototypes of these devices exist and are working in labs. The device will be personalized and will contain your credit card and other key information. It will be your little personalized wallet, or global travel experience, or Dick Tracy handset, or whatever. The world of technology is evolving and evolving rapidly. It's a race that has no end.

Plant: Thank you for sharing your insights.

Executive Interview #5: Healthcare Services

SoftAid Medical Management Systems (manage.MD)

www.manage.md
Founder, CEO, & President: *Jose Valero*
Vice President: *Jim Clark*

Summary

A leading e-health company, SoftAid delivers office management applications to healthcare providers nationwide. The company was founded in 1992 and now has over 250 clients. SoftAid is one of the first firms to deliver Internet-based applications that help providers improve efficiencies by automating error-prone data entry processes, improving documentation and eliminating redundant patient care.

Plant: Gentlemen, perhaps you could tell me about your company and how the Internet has impacted your strategic thinking.

Clark: We started as a software company about 9 years ago as a medical billing software vendor writing custom applications for healthcare. We have evolved from the DOS-based world to the Windows-based world as a software company, and we saw the Internet as the new revolution in application deployment. And a couple of years ago we decided to move in that direction.

In the past we had looked at the Internet and thought of ways of getting involved, apart from the software, in the healthcare side, and we discussed starting our own ISP and other different ways that we could get involved in the Internet. It has always remained upon our minds.

Valero: We always looked for opportunities that would be available and realistic within our financing model.

We saw the Internet as a means of leveraging our knowledge base and differentiating ourselves in a crowded market for billing systems. The Internet strongly suits itself to the healthcare industry. As the data in healthcare is locked behind walls of proprietary systems, the systems are very disparate and do not facilitate the interchange of data, so *that*, we felt, lent itself to an Internet solution. One of the offerings we saw evolving was data and system hosting through the Internet for healthcare organizations. This lowers their total cost of ownership, decreasing the maintenance burden. As we can update our software instantly, we can keep the software at one location instead of at many locations across the nation. Plus we can simply offer the doctor a simple way to log on and have all the functionality he needs, and all he needs on the other side is a modem and a connection to the Internet. So he does not have to have a very powerful machine.

In the application service provider model, our goal is to come into a client and allow them to use our software, our services, and our hosting facilities for no more than they pay for support for their legacy system. We can do that by the efficiencies that we gain from the maintenance and support of our Internet product. We have already developed the product and customers purchase the licenses. The marginal cost for distribution is nominal when it is sitting on our servers.

Plant: What do you consider were your core strategic strengths that you felt could be leveraged as you moved in that direction?

Valero: We had a vertical application that was in very high demand within a niche industry, so we had a niche application within a niche industry that was growing fast. So our core was our experience and the product that we had developed over the years. Also keep in mind that our industry-specific knowledge together with a true understanding of what our market required and where the inefficiencies lie within our market enabled us to understand how we could use the Internet to eradicate those inefficiencies.

Plant: You come from a healthcare background, but, being in an entrepreneurial mode as a youthful, private company, what was the motivator and driver behind your move into the Internet space?

Clark: The healthcare industry has traditionally lagged behind other industries in terms of its redemption of technology, so it was fortunate for us to be in the healthcare technology industry and to see what was occurring early. We have continuously followed the Internet and its technologies from the very outset. So when we began planning our Internet strategy in 1997 for Internet-based healthcare systems, we were extremely early and there were no other organizations in the space. Patient confidentiality of records, privacy, and the security issues were a prohibitive factor. So we were able to see what was going on in other industries and see how that was going to affect us in healthcare. As entrepreneurs, we are always looking for new applications and new ways of reducing inefficiencies and looking for new ways of capitalizing upon that.

Valero: At the same time we continued to develop our current product. What is happening is that healthcare is slowly adopting these ideas, using the Internet to save time and money, and we are seeing some competition in the field come with one or two applications, but we are entering the market with a holistic approach. We are looking past all the current problems and have attempted to gain a vision of what it is going to look like 2 plus years out; with the speed of technological advance, 2 years is a long time.

Plant: How do you feel going forward regarding governmental and regulatory issues? What will be the impact upon the healthcare industry?

Valero: For us, it affects us in one major way: that is the electronic billing of claims and that the government, through HCFA—the Health Care Finance Administration—they regulate a lot of these issues relating to transmitting the electronic data and the format, etc., and they are moving towards the Internet also, but not at a fast pace, so it has really not affected us in that sense. We are somewhat ahead of the game through the experience we have gained in our previous products, when it comes to government regulations. However, they are going to follow suit and are heading in the same direction.

Clark: The government influence is a wonderful thing for software vendors in healthcare because it antiquates those systems very quickly so they have to have a good relationship with a technology vendor. They can't just run off and develop a proprietary system that will live forever. It has been good for us, the government influence; we have to move with the technology, obviously. It is even more important with things like HIPA [Health Insurance Portability and Accountability Act] which is a Congress mandate which deals with how the Internet is used in healthcare, so as vendors we have to meet those guidelines and have it work for us.

Plant: With this background, perhaps you could share with us some of your insights as to the challenges faced going forward by e-commerce strategists, both within your industry and in general.

Clark: As far as implementation goes, there is an adoption curve, and healthcare has traditionally been a laggard with respect to the adoption of technology. So we have those barriers to entry to overcome. Healthcare spends in general about half of the amount other industries spend on information technology—7% as compared to 14%. So it's a challenge there. So, having said that, the Internet and healthcare are converging rapidly, and there are a lot of firms coming out, some very well funded—a lot of players from other industries entering the space because they see the opportunities. It's a $250–400 billion industry, depending upon which market study you read. So there are a lot of inefficiencies to address, and our biggest impediment to going forward is not going to be the adoption of the technology but the competition as it comes in. There are a lot of strategic alliances being formed, and one of the keys for us to our long-term growth is the ability to form long-term alliances and develop a product that is going to last.

Valero: That may also help us, however, because at the moment only 5% of the doctors are interested in an Internet-based solution, and that is growing rapidly. But having some of the larger players in the market tout this technology will also assist in the move to an Internet-type solution. There are also some barriers that we have to get past, such as physicians' concern with security. You can imagine that security is an issue that we have dealt with in the past from a technology perspective, but there is an educational learning curve to be passed through by the user base.

Plant: As businessmen what are the major challenges? Is it a human resource issue? Is it a regulatory issue? Is it an issue of keeping up with the technology or a standardization of technology issue? What, as an entrepreneur, as a private company, do you still face?

Clark: From the positioning and marketing perspective, it is vitally important to position and present your product to the target market correctly, decide upon how the customers are going to adapt this technology. And again it is a very small percentage of the market that is ready for this technology. It is finding the right positioning of the product by partnering with the right vendors to get the product in front of the right eyes.

Plant: So the partnering role and the fact that you can focus upon a narrow marketspace at the moment is a benefit to you in the sense of cutting through the competition?

Valero: Exactly; that is going to make it a little more efficient to work through those large numbers.

Plant: Do you feel that, for start-ups in general, one of the challenges is to find the right partners and move forward with them?

Valero: Yes, absolutely.

Plant: What other areas are challenging organizations developing e-commerce strategies?

Clark: One issue is human resources. The talent pool is so tight—it is very difficult to find the right talent.

From a technology perspective, what is interesting about coming to market with an Internet-based product against an industry of legacy systems is that the Internet products are in their infancy stage. That goes from the infrastructure, the bandwidth issues, the applications, and how robust they are. In terms of actually using them in a day-to-day setting, a Web-based application will have some limitations to it against, say, a Windows-based application or a UNIX application, but that will change as the bandwidth changes. That's also an impediment that we have to address and time will work that out.

Valero: Clearly the strengths we have built up come from the challenges entrepreneurs face in the Internet marketspace: Time to market is key, continual adaptation to the technology, meeting the customer's needs, providing a better mechanism for performing a task than the customer already has, and preempting regulatory issues. These strengths have allowed us to position ourselves effectively in the Internet space, to grow our market share, and to develop as a major force in the online medical management systems arena.

Plant: Thank you for sharing your insights.

Future Steps: Epilogue

The interviews with executives as presented in this section indicate that the future of e-commerce is going to be more taxing than the past and that it is more important than ever to be creative and innovative.

Office Depot

www.OfficeDepot.com
Executive Director, Marketing & Merchandising: *Keith Butler*
Summarizes that the four most important issues facing e-commerce strategists going forward are

- Adjusting to the new playing field (read: AOL–Time Warner)
- Making e-commerce as seamless as offline commerce, so that it includes customer service, inventory management, fulfillment, delivery management
- Adjusting to the new playing field created by the merger of AOL and Time Warner, since they can and will control substantial access to large quantities of consumers, keeping technology in the background to make e-commerce intuitive and easy to use.

The first wave of e-commerce to a large extent ended at the end of the twentieth century. The second wave of systems and entrepreneurship has commenced. This second wave is going to have severe implications for the weak survivors of the first wave and for subsequent new start-ups. The weaker organizations from the first e-commerce wave of development are either going to

1. Disappear. They will disappear due to their inability to maintain their financial debt base of operations. These include many of the third-mover companies in specific verticals as well as portals that have low customer liquidity.

2. Be acquired. Some of the branded sites may survive, but they will become targets for acquisition; they will then become the engine behind an e-consortium or information hub.

3. Reposition. There will still be a large dynamic set of undercurrents in the electronic commerce marketspace with the emergence of different "strains" of e-commerce, such as B2B, B2G, and so on. This will allow the B2C companies that did not make the grade in the first wave to recreate

themselves in a more favorable marketspace, building on their knowledge and strengths from the first wave and discarding their weaknesses where possible.

The capital markets are also going to change:

1. Venture capital (VC) is going to become much harder to acquire. The *concept plan* has already given way to the *e-business plan*, and the pattern is for the "screws to be tightened" by the VCs upon the entrepreneurs toting these plans around Wall Street. Subsequent rounds of funding capital will require strong financial analysis that identifies metrics, returns, earning projections (with positive earnings), and plans to IPO that include true realism and measurable deliverables at every milestone. The valuation metrics for the investment banks and VCs are also becoming more refined.

2. So-called Angel investors will continue to invest, but whether the nature of returns in the e-commerce space will interest them for the considerable future remains to be seen. A new technology future may be starting tomorrow with a breakthrough in biotechnology or wireless communications, leading the investor community down different avenues.

Even for the so-called success stories of the late twentieth century, in the dawn of the early twenty-first century their future looks more and more conservative. AOL merged with Time Warner and, as Keith Butler of Office Depot points out, this changes the playing field considerably. As the original brands of the Internet move to stabilize, the Internet could grow into an oligarchy dominated by AOL and e-consortia information hubs as 'viewers' move toward focused content and away from generalist *low value-added sites*. The speed to locate information of a quality nature will become the key component by which sites and organizations are going to be judged by customers of the future. Other first-wave success stories are already changing models. They have realized all the gains from the first wave and internally acknowledge that, for them, it is over. They know that their current models are unsustainable and are thus selling their content channels to the highest bidders. They then ask for a percentage of the revenues produced by the purchaser and content users going forward—an incredible turnaround from the days when content was king. These organizations then have a relatively low risk and a potential for massive future gains if they have sold out to the right company. Ironically this company may be a former traditional player wishing to enter the market for the first time.

So, What of the Future?

1. For those still wanting to be born on the Internet, the criteria for success remain the same—be creative, differentiate, don't get caught in a vertical market without a large amount of information provision, and quality free content. Think "new model"—the money flows to the creative.

2. The future looks increasingly wireless, and the creative issues will be how to harness that technology to give customers that next "gee whiz, how could I ever have lived without this" factor.

3. The future looks increasingly global—how do I sell product to Asia and Latin America? It is still interesting to note that only half the population of the world has ever placed a telephone call. The challenge is to open these new markets.

4. How does the technology, if harnessed correctly, reposition other emerging industries? Can the information hub portal concept be applied to biotechnology, genetic engineering, and so on? What lessons have been learned and what can be transferred to generate growth in other information-based industries?

5. For organizations moving to the Net from traditional models, careful consideration needs to be made of the strategy to be adopted. Total online? Clicks and mortar? Bricks and mortar? Continue to be offline? The strategy will, as has been discussed throughout this book, be centered on developing new business models, models based on modification of existing strengths, shedding the weaknesses inherited from the past and transforming the organization so that the core competencies and brands built upon over the years still add to the equity of the organization and generate continuance and relevance in the marketplace.

6. Key to all new models will be balance—unless a true inflection point occurs, companies will generally be advised to not follow paths of extreme strategic movement.

7. The new organizational form may in many instances come from the old in the form of the e-consortia. The strength of powerful groupings will be important in the next e-commerce wave. The e-consortium is a mechanism for old organizations to refresh their strategies while simulta-

neously allowing them to defer risk. The e-consortia will allow the large, rich, and previously dominant organizations to leverage their old cachet and competencies in a changing arena, which initially they may not have been lithe enough to adapt to.

❦ ❦ ❦ ❦ ❦ ❦

We hope that the discussions and models presented herein have allowed you to create a new model in your mind and that the model generates *value* for you, your organization, or your state. Our goal was to make the frameworks broadly applicable so that the principals can be applied to the broadest spectrum of industries and situations, ultimately helping you to become more agile, nimble, and innovative in your thought processes, developing an excitement for the art of the possible and casting off the lethargies of the past.

United States Department of Commerce

Patent and Trademark Office Guide to Internet Trademarks[1]

UNITED STATES DEPARTMENT OF COMMERCE
Patent and Trademark Office
OFFICE OF ASSISTANT COMMISSIONER FOR TRADEMARKS
2900 Crystal Drive
Arlington, Virginia 22202-3513

EXAMINATION GUIDE NO. 2-99

September 29, 1999

MARKS COMPOSED, IN WHOLE OR IN PART, OF DOMAIN NAMES

I. Introduction And Background

A domain name is part of a Uniform Resource Locator (URL), which is the address of a site or document on the Internet. In general, a domain name is comprised of a second-level domain, a "dot," and a top-level domain (TLD). The wording to the left of the "dot" is the second-level domain, and the wording to the right of the "dot" is the TLD.

---

1. www.uspto.gov/web/offices/tac/notices/guide299.htm

Example: If the domain name is "XYZ.COM," the term "XYZ" is a second-level domain and the term "COM" is a TLD.

A domain name is usually preceded in a URL by "http://www." The "http://" refers to the protocol used to transfer information, and the "www" refers to World Wide Web, a graphical hypermedia interface for viewing and exchanging information. There are two types of TLDs: generic and country code.

Generic TLDs

Generic TLDs are designated for use by the public. Each generic TLD is intended for use by a certain type of organization. For example, the TLD ".com" is for use by commercial, for profit organizations. However, the administrator of the .com, .net, .org and .edu TLDs does not check the requests of parties seeking domain names to ensure that such parties are a type of organization that should be using those TLDs. On the other hand, .mil, .gov, and .int TLD applications are checked, and only the U.S. military, the U.S. government, or international organizations are allowed in the domain space. The following is a list of the current generic TLDs and the intended users:

.com	commercial, for profit organizations
.edu	4 year, degree granting colleges/universities
.gov	U.S. federal government agencies
.int	international organizations
.mil	U.S. military organizations, even if located outside the U.S.
.net	network infrastructure machines and organizations
.org	miscellaneous, usually non-profit organizations and individuals

Country Code

Country code TLDs are for use by each individual country. Each country determines who may use their code. For example, some countries require that users of their code be citizens or have some association with the country, while other countries do not. The following are examples of some of the country code TLDs currently in use:

.jp	for use by Japan
.tm	for use by Turkmenistan
.tv	for use by Tuvalu
.uk	for use by the United Kingdom

Proposed TLDs

Due to growing space limitations, several new TLDs have been proposed, including the following:

.arts	cultural and entertainment activities
.firm	businesses

.info	entities providing information services
.nom	individual or personal nomenclature
.rec	recreation or entertainment activities
.store	businesses offering goods to purchase
.web	entities emphasizing activities related to the web

While these proposed TLDs are not currently used on the Internet as TLDs, applicants may include them in their marks.

Applications for registration of marks composed of domain names

Since the implementation of the domain name system, the Patent and Trademark Office (Office) has received a growing number of applications for marks composed of domain names. While the majority of domain name applications are for computer services such as Internet content providers (organizations that provide web sites with information about a particular topic or field) and online ordering services, a substantial number are for marks used on other types of services or goods.

When a trademark, service mark, collective mark or certification mark is composed, in whole or in part, of a domain name, neither the beginning of the URL (http://www.) nor the TLD have any source indicating significance. Instead, those designations are merely devices that every Internet site provider must use as part of its address. Today, advertisements for all types of products and services routinely include a URL for the web site of the advertiser. Just as the average person with no special knowledge recognizes "800" or "1-800" followed by seven digits or letters as one of the prefixes used for every toll-free phone number, the average person familiar with the Internet recognizes the format for a domain name and understands that "http," "www," and a TLD are a part of every URL.

Applications for registration of marks consisting of domain names are subject to the same requirements as all other applications for federal trademark registration. This Examination Guide identifies and discusses some of the issues that commonly arise in the examination of domain name mark applications.

II. Use as a Mark

A. Use Applications

A mark composed of a domain name is registrable as a trademark or service mark only if it functions as a source identifier. The mark as depicted on the specimens must be presented in a manner that will be perceived by potential purchasers as indicating source and not as merely an informational indication of the domain name address used to access a web site. See In re Eilberg, 29 USPQ2d 1955 (TTAB 1998).

B. Advertising One's Own Products or Services on the Internet is not a Service

Advertising one's own products or services is not a service. See In re Reichhold Chemicals, Inc., 167 USPQ 376 (TTAB 1970); TMEP §1301.01(a)(ii). Therefore, businesses that create a web site for the sole purpose of advertising their own products or services cannot register a domain name used to identify that activity. In examination, the issue usually arises when the applicant describes the activity as a registrable service, e.g., "providing information about [a particular field]," but the specimens of use make it clear that the web site merely advertises the applicant's own products or services. In this situation, the examining attorney must refuse registration because the mark is used to identify an activity that does not constitute a "service" within the meaning of the Trademark Act. Trademark Act §§1, 2, 3 and 45, 15 U.S.C. §§1051, 1052, 1053 and 1127.

C. Agreement of Mark on Drawing with Mark on Specimens of Use

In a domain name mark (e.g., XYZ.COM or HTTP://WWW.XYZ.COM), consumers look to the second level domain name for source identification, not to the TLD or the terms "http://www." or "www." Therefore, it is usually acceptable to depict only the second level domain name on the drawing page, even if the specimens of use show a mark that includes the TLD or the terms "http://www." or "www." Cf. Institut National des Appellations D'Origine v. Vintners Int'l Co., Inc., 954 F.2d 1574, 22 USPQ2d 1190 (Fed. Cir. 1992) (CHABLIS WITH A TWIST held to be registrable separately from CALIFORNIA CHABLIS WITH A TWIST); In re Raychem Corporation, 12 USPQ2d 1399 (TTAB 1989) (refusal to register "TINEL-LOCK" based on specimens showing "TRO6AI-TINEL-LOCK-RING" reversed). See also 37 C.F.R. §2.51(a)(1) and TMEP §807.14 et. seq.

> Example: The specimens of use show the mark HTTP://WWW.XYZ.COM. The applicant may elect to depict only the term "XYZ" on the drawing page.

Sometimes the specimens of use fail to show the entire mark sought to be registered (e.g., the drawing of the mark is HTTP://WWW.XYZ.COM, but the specimens only show XYZ). If the drawing of the mark includes a TLD, or the terms "http://www.," or "www.," the specimens of use must also show the mark used with those terms. Trademark Act §1(a)(1)(C), 15 U.S.C. §1051(a)(1)(C).

> Example: If the drawing of the mark is XYZ.COM, specimens of use that only show the term XYZ are unacceptable.

D. Marks Comprised Solely of TLDs for Domain Name Registry Services

If a mark is composed solely of a TLD for "domain name registry services" (e.g., the services currently provided by Network Solutions, Inc. of registering .com domain names), registration should be refused under Trademark Act §§1, 2, 3 and 45, 15 U.S.C. §§1051, 1052, 1053 and 1127, on the ground that the TLD would not be perceived as a mark. The examining attorney should include evidence from the NEXIS® database, the Internet, or other sources to show that the proposed mark is currently used as a TLD or is under consideration as a new TLD.

If the TLD merely describes the subject or user of the domain space, registration should be refused under Trademark Act §2(e)(1), 15 U.S.C. §2(e)(1), on the ground that the TLD is merely descriptive of the registry services.

E. Intent-to-Use Applications

A refusal of registration on the ground that the matter presented for registration does not function as a mark relates to the manner in which the asserted mark is used. Therefore, generally, in an intent-to-use application, a mark that includes a domain name will not be refused on this ground until the applicant has submitted specimens of use with either an amendment to allege use under Trademark Act §1(c), or a statement of use under Trademark Act §1(d), 15 U.S.C. §1051(c) or (d). However, the examining attorney should include an advisory note in the first Office Action that registration may be refused if the proposed mark, as used on the specimens, identifies only an Internet address. This is done strictly as a courtesy. If information regarding this possible ground for refusal is not provided to the applicant prior to the filing of the allegation of use, the Office is in no way precluded from refusing registration on this basis.

III. Surnames

If a mark is composed of a surname and a TLD, the examining attorney must refuse registration because the mark is primarily merely a surname under Trademark Act §2(e)(4), 15 U.S.C. §1052(e)(4). A TLD has no trademark significance. If the primary significance of a term is that of a surname, adding a TLD to the surname does not alter the primary significance of the mark as a surname. Cf. In re I. Lewis Cigar Mfg. Co., 205 F.2d 204, 98 USPQ 265 (C.C.P.A. 1953) (S. SEIDENBERG & CO'S. held primarily merely a surname); In re Hamilton Pharmaceuticals Ltd., 27 USPQ2d 1939 (TTAB 1993) (HAMILTON PHARMACEUTICALS for pharmaceutical products held primarily merely a surname); In re Cazes, 21 USPQ2d 1796 (TTAB 1991) (BRASSERIE LIPP held primarily merely a surname where "brasserie" is a generic term for applicant's restaurant services). See also TMEP §1211.01(b).

IV. Descriptiveness

If a proposed mark is composed of a merely descriptive term(s) combined with a TLD, the examining attorney should refuse registration under Trademark Act §2(e)(1), 15 U.S.C. §1052(e)(1), on the ground that the mark is merely descriptive. This applies to trademarks, service marks, collective marks and certification marks.

> Example: The mark is SOFT.COM for facial tissues. The examining attorney must refuse registration under §2(e)(1).

Example: The mark is NATIONAL BOOK OUTLET.COM for retail book store services. The examining attorney must refuse registration under §2(e)(1).

The TLD will be perceived as part of an Internet address, and does not add source identifying significance to the composite mark. Cf. In re Page, 51 USPQ2d 1660 (TTAB 1999) (addition of a telephone prefix such as "800" or "888" to a descriptive term is insufficient, by itself, to render the mark inherently distinctive); In re Patent & Trademark Services Inc., 49 USPQ2d 1537 (TTAB 1998) (PATENT & TRADEMARK SERVICES INC. is merely descriptive of legal services in the field of intellectual property; the term "Inc." merely indicates the type of entity that performs the services and has no significance as a mark); In re The Paint Products Co., 8 USPQ2d 1863 (TTAB 1988) (PAINT PRODUCTS CO. is no more registrable as a trademark for goods emanating from a company that sells paint products than it would be as a service mark for retail paint store services offered by such a company); In re E.I. Kane, Inc., 221 USPQ 1203 (TTAB 1984) (OFFICE MOVERS, INC. incapable of functioning as a mark for moving services; addition of the term "Inc." does not add any trademark significance to matter sought to be registered). See also TMEP §1209.01(b)(12) regarding marks comprising in part "1-800," "888," or other telephone numbers.

V. Generic Refusals

If a mark is composed of a generic term(s) for applicant's goods or services and a TLD, the examining attorney must refuse registration on the ground that the mark is generic and the TLD has no trademark significance. See TMEP §1209.01(b)(12) regarding marks comprised in part of "1-800" or other telephone numbers. Marks comprised of generic terms combined with TLDs are not eligible for registration on the Supplemental Register, or on the Principal Register under Trademark Act §2(f), 15 U.S.C. §1052(f). This applies to trademarks, service marks, collective marks and certification marks.

Example: TURKEY.COM for frozen turkeys is unregistrable on either the Principal or Supplemental Register.

Example: BANK.COM for banking services is unregistrable on either the Principal or Supplemental Register.

The examining attorney generally should not issue a refusal in an application for registration on the Principal Register on the ground that a mark is a generic name for the goods or services unless the applicant asserts that the mark has acquired distinctiveness under §2(f) of the Trademark Act, 15 U.S.C. §1052(f). Absent such a claim, the examining attorney should issue a refusal on the ground that the mark is merely descriptive of the goods or services under §2(e)(1), and provide an advisory statement that the matter sought to be registered appears to be a generic name for the goods or services. TMEP §1209.02.

VI. Marks Containing Geographical Matter

The examining attorney should examine marks containing geographic matter in the same manner that any mark containing geographic matter is examined. See generally TMEP §§1210.05 and 1210.06. Depending on the manner in which it is used on or in connection with the goods or services, a proposed domain name mark containing a geographic term may be primarily geographically descriptive under §2(e)(2) of the Trademark Act, 15 U.S.C. §1052(e)(2), or primarily geographically deceptively misdescriptive under §2(e)(3) of the Trademark Act, 15 U.S.C. §1052(e)(3), and/or merely descriptive or deceptively misdescriptive under §2(e)(1) of the Trademark Act, 15 U.S.C. §1052(e)(1).

Geographic matter may be merely descriptive of services provided on the Internet

When a geographic term is used as a mark for services that are provided on the Internet, sometimes the geographic term describes the subject of the service rather than the geographic origin of the service. Usually this occurs when the mark is composed of a geographic term that describes the subject matter of information services (e.g., NEW ORLEANS.COM for "providing vacation planning information about New Orleans, Louisiana by means of the global computer network"). In these cases, the examining attorney should refuse registration under Trademark Act §2(e)(1) because the mark is merely descriptive of the services.

VII. Disclaimers

Trademark Act §6(a), 15 U.S.C. §1056(a), provides for the disclaimer of "an unregistrable component" of a mark. The guidelines on disclaimer set forth in TMEP §1213 et. seq. apply to domain name mark applications.

If a composite mark includes a domain name composed of unregistrable matter (e.g., a merely descriptive or generic term and a TLD), disclaimer is required. See examples below and TMEP §§1213.03.

If a disclaimer is required and the domain name includes a misspelled or telescoped word, the correct spelling must be disclaimed. See examples below and TMEP §§1213.04(a) and 1213.09(c).

A compound term composed of arbitrary or suggestive matter combined with a "dot" and a TLD is considered unitary, and therefore no disclaimer of the TLD is required. See examples below and TMEP §1213.04(b).

Mark	Disclaimer
XYZ BANK.COM	BANK.COM
XYZ FEDERALBANK.COM	FEDERAL BANK.COM
XYZ GROCERI STOR.COM	GROCERY STORE.COM
XYZ.COM	no disclaimer
XYZ.BANK.COM	no disclaimer
XYZBANK.COM	no disclaimer

VIII. Material Alteration

Amendments may not be made to the drawing of the mark if the character of the mark is materially altered. Trademark Rule 2.72, 37 C.F.R §2.72. The test for determining whether an amendment is a material alteration was articulated in Visa International Service Association v. Life-Code Systems, Inc., 220 USPQ 740 (TTAB 1983):

> The modified mark must contain what is the essence of the original mark, and the new form must create the impression of being essentially the same mark. The general test of whether an alteration is material is whether the mark would have to be republished after the alteration in order to fairly present the mark for purposes of opposition. If one mark is sufficiently different from another mark as to require republication, it would be tantamount to a new mark appropriate for a new application.

Id. at 743–44.

Each case must be decided on its own facts. The controlling question is always whether the new and old form of the marks create essentially the same commercial impression. TMEP §807.14(a).

> Example: Amending the mark PETER, used on kitchen pots and pans, from PETER to PETER PAN would materially change the mark because adding the generic word PAN dramatically changes the meaning of the mark—from a person's name, to a well known storybook character's name.

Adding or deleting TLDs in domain name marks

Generally, for domain name marks (e.g., COPPER.COM), the applicant may add or delete a TLD to the drawing of the mark without materially altering the mark. A mark that includes a TLD will be perceived by the public as a domain name, while a mark without a TLD will not. However, the public recognizes that a TLD is a universally-used part of an Internet address. As a result, the essence of a domain name mark is created by the second level domain name, not the TLD. The commercial impression created by the second level domain name usually will remain the same whether the TLD is present or not.

> Example: Amending a mark from PETER to PETER.COM would not materially change the mark because the essence of both marks is still PETER, a person's name.

Similarly, substituting one TLD for another in a domain name mark, or adding or deleting a "dot" or "http://www." or "www." to a domain name mark is generally permitted.

> Example: Amending a mark from XYZ.ORG to XYZ.COM would not materially change the mark because the essence of both marks is still XYZ.

Adding or deleting TLDs in other marks

If a TLD is not used as part of a domain name, adding or deleting a TLD may be a material alteration. When used without a second level domain name, a TLD may have trademark significance. See TMEP §807.14(a).

> Example: Deleting the term .COM from the mark .COM ? used on sports magazines would materially change the mark.

IX. Likelihood of Confusion

In analyzing whether a domain name mark is likely to cause confusion with another pending or registered mark, the examining attorney must consider the marks as a whole, but generally should accord little weight to the TLD portion of the mark. See TMEP §1207.01(b) et. seq.

X. Marks Containing The Phonetic Equivalent of A Top Level Domain

Marks containing the phonetic equivalent of a TLD (e.g., XYZ DOTCOM) are treated in the same manner as marks composed of a regular TLD. If a disclaimer is necessary, the disclaimer must be in the form of the regular TLD and not the phonetic equivalent. See TMEP §1213.09(c).

> Example: The mark is INEXPENSIVE RESTAURANTS DOT COM for providing information about restaurants by means of a global computer network. Registration should be refused because the mark is merely descriptive of the services under Trademark Act §2(e)(1), 15 U.S.C. §1052(e)(1).

> Example: The mark is XYZ DOTCOM. The applicant must disclaim the TLD ".COM" rather than the phonetic equivalent "DOTCOM."

Featured IBM Technology in Charles Schwab Case Study

WebSphere Application Server	WebSphere Application Server is a reliable and robust platform for Java servers, using open, cross-platform Java and XML/XSL technologies. www.ibm.com/software/websphere
CICS	CICS is an application server that provides industrial-strength, online transaction management for mission-critical applications. Already proven in the market for over 30 years with many of the world's leading businesses, CICS enables customers to modernize and extend their existing applications, efficiently create exciting new ones, and so take advantage of the opportunities provided by e-business while fully leveraging their existing investments. www.ibm.com/software/ts/cics
RS/6000	A UNIX enterprise server from IBM. RS/6000 support applications and networks for e-business. www.rs.6000.ibm.com

Index

Back | Forward | Home | Reload | Images | Open | Print | Find | Stop

http://www.phptr.com/

What's New? | What's Cool? | Destinations | Net Search | People | Software

PRENTICE HALL

Professional Technical Reference
Tomorrow's Solutions for Today's Professionals.

Keep Up-to-Date with
PH PTR Online!

We strive to stay on the cutting-edge of what's happening in professional computer science and engineering. Here's a bit of what you'll find when you stop by **www.phptr.com**:

@ **Special interest areas** offering our latest books, book series, software, features of the month, related links and other useful information to help you get the job done.

Deals, deals, deals! Come to our promotions section for the latest bargains offered to you exclusively from our retailers.

$ **Need to find a bookstore?** Chances are, there's a bookseller near you that carries a broad selection of PTR titles. Locate a Magnet bookstore near you at www.phptr.com.

! **What's New at PH PTR?** We don't just publish books for the professional community, we're a part of it. Check out our convention schedule, join an author chat, get the latest reviews and press releases on topics of interest to you.

✉ **Subscribe Today!** **Join PH PTR's monthly email newsletter!**

Want to be kept up-to-date on your area of interest? Choose a targeted category on our website, and we'll keep you informed of the latest PH PTR products, author events, reviews and conferences in your interest area.

Visit our mailroom to subscribe today! **http://www.phptr.com/mail_lists**